I0886148

ALFRED WERTHEIMER

ELVIS AND THE BIRTH OF ROCK AND ROLL

TASCHEN

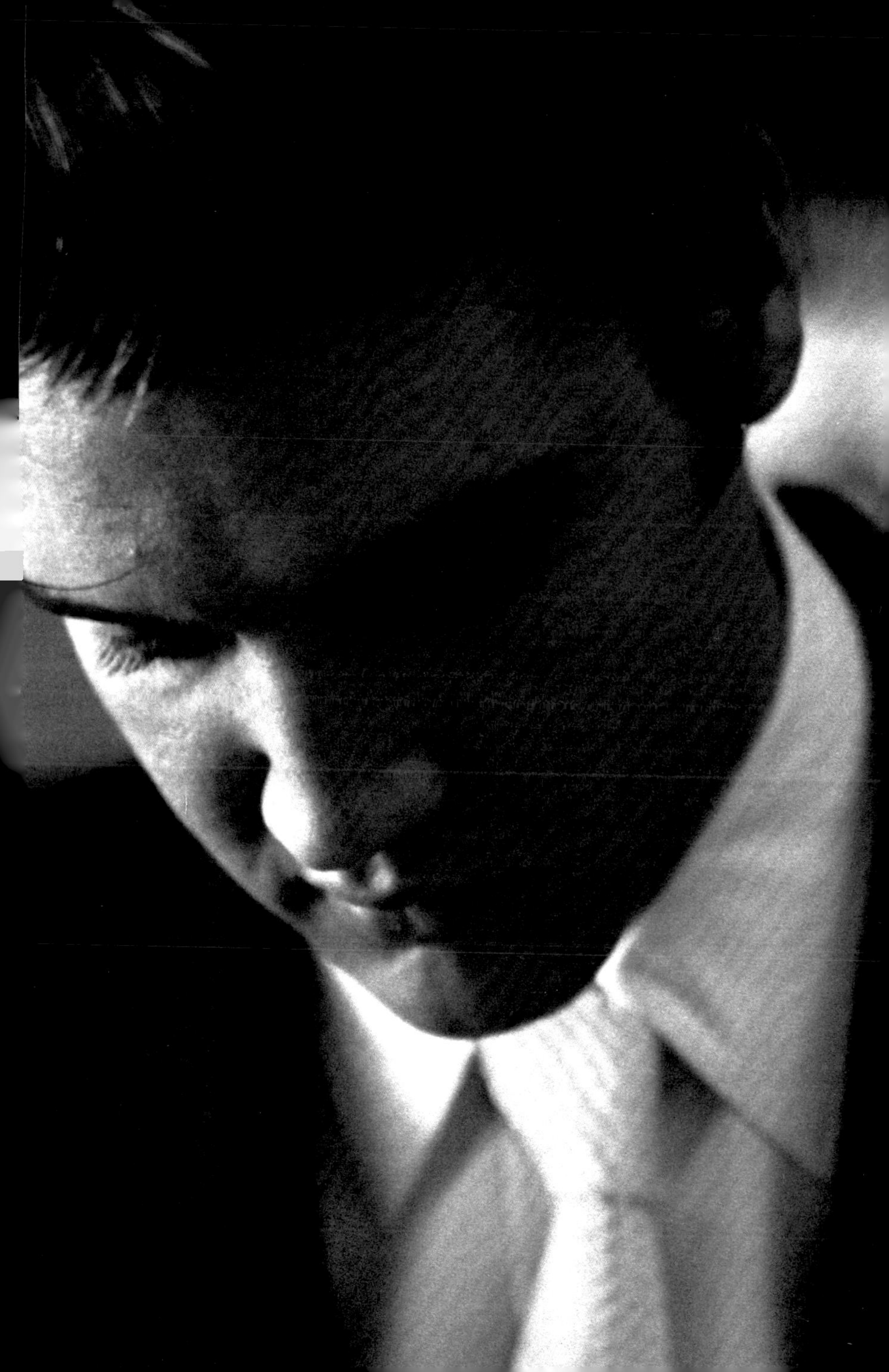

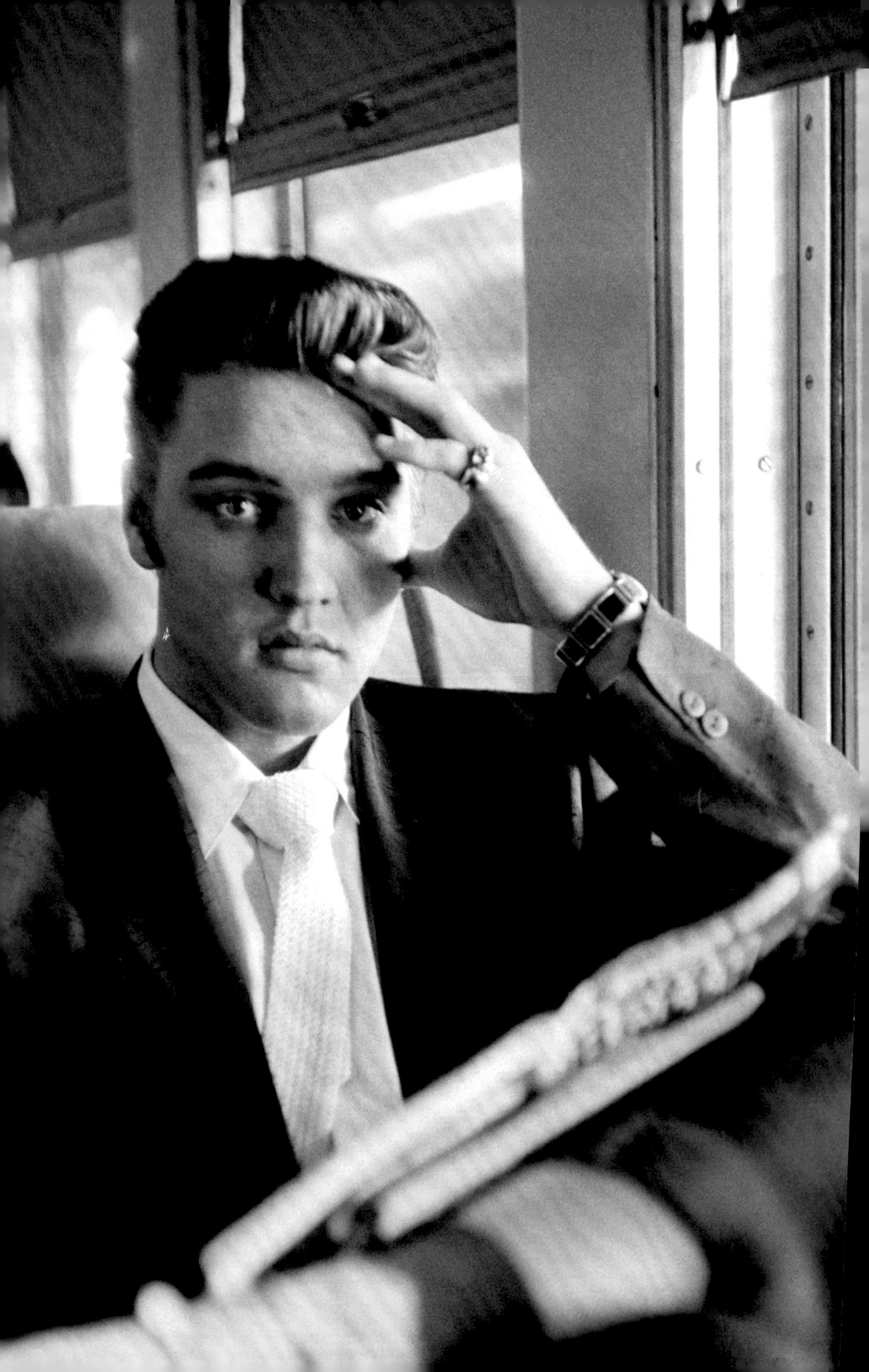

ALFRED WE

EL

A

THE BIRTH OF R

★ ED. BY CHRIS MURRAY ★ E

TASCHEN ★ ART DIRECTION BY JO

ERTHEIMER

VIS

D

CK AND ROLL

AY BY ROBERT SANTELLI ★

AKER ★ POSTERS BY ★ *Hatch Show Print*

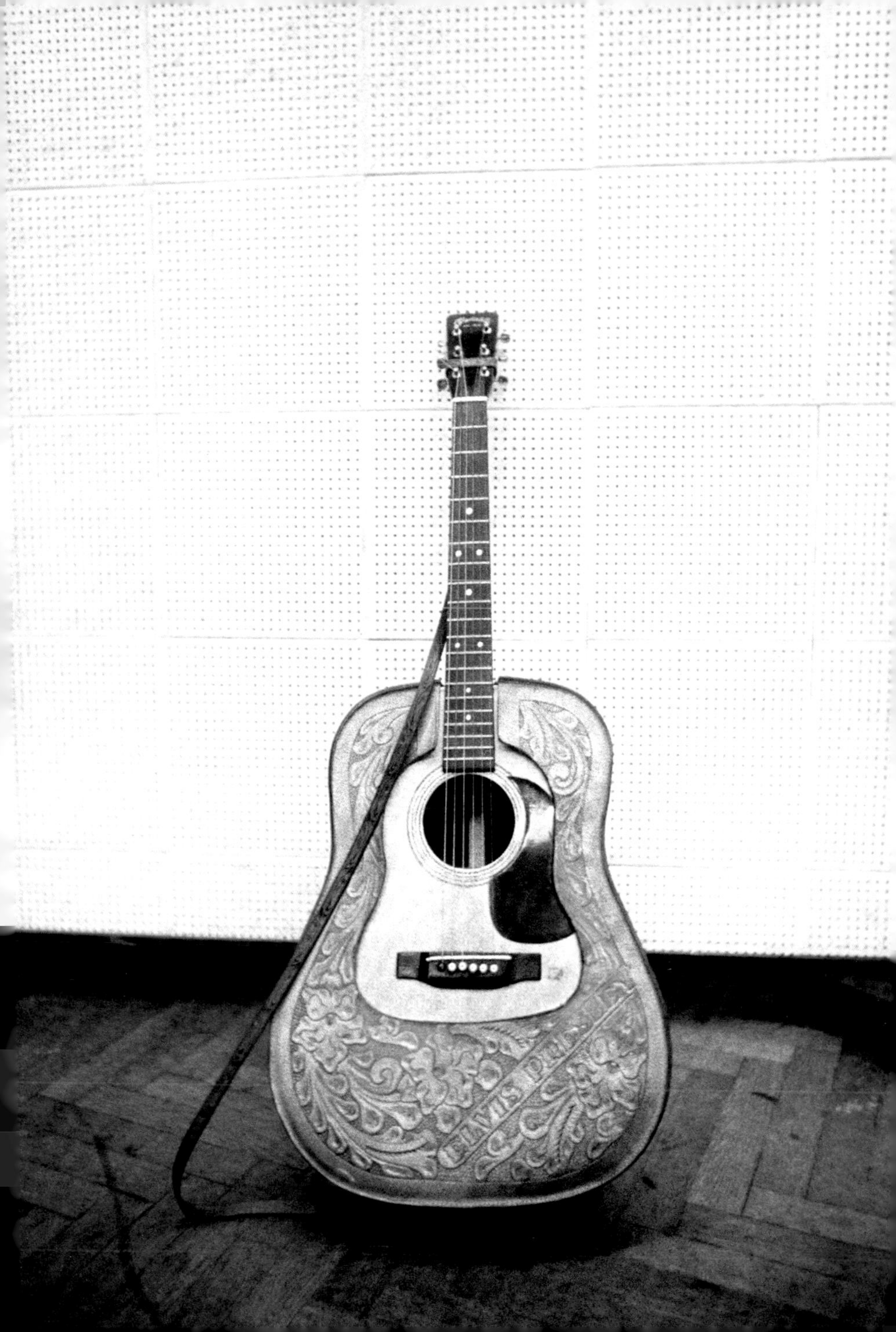
ELVIS PR

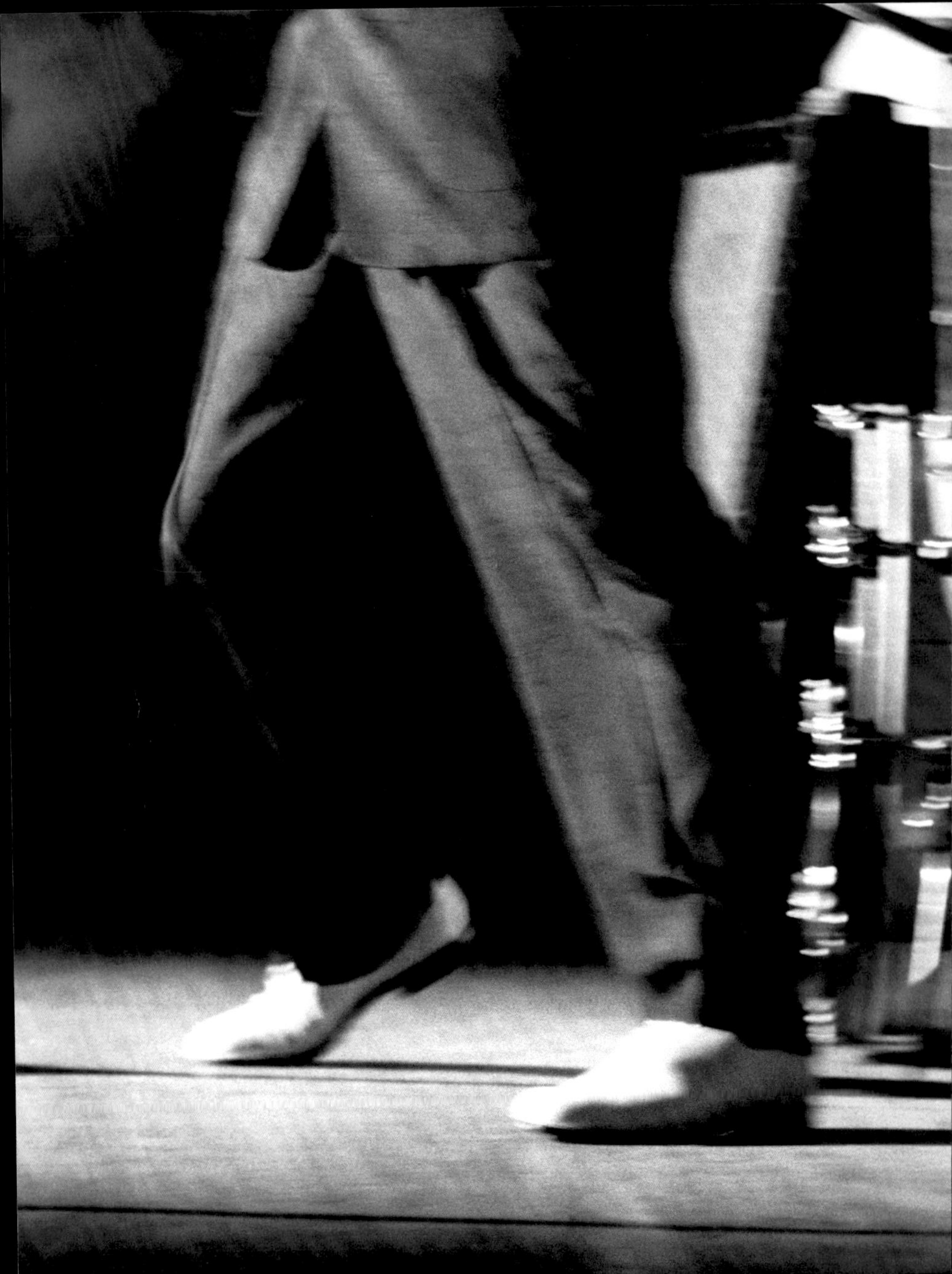

In the Beginning

★

ALFRED WERTHEIMER

THE YEAR WAS 1956, and I was working as a freelance photographer in New York City when RCA Victor publicist Anne Fulchino hired me to shoot a newly signed singer by the name of Elvis Presley. I remarked, "Elvis who?"

That was one of the last times anyone had to ask that question again. The 21-year-old singer shot to stardom shortly after I photographed him that Saturday night, March 17, on *Stage Show* hosted by Tommy and Jimmy Dorsey. Once I stumbled into that assignment and met Elvis, I felt that this guy had something that was unique, and had an interesting story that had to be told. So I followed him on the road and everywhere else for two weeks, taking over 2,500 photographs of the singer who would later be known to the world as the King of Rock and Roll.

Most of the time, Elvis never even knew I was taking his picture. He was laser-focused on whatever he did, so I would wait until he was engaged—and he was always immersed in being Elvis—whether rehearsing, flirting with women, combing his hair, buying a ring, or talking to his father about why the plumbing wasn't working and they had to fill the pool with a hose from the kitchen sink. Elvis gave me complete access to his life—I would even follow him into the bathroom.

My feeling was that the closer I could come to being a fly on the wall and still produce high-quality work, I didn't necessarily have to worry about what photographer Henri Cartier-Bresson called the "decisive

White Bucks, onstage at the Mosque Theater,
Richmond, Virginia, June 30, 1956.

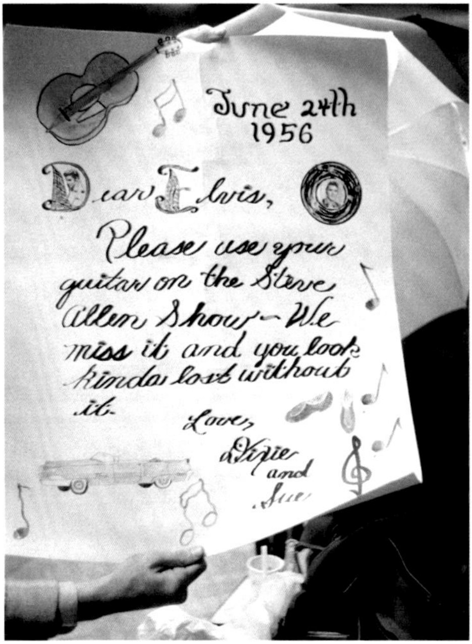

Scroll signed by fans, imploring Elvis to play his guitar on the show.

moment." I wanted to be an unobtrusive observer—like a good psychiatrist with a camera. Obviously, the decisive moment is graphically strong, but the moments before and after—those images are unusual and there's often a strangeness involved that I like. And from the thousands of pictures I took of Elvis, what I find most appealing are the immediate pre- and post-decisive moments.

I can recall Elvis busy washing up at the Warwick Hotel in New York—he had a towel over his shoulder, a toothbrush in his hand and toothpaste on the brush, and the water was running in the sink—and he's ready to stick the toothbrush in his mouth, in a pre-decisive moment that everyone who has ever brushed their teeth has experienced. And I just love that picture of Elvis with a couple of pimples on his back.

There are a lot of iconic images that came out of that bathroom session, pictures I wouldn't have ever captured had I not asked to follow Elvis into his inner sanctum. This was my first year in professional photography, and fortunately I didn't know any better. So as far as I was concerned, everything was fair game if Elvis would allow me in. I was experimenting and making up my rules as I went along, whatever it took to come up with some money shots that could be published.

Here I was with somebody who I didn't know was going to become famous. But I did know two things: I knew that he was not shy—I mean, Elvis was shy in the sense that he was introverted, but he was not shy to the camera. He permitted closeness. And when you get close there is a whole different dynamic to a picture. As I remember Robert Capa saying,

"If your pictures are boring, it means you're not close enough." Closeness allows you to capture a certain texture, which creates a presence and makes a photograph interesting. The other thing I knew that Elvis had in his favor was that he made the girls cry.

YOU'RE EITHER A NOTE TAKER, a writer, or, in my case, a photographer—an observer ready to freeze moments that you see and then piece them together. And it's not a simple process, because the subject does not tell you what he's doing. But it's just as well—because the moment it becomes a verbal process, it's no longer a visual process. The main subject does not know what you're going to do, because you do not know what you're going to do. You react to an event as it unfolds without having control over it.

As a photojournalist, the game that I would play with myself was, how can I not intrude on what the subject wants to do? And how can I keep the background organized not to interfere too much with foreground? And how can I compose it in such a way where I won't have a lot of ambiguity between the foreground and the background? That was my style, and this is just an example of how those things worked in my mind.

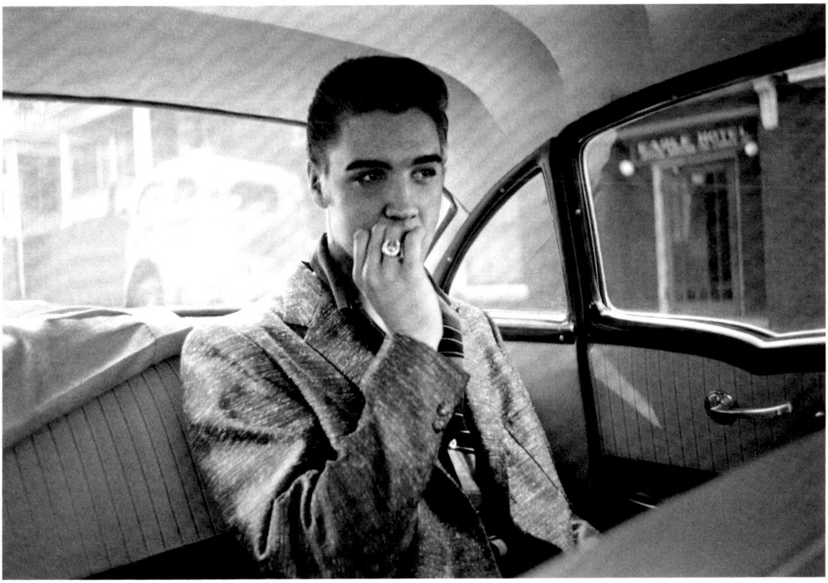

Taxi cab to the Jefferson Hotel, Richmond.

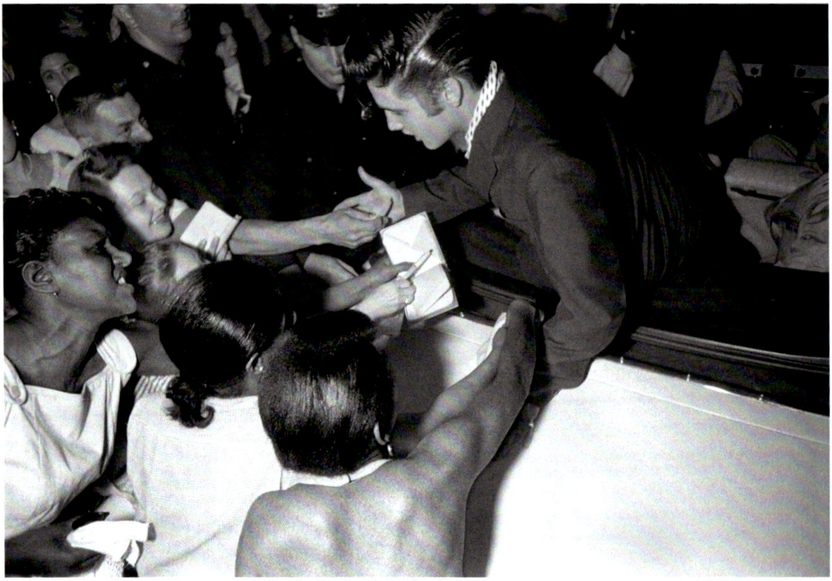

Photographers tend to practically engrave their photographs on their brains, or at least I do with most every image that has any significance. Some things appear in photographs that you don't see with your eyes. I mean photography picks up things that are not reality—they're photo-reality. For example, while shooting the concert at Russwood Park, somebody's flashbulb went off in the audience at the exact moment my shutter opened to photograph the crowd. It created a flare in my lens that produced a magnificent spray of light in front of Elvis and backlit the crowd. It's what Kodak tells you never to do, but it was a wonderful accident, and the photograph *Starburst* was born.

Another moment: On the 27-hour train ride to Memphis, Elvis was bored. In an attempt to entertain himself, he picked up a stuffed panda and put it on his left hip and walked down to the other end of the car. I picked up my camera and followed him. The passengers on the train didn't know what to make of Elvis. I mean, 21-year-old men don't normally walk around with four-foot pandas. But Elvis paid them no mind. Halfway back up the aisle he made a sharp left and looked two teenage girls straight in

Outside *The Steve Allen Show's* Hudson Theatre,
desperate fans reach for an autograph.

the eyes, and said, "Are you coming to my concert tonight?" Well, they said, "Who are you...what concert?" He then said, "I'm Elvis Presley, I have got a concert at Russwood Park." Well, they said, "How do we know you're Elvis Presley?" He said, "You see that photographer over there? Do you think he would be taking my picture if I wasn't Elvis Presley?" That whole time I had been standing on one of the seats shooting him chatting it up with the girls and that explanation seemed to satisfy them.

This was the young Elvis, the one who permitted closeness and might have said to himself, "Well, look, how is anybody ever going to know what I am all about if there is no record of me except my music? We're living in photographic times, so why not cooperate? After all, I don't even know when this guy is taking pictures." Every once in a while, if I was in his face, well then he would be aware, but in the whole collection there are only one or two pictures where Elvis was posing. The rest are just Elvis living his life—and all I was doing was recording that life. I wasn't asking him to do anything for me and he couldn't have cared less about somebody following him with a camera. I believe the uniqueness of my photographs of Elvis lies in the fact that I accepted he was the director of his own life.

YOU WILL FIND THAT WHEN people are intensely involved in something that's important to them, they're pretty much oblivious to the camera. That's when you get your best pictures, because your subjects are not hamming it up. If you can get in close and frame it properly with the available light and operate at slow shutter speeds—and manage not to trip over your own feet—you will get what I find to be very interesting photographs.

I used two 35mm split range-finder black Nikon S-2 cameras to shoot Elvis—one with a 105mm lens and the other with a 35mm lens. I think I used supplemental light in only 25 or 30 photographs. I stayed away from using a flash for the most part, because I thought that the flash effect was always so artificial. It kills the mood and the tonality of the lighting that exists. Since I was more or less into the available-light category of photography, I coined the phrase, "available-darkness photography," with the idea that you can find people in their more natural state the darker the place they're in. For example, if you go into a bar, people will be a lot more themselves than they would in a fluorescent-lit office. It's just the way it is!

I was basically self-taught in photography, except for one class I took from Josef Breitenbach at Cooper Union, during which time I experimented with what I like to call the New York Ashcan School of Photography. Once I had a camera in my hand, I had no shame. I was fearless. Without a camera, I was a milquetoast…

I admired the work of W. Eugene Smith—he was one of my heroes. So were David Douglas Duncan, Margaret Bourke-White, Dorothea Lange, and the whole Stryker group during the WPA (Works Progress Administration) days. I was intrigued by the photographs of Walker Evans, and if you go back a way, certainly Talbot, Daguerre, Mathew Brady, and Muybridge—and by all means the master of them all, whom I didn't discover until years after I got into photography, Erich Salomon. However, it was my good friend Paul Schutzer—another photographer who was killed in the Gaza Strip working for *Life* magazine covering the Six-Day War—who introduced me to Anne Fulchino. She was my connection to Elvis.

In 1956 I was not publishing my work very much, but I did go back to photograph Elvis one last time in September of 1958 when he was in the Army and giving a press conference before shipping out on the troop ship USS *Randall*, from the Brooklyn Port of Embarkation for Germany with 6,000 other soldiers. It was the last time I saw him.

Thereafter, I got into motion picture camera work, where I covered the 1960 John F. Kennedy–Richard Nixon presidential election, was a staff cinematographer for Granada Television, and later, a cameraman for the original Woodstock Music Festival. The irony of all this is that I did not get one single phone call for an Elvis Presley photograph for 19 years from the time I last saw him alive until the day he died, on August 16, 1977.

That day I got a call from Robert Pledge of Contact Press Images, a photo agency in New York, who suggested I go see John Durniak at *Time* magazine with my photographs of Elvis. When all was said and done he wanted an exclusive for one week before any other publication would get their hands on my work. For this he was willing to pay what I considered a huge sum of money for 1977. It was more money than I made on all of my Elvis Presley photos in the previous 21 years. I believe when the artist dies, then the public wants to know!

Two years after Elvis's death my first book on the subject was published and my work has been all about Elvis ever since—it's been the longest assignment of my life.

Elvis returns to the Warwick Hotel between the afternoon rehearsal and evening performance of *Stage Show*, March 17, 1956.

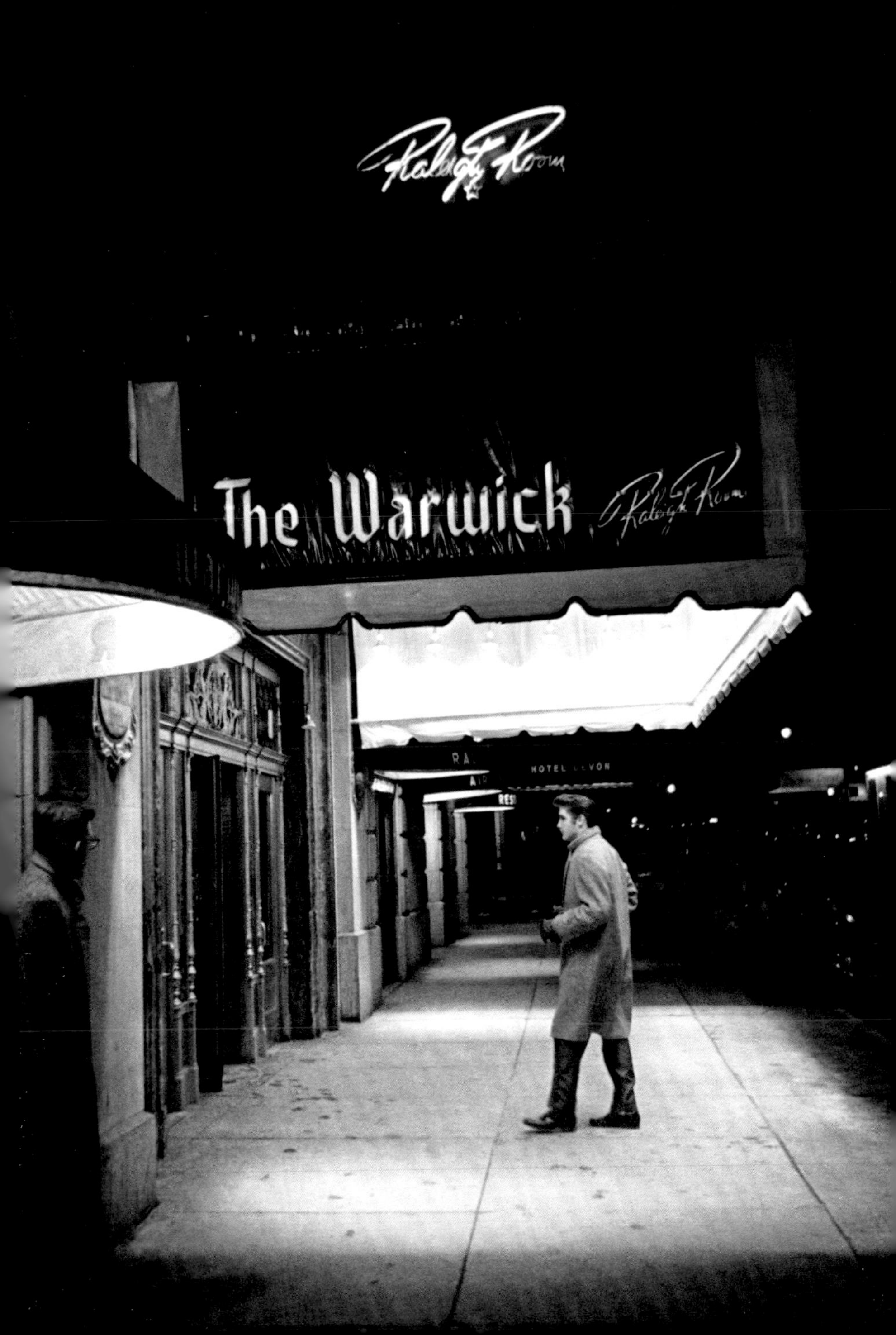
Raleigh Room
The Warwick
Raleigh Room
HOTEL DEVON

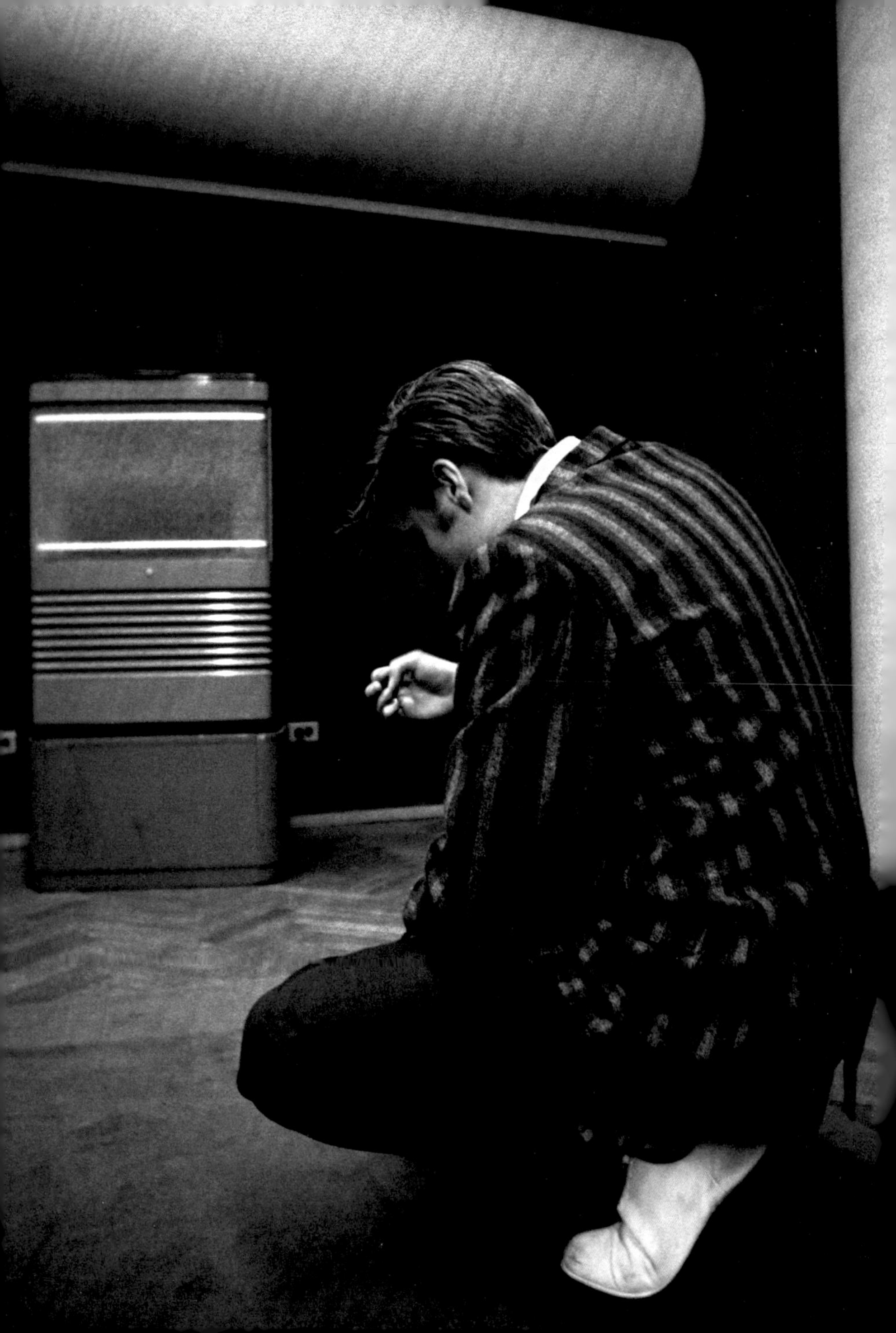

Elvis: The Life and Legacy

★

ROBERT SANTELLI

THEY CALLED HIM THE KING OF ROCK AND ROLL. Elvis Presley, the young man with the swiveling hips and sexy smile, the one who put the music on the map and unleashed a cultural revolution that changed the world. More a rebel than a royal, he rose up against conformity and sneered at popular convention. He used music to punch a hole through both poverty and prejudice. With those looks, that voice, and a bucking restlessness that made every song he sang an anxious statement about a changing America, he blazed the path we were all bound to follow.

Until 1956 Elvis was hardly known by America outside the South, where for the past couple of years he'd been barnstorming with his band, melting girls' hearts, testing the laws of decency (at least that's what civic leaders and pastors claimed), and generally remaking the arch and angles of American music. In January of that year, RCA Victor Records, the New York–based recording company that now had him under contract, released "Heartbreak Hotel," a shivering, seductive tale of primitive rock-and-roll angst, and with it, The Year of Elvis officially began. Over the ensuing months, RCA released more Presley singles—all of them racking up record sales. Hollywood beckoned and Elvis became a movie star. By year's end, the young singer was a millionaire, rock and roll had taken up residence on the pop charts, and America's youth felt the tug of change and the stirrings of freedom.

Listening to a playback at
RCA Victor Studio 1.

There with his camera to capture Elvis's most precious moments—those we'd come to cherish, thanks to the startling pictures he made—was the photographer Alfred Wertheimer. Though he knew next to nothing about this young singer when first assigned the task of taking photos of Elvis—except that he made an exceptional subject to shoot—Wertheimer would document his meteoric rise like no one else. The pictures are beautiful and revealing, historic and artistic. They resonate with Presley's youthful passion, and pose the question: If Elvis had not come along, what would have become of America?

ELVIS PRESLEY WAS BORN POOR IN TUPELO, Mississippi, on January 8, 1935, in the midst of the Great Depression. The only child of Gladys and Vernon Presley, young Elvis loved the gospel, blues, country, and pop sounds he heard as a boy. His family scraped by, its condition made worse when Vernon went to prison for writing bad checks. Young Elvis found solace in the music he heard on the radio and blaring from churches and juke joints. When the Presley family moved to Memphis in 1948, eager for a new start, Elvis took his love of music with him, for now it was deep within his soul, searching for a release.

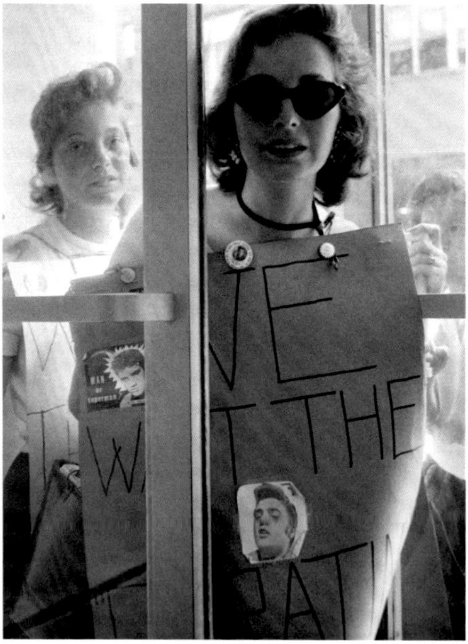

Fans speak out: "We want Elvis on TV with his guitar—not without it."

Elvis took advantage of his new surroundings. Beale Street—where black bluesmen, gamblers, loan sharks, con men, and hookers plied their trades— fascinated him. He graduated from Humes High School in 1953 and got a job driving a truck for Crown Electric. But music was always on his mind. He embraced the blues and rhythm and blues

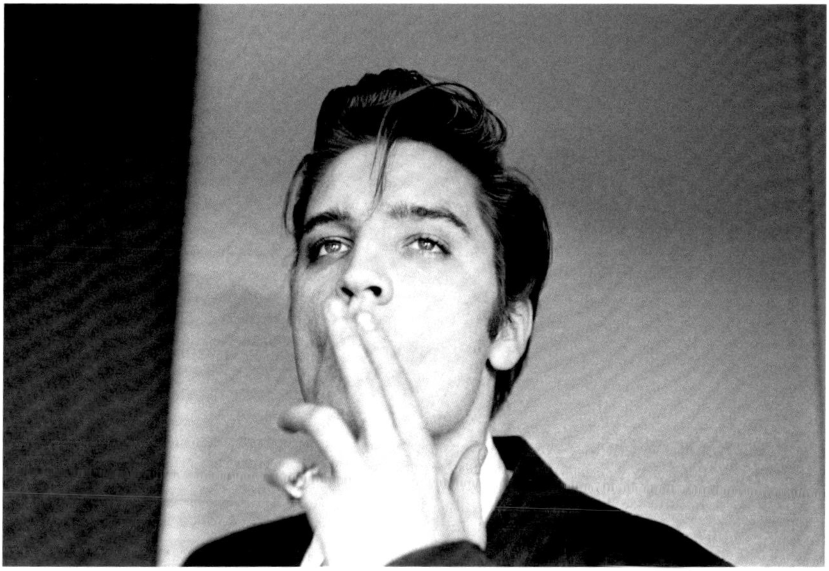

and felt the sacred touch of both black and white gospel. He sang and strummed some simple guitar chords, but he never could have thought or even dreamed of what was to come.

In July 1954, he entered the Memphis Recording Service on Union Avenue, where less than a year earlier he had cut two songs that he made into a record for his mother. Studio owner Sam Phillips took special notice of the handsome, pompadoured young man who was white, but sang black. Phillips, barely making ends meet, thought that just maybe the Presley kid was the ticket for which he'd been hoping. That hot summer, Phillips brought Elvis back to his studio, along with honky-tonk musicians Scotty Moore, who played guitar, and Bill Black, a bass player. Together, the three stumbled upon a sound so rich and new that it couldn't be described in conventional terms. Part blues and part country, with gospel strains running through Elvis's vocals, this hybrid music was like nothing anyone had ever heard before. Sam Phillips had no name for it; neither did Elvis or Scotty or Bill. Not long after, it would be defined as rock and roll, but that July in Memphis it sounded like musical sex.

Heading back to Memphis from New York City on the Southern Railway, Elvis, in animated pose, July 3, 1956.

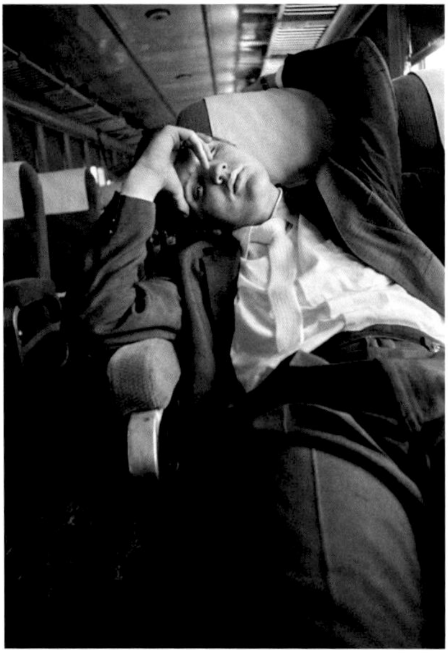 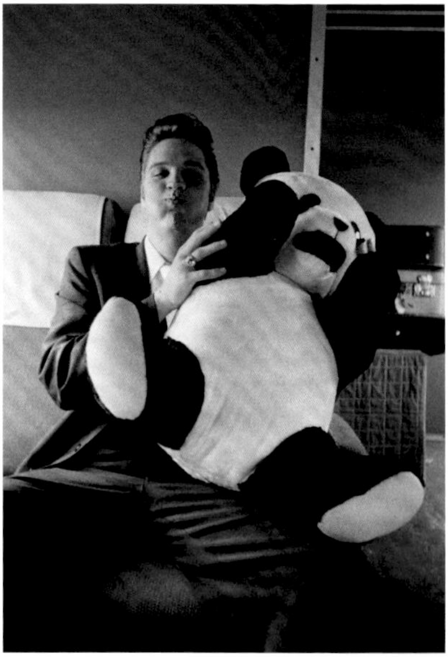

That historic turn at the Memphis Recording Service was presented to the rest of America when Phillips released Presley's versions of "That's Alright Mama" (written by bluesman "Big Boy" Arthur Crudup) and "Blue Moon of Kentucky" (written by country bluegrass pioneer Bill Monroe) on his small, independent Sun Records label. Prior to Elvis, most of those who recorded for Sun were black blues singers, and the label barely made money. When Elvis sang his special kind of blues with a country twist, the songs shed their earlier identities and simply rocked. There was no other way to put it or say it: They rocked. Things would never be the same.

RCA Victor Records only heard the sound of the cash register ringing when they offered Sam Phillips the then-unheard-of sum of $35,000 for Presley's contract, plus $5,000 more so Elvis could buy a Cadillac for his beloved mother. Everyone benefited. Presley released his first RCA singles in early 1956; by year's end, he had earned a million dollars, his name was on the lips and in the dreams of every American adolescent female, and he was known simply as Elvis. The hits rolled from the recording studio to the radio and finally onto record players across America: "I Want You, I Need

Hours into the journey, Elvis drifted between sleep, reading, and clowning around with a giant stuffed panda. The 27-hour ride to Memphis, Tennessee, ran from July 3 to July 4, 1956.

You, I Love You"; "Hound Dog"; "Don't Be Cruel"; and "Love Me Tender." They all shot to number one. Elvis performed on *The Ed Sullivan Show*, the Dorsey Brothers' *Stage Show*, and *The Steve Allen Show*. The country buzzed Elvis Presley.

He made his acting debut in the movie *Love Me Tender*. Being on the big screen only elevated his star status. That he couldn't really act mattered little. His part in the film only confirmed what most of teen America already knew: Elvis was a hunk, a heartthrob. Teenage boys wanted to be like him; girls just plain wanted him. Elvis's hits continued in the late '50s, but by this time there were plenty more young rock and roll stars competing for the same spotlight that once shone only on him. Still, Elvis was the King. When he traded his slick-combed jet-black hair for a GI crew cut in 1958 and shipped off to Germany, his fans still got their share of Elvis music, thanks to the shrewd work of his manager, Colonel Tom Parker. Maintaining Elvis's fan base was Parker's number one priority while his boy served Uncle Sam, and he saw to it that Elvis had stockpiled plenty of songs before heading to boot camp.

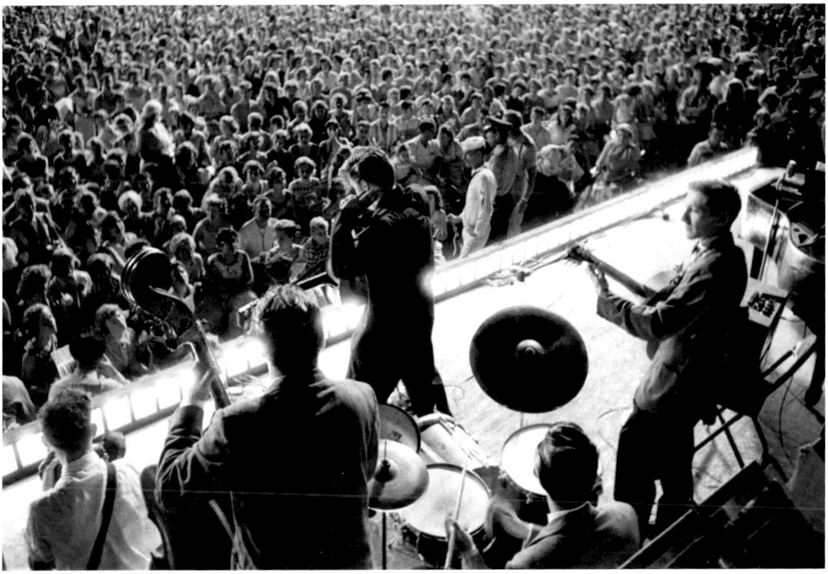

Russwood Park, July 4, 1956. Among the audience were Elvis's parents, Gladys and Vernon, uncle Vespa, grandmother Minnie Mae, and ex-girlfriend Barbara Hearn, who watched from the side of the stage.

WHEN PRESLEY BECAME A CIVILIAN AGAIN, rock and roll had changed, and so had he. Rather than regain the music territory he once exclusively ruled, Elvis spent most of his creative time making movies, few of them good. The Beatles, the Rolling Stones, the Beach Boys, Bob Dylan, Motown, and many more had inspired a new generation of music fans to press past Elvis, as "rock and roll" became simply "rock" and fueled a new revolution—one far more potent than anything witnessed in the 1950s.

Elvis returned for one more magical music moment. It occurred on television in 1968, seven years after his last public performance. History calls it the "Comeback Special." It was certainly special; his performance recalled the raw exuberance of his early sound and proved it could still topple giants. Suddenly Elvis was with us again, but he didn't stay, despite three more hit singles the following year: "In the Ghetto," "Suspicious Minds," and "Don't Cry Daddy." His voice was still crisp, but it had lost the magic. He toured the U.S. and sold out everywhere, and he even had one more number one album in 1973. But Elvis was more relic than rocker. Fans came for the memories. There was little else Elvis could give them.

On August 16, 1977, he was found dead in a bathroom of his lavish home, Graceland. Congestive heart failure was the official culprit. He was just 42 years old. From that point on, the myth took over. America and the rest of the world grieved, and when the tears dried Elvis was bigger than ever. His records rebounded to the top of the charts, documentaries gave us new insight into the fallen star, and Graceland became the most visited residence in America, other than the White House.

Today when we hear his music or see photographs of him—especially the realism and intimacy found in Wertheimer's photographs of the beginning of Elvis's career in 1956—it brings us back to another place and time. Wertheimer's photographs not only document a crucial year in Elvis's storied career, but they also capture the metamorphosis of pop music and the cultural transformation of America. Rich with raw emotion and uncut honesty, Wertheimer's images show Elvis unguarded and innocent, confident and scared, sexy and silly. We would never see him like that again, and without these photos we'd never have had that inside view of his life at all—and for that we have Al Wertheimer to thank.

Back home with his family in Memphis on the Fourth of July, Elvis signs autographs for neighbors while sitting on his Harley-Davidson, 1034 Audubon Drive.

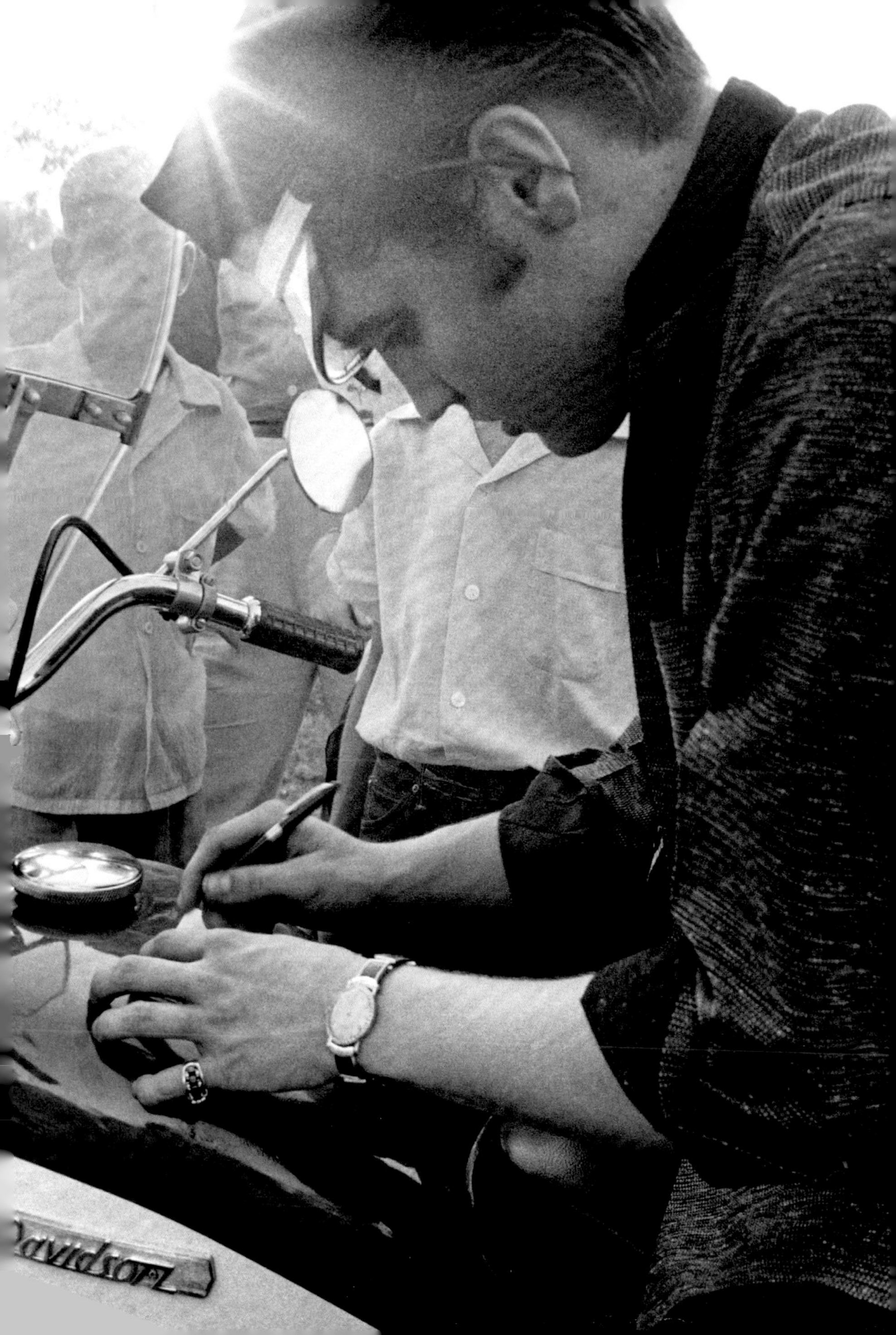

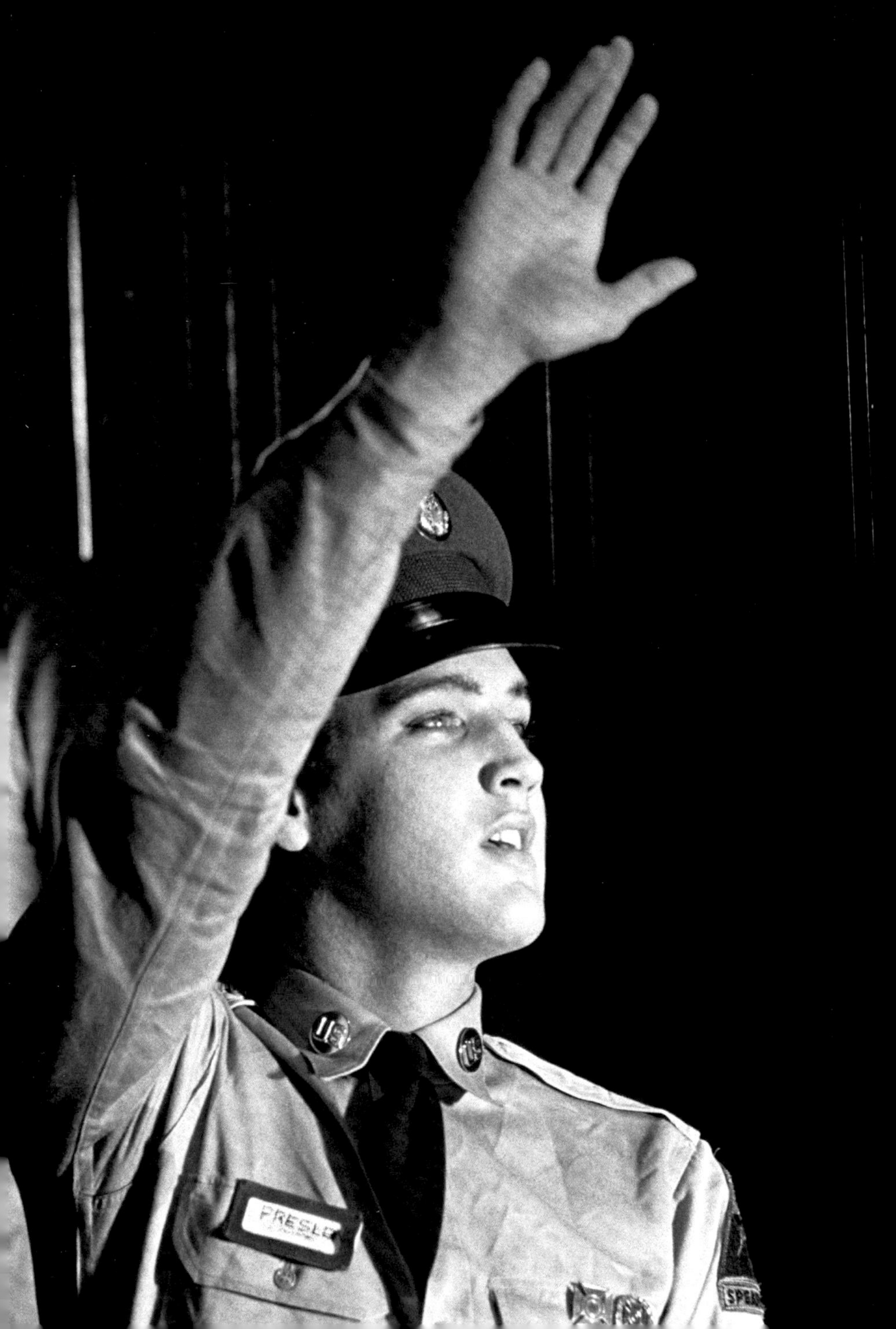

It all happened so fast till,
I don't know, I'm afraid to wake up, afraid
it's liable to be a dream, you know.

ELVIS PRESLEY
Robinson Auditorium, Little Rock, Arkansas,
May 16, 1956

Private Presley waves to the crowd. This would be the last day Wertheimer would see his subject.

ELVIS PRESLEY

THE DORSEY BROTHERS

STAGE SHOW

CBS STUDIO 50

MARCH 17, 1956

NEW YORK CITY

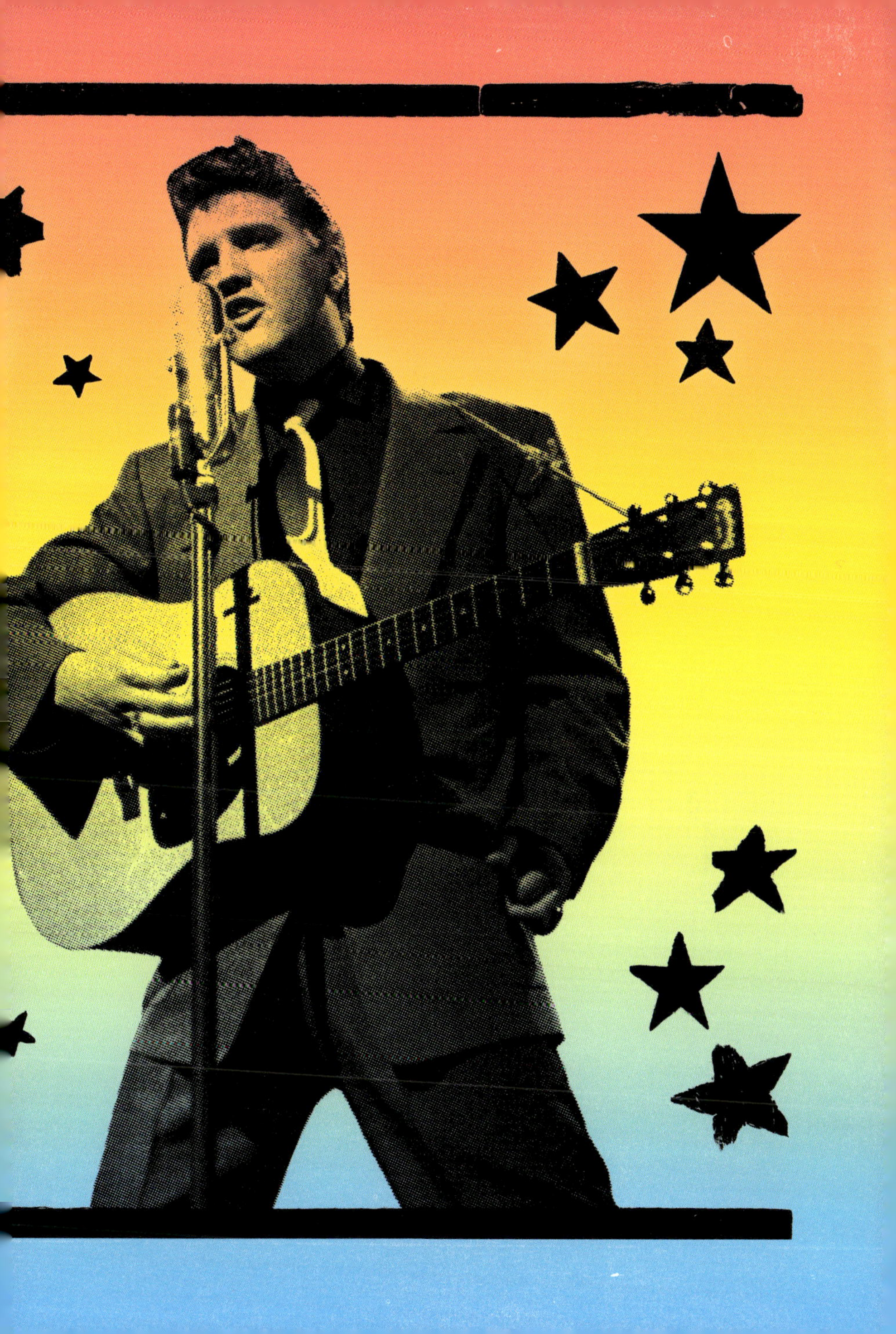

ANNE FULCHINO OF RCA VICTOR'S POP RECORD DIVISION called me to photograph some publicity shots of Elvis Presley during his performance on *Stage Show*, a variety show hosted by Tommy and Jimmy Dorsey. My first words were "Elvis who?" Despite this reaction, I headed down to CBS's Studio 50 to meet the singer and watch him rehearse "Heartbreak Hotel" and "Blue Suede Shoes." The studio was packed. Joining Elvis were his guitar player Scotty Moore, bass player Bill Black, drummer D.J. Fontana, the June Taylor Dancers, magicians, and the complete Dorsey band of at least 30 musicians. Let's not forget the publicity people, reporters, and an entourage of production staff. As I said in the preface to this book, what I learned about Elvis that day was that he permitted closeness. He wasn't shy to the camera. I was able to shoot him up close: during rehearsal, with the ring salesman, back at the Warwick Hotel, reading fan mail, and falling asleep before taking a shower. Closeness is the difference between being able to get a good photograph versus an ordinary one. I then followed him on his return to the theater, and to shoot his final performance.

Stage door, CBS TV Studio 50, New York City.

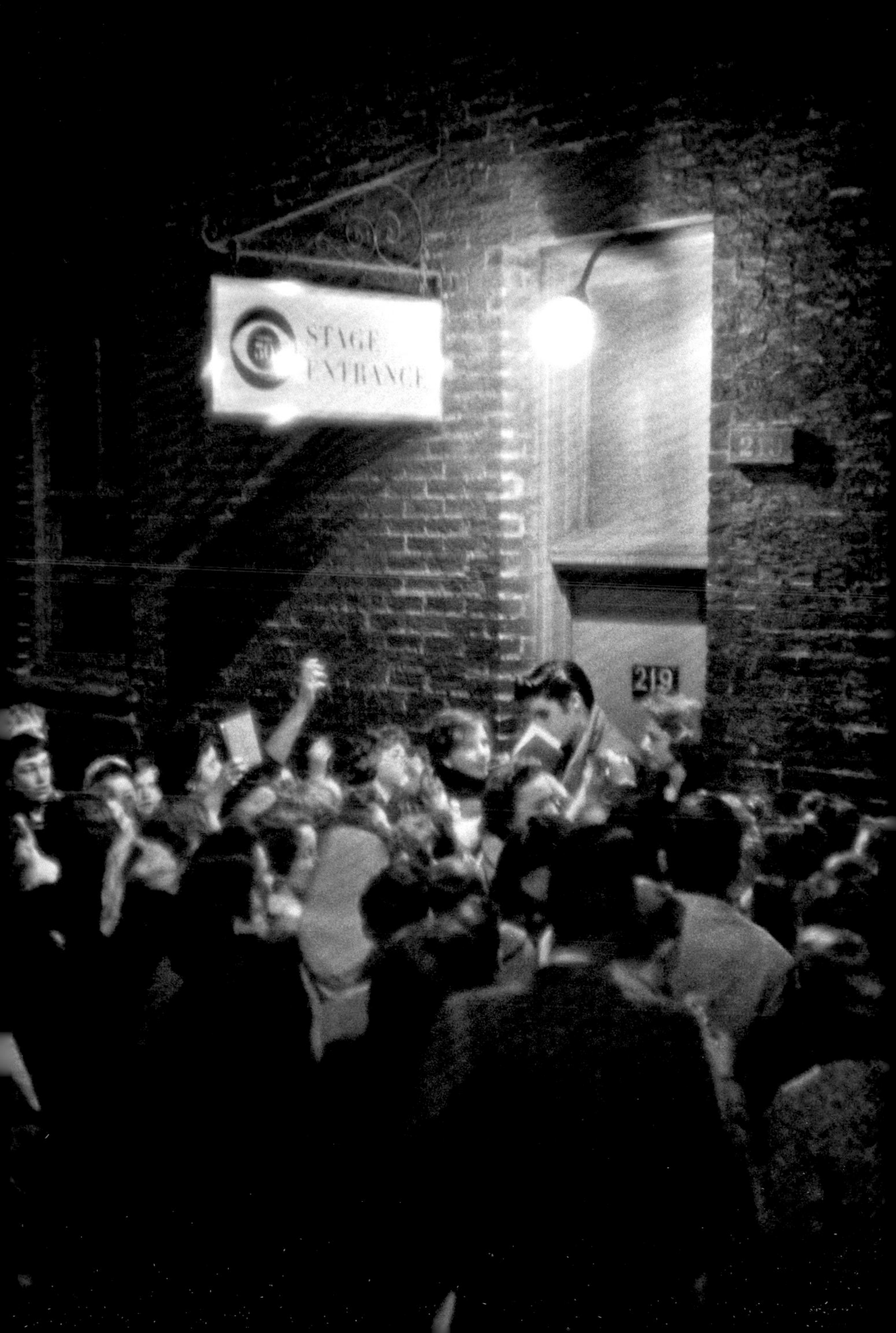
STAGE
ENTRANCE
219

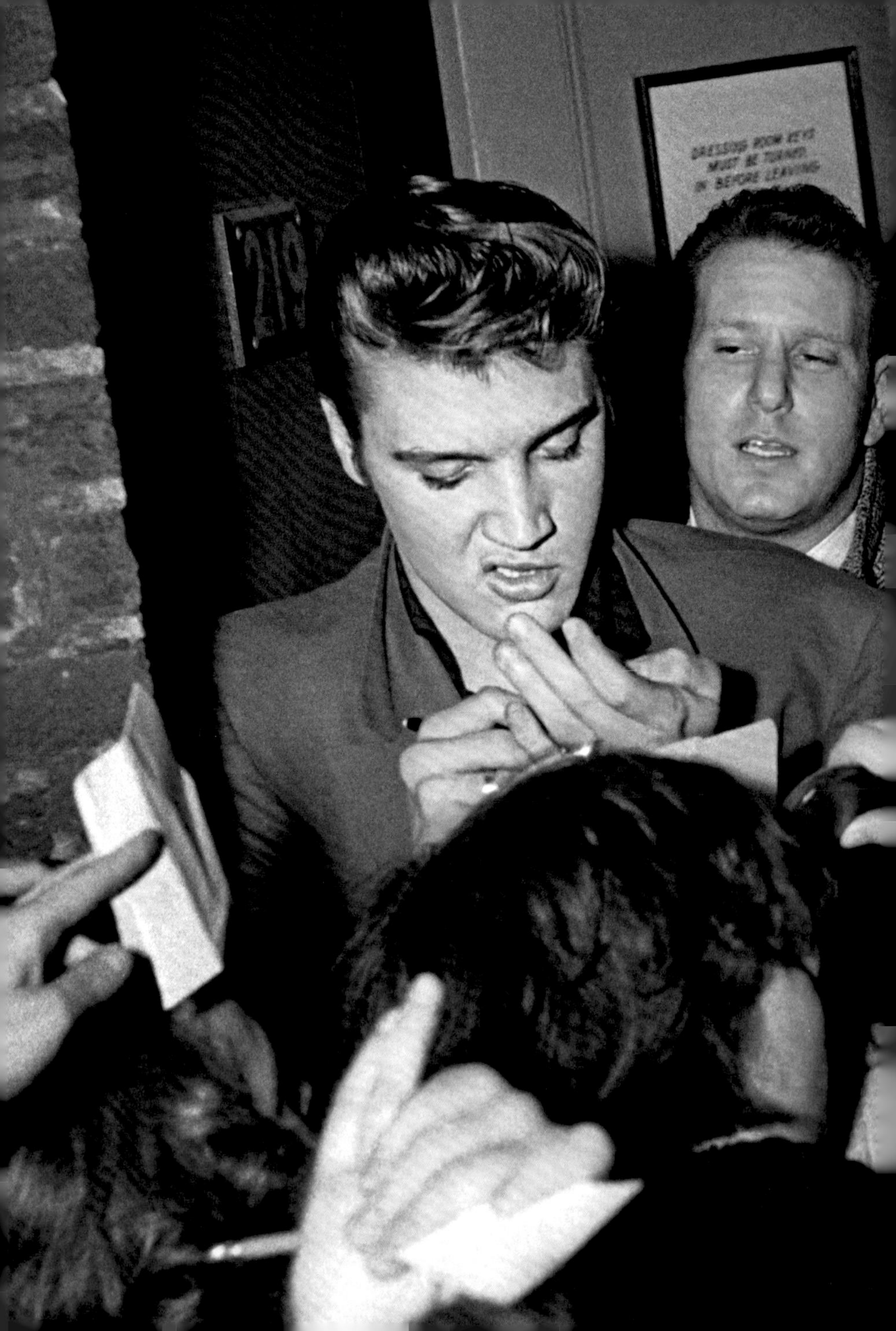

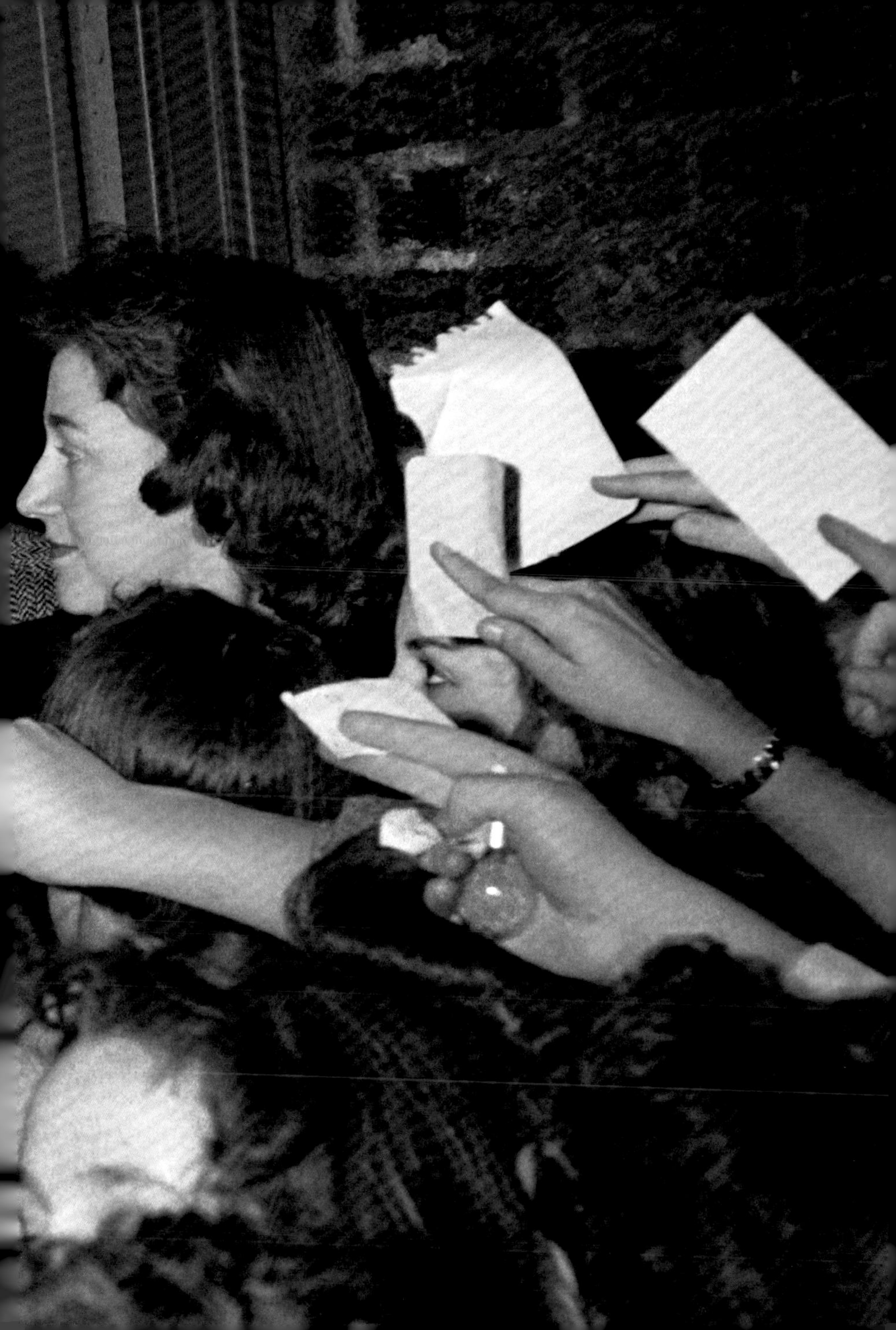

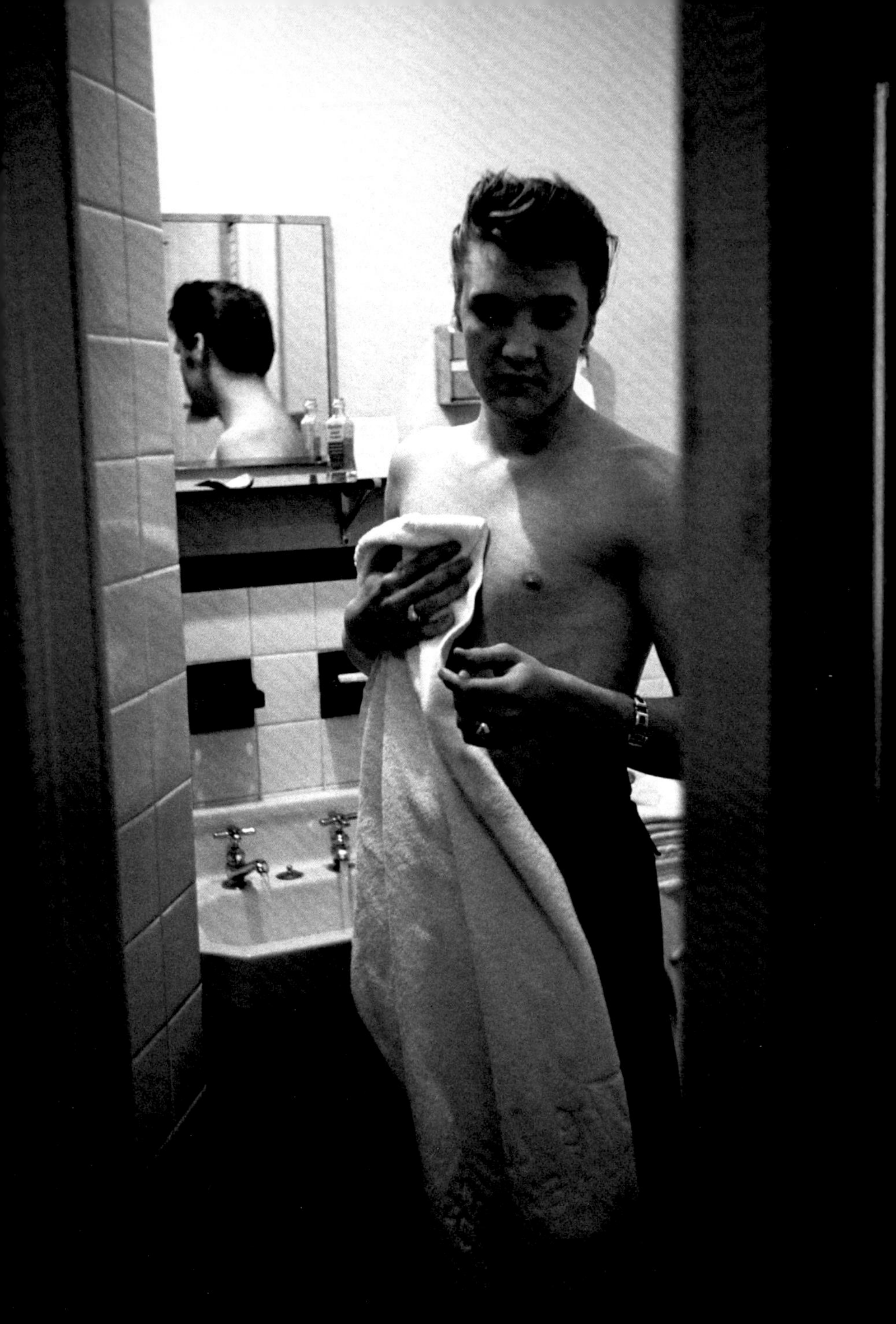

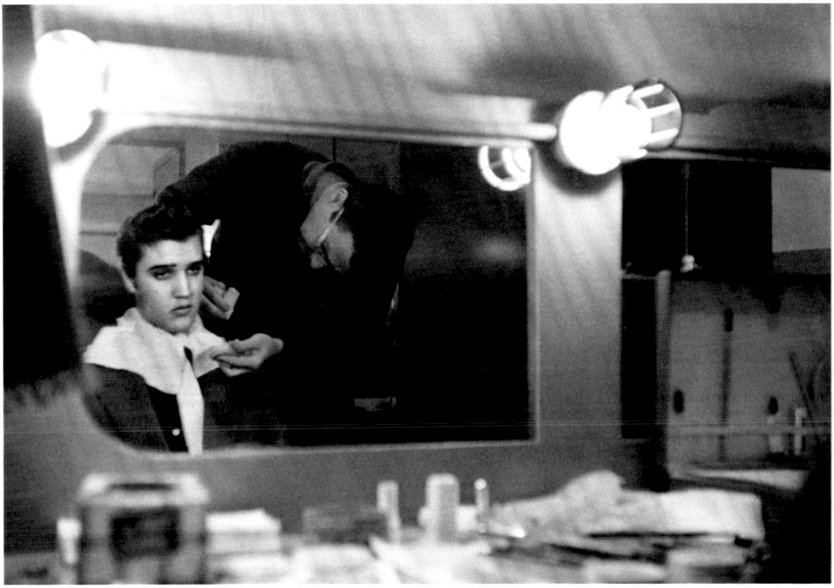

PREVIOUS SPREAD
Elvis delivers autographs and his trademark sneer to the crowd. First booked by producer Jackie Gleason to appear on the show on January 28, 1956, Elvis was so popular that five more appearances were lined up for February and March.

OPPOSITE
Backstage, CBS TV Studio 50.

ABOVE
Elvis gets made up for the dress rehearsal of *Stage Show*.

FOLLOWING SPREAD
Shopping for shirts at the Supreme Men's Shop on Broadway, New York City.

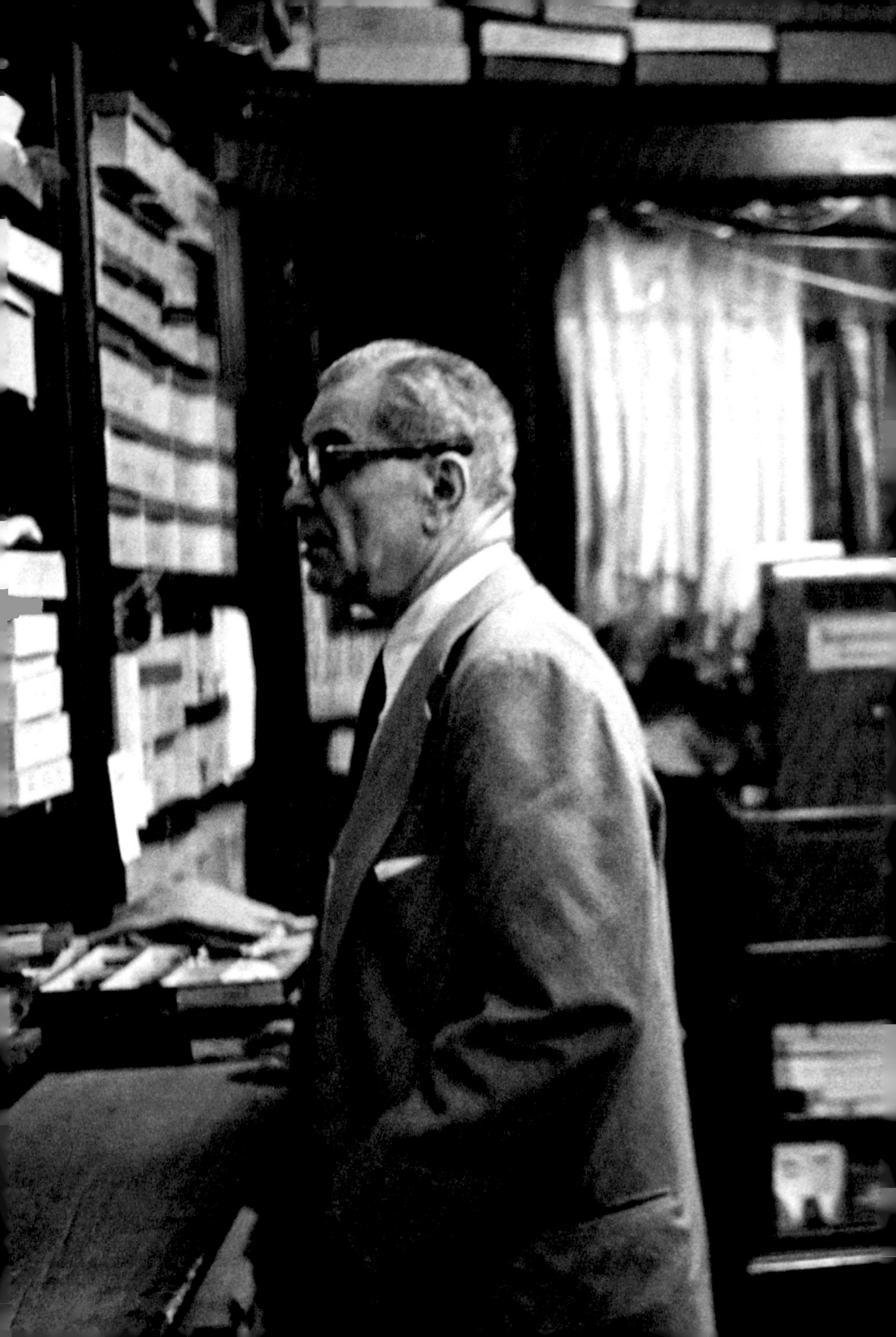

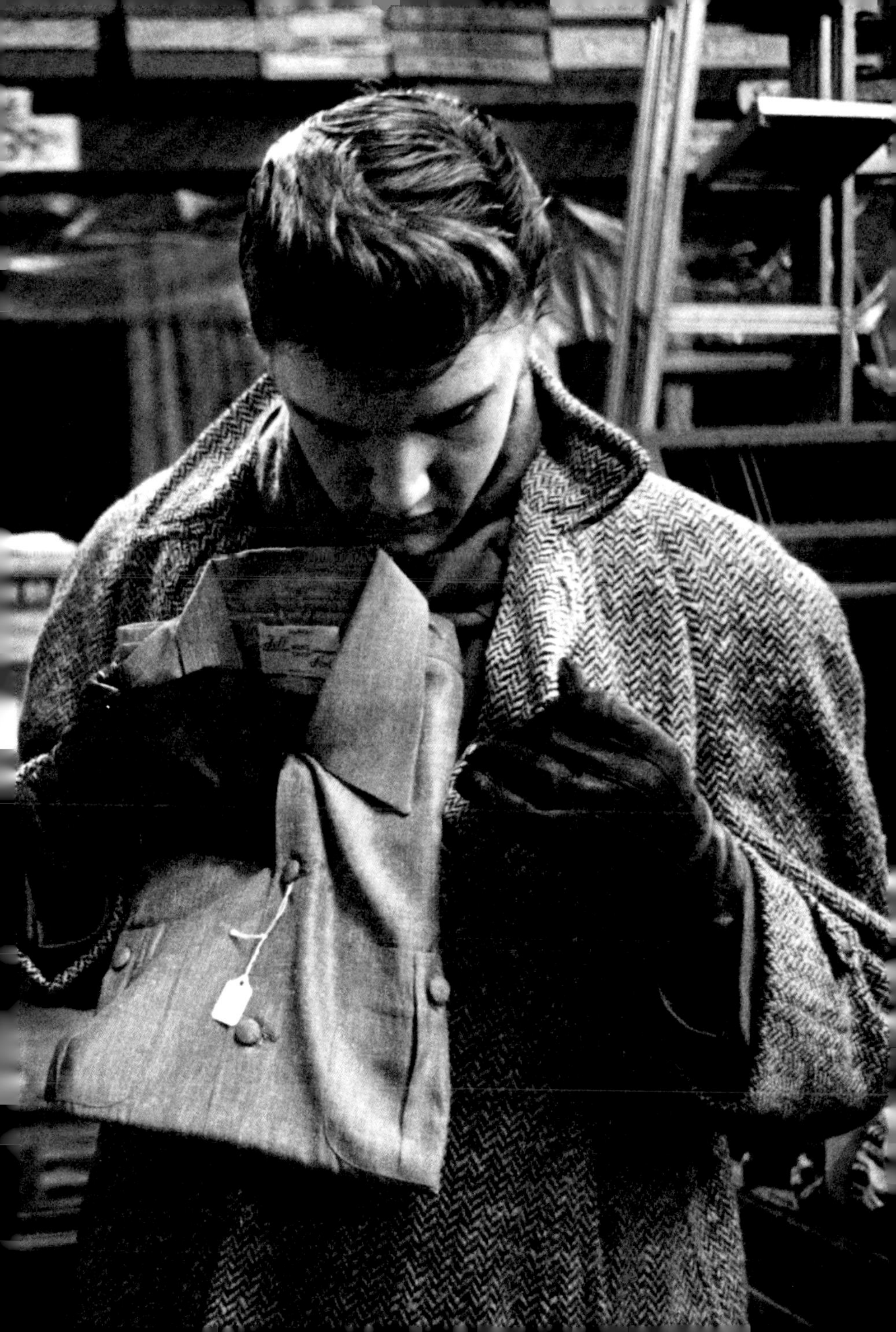

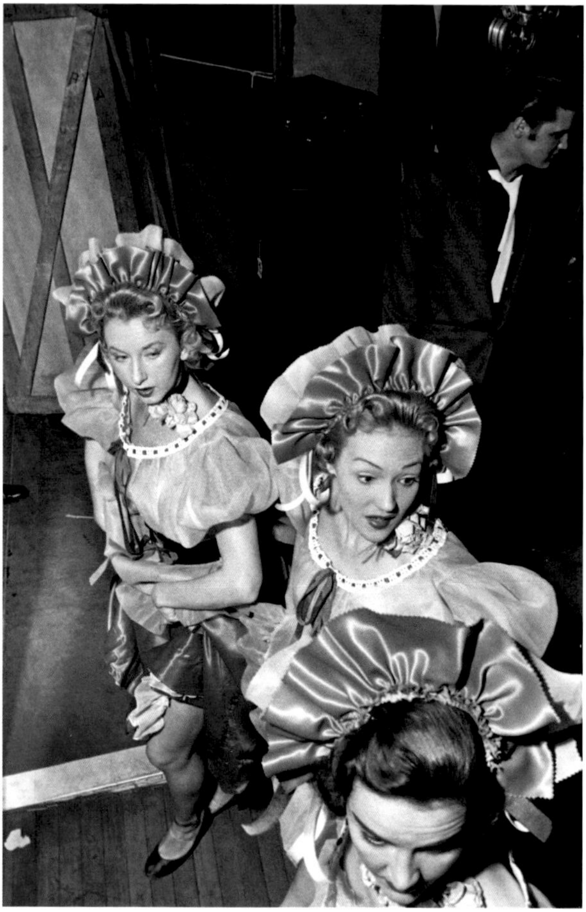

ABOVE
The June Taylor Dancers, who were favorites of producer Jackie Gleason, backstage at *Stage Show*.

OPPOSITE
Between the acts, Elvis gives the photographer a smile.

FOLLOWING SPREAD
Cue cards set the pace during the run-through.

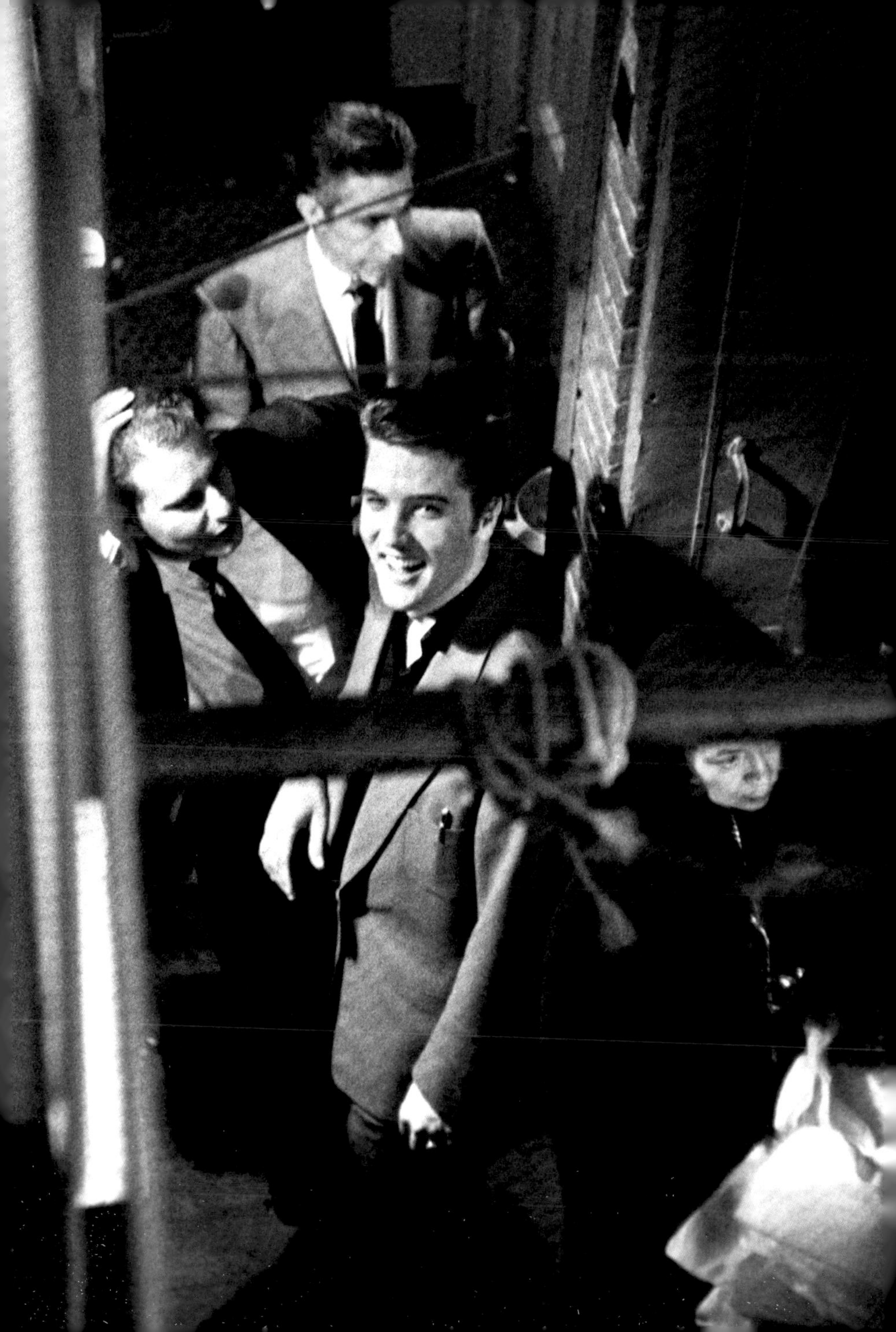

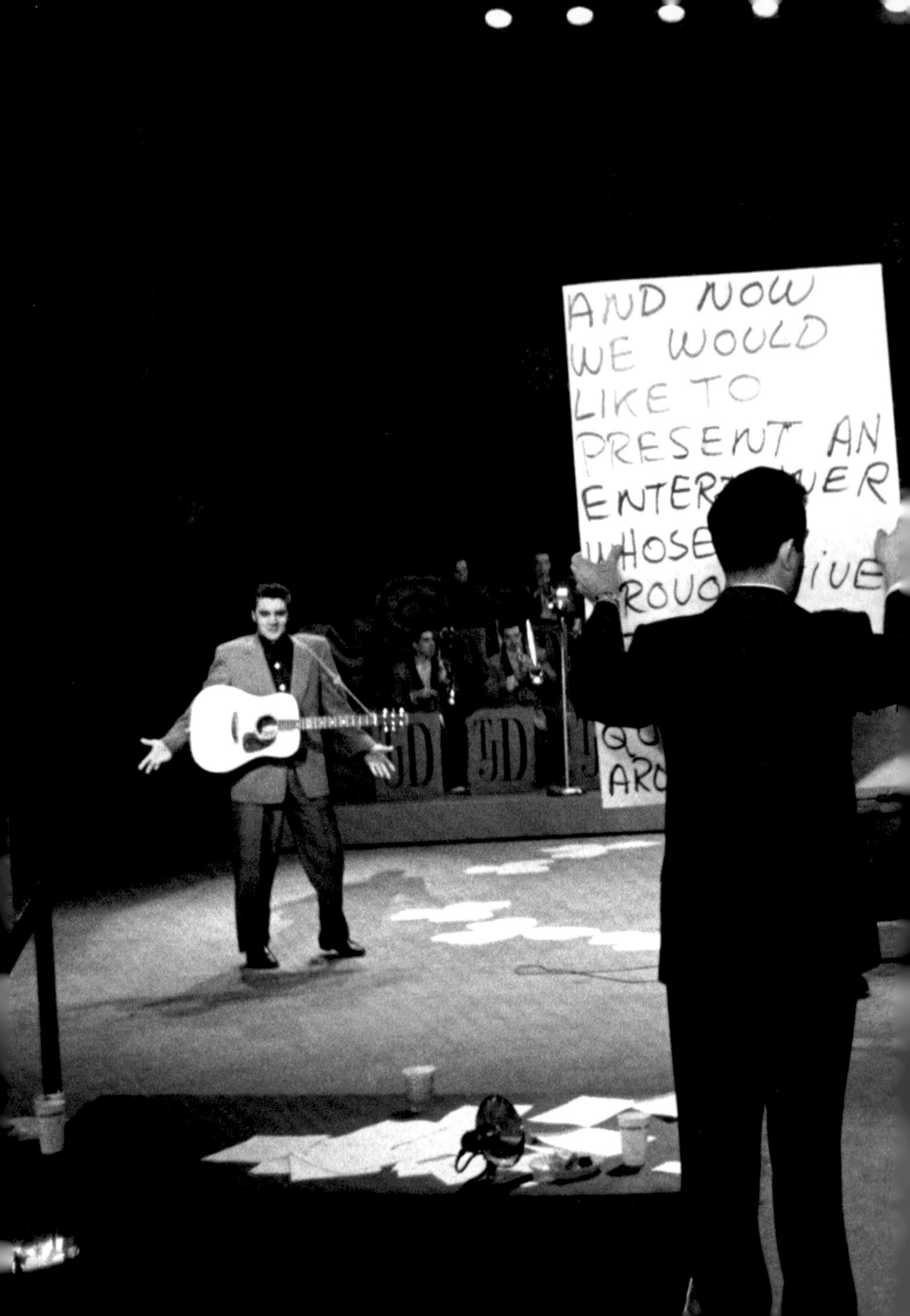
AND NOW
WE WOULD
LIKE TO
PRESENT AN

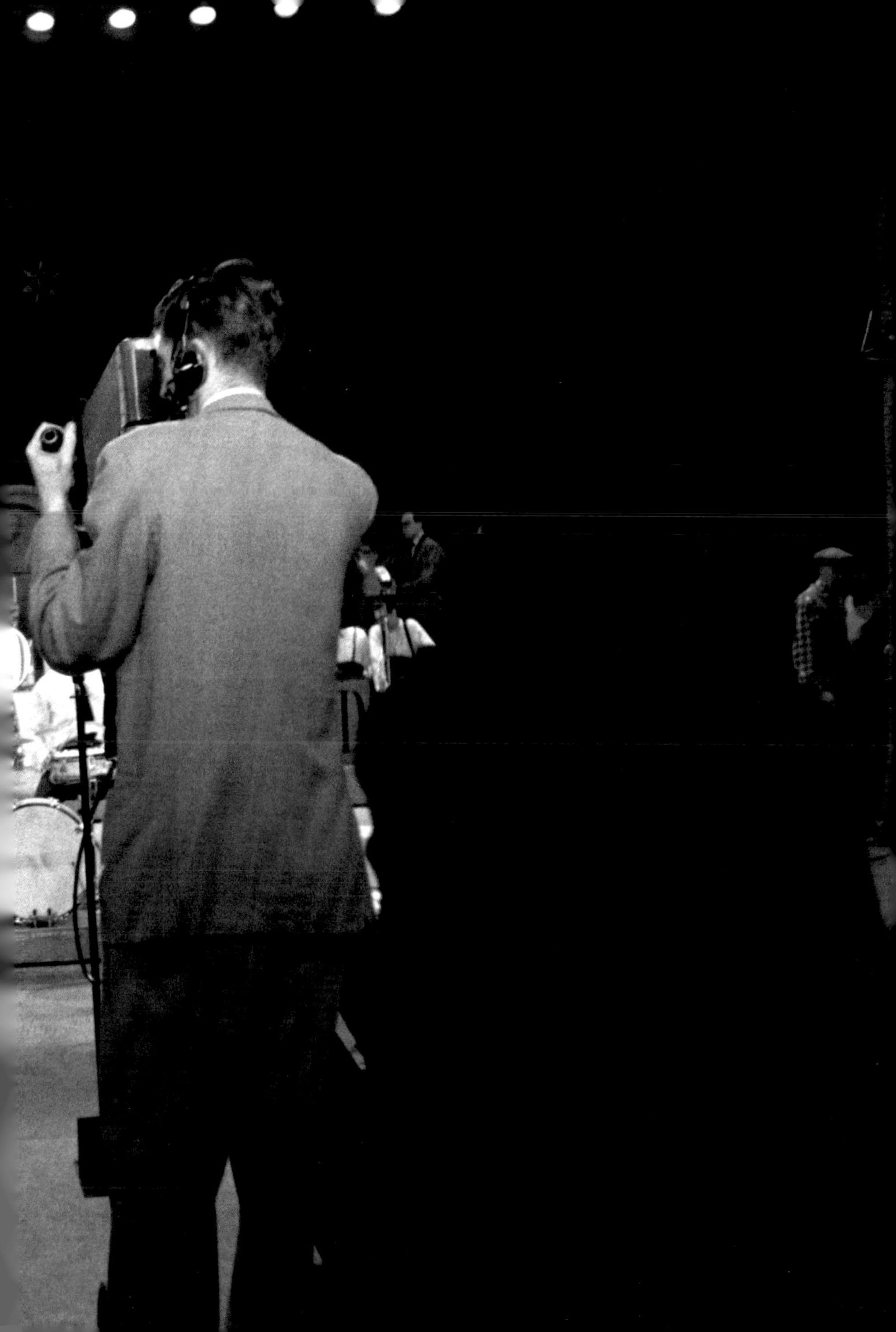

Without Elvis none of us could have made it.

BUDDY HOLLY

My crushing ambition in life was to be like Elvis Presley.

JOHN LENNON

OPPOSITE
Stand By, *Stage Show* rehearsal, New York City, March 17, 1956.

FOLLOWING SPREAD
His necktie now on for the cameras and live audience, Elvis performs "Heartbreak Hotel" and "Blue Suede Shoes" with Scotty Moore, Bill Black on bass, and D.J. Fontana on drums.

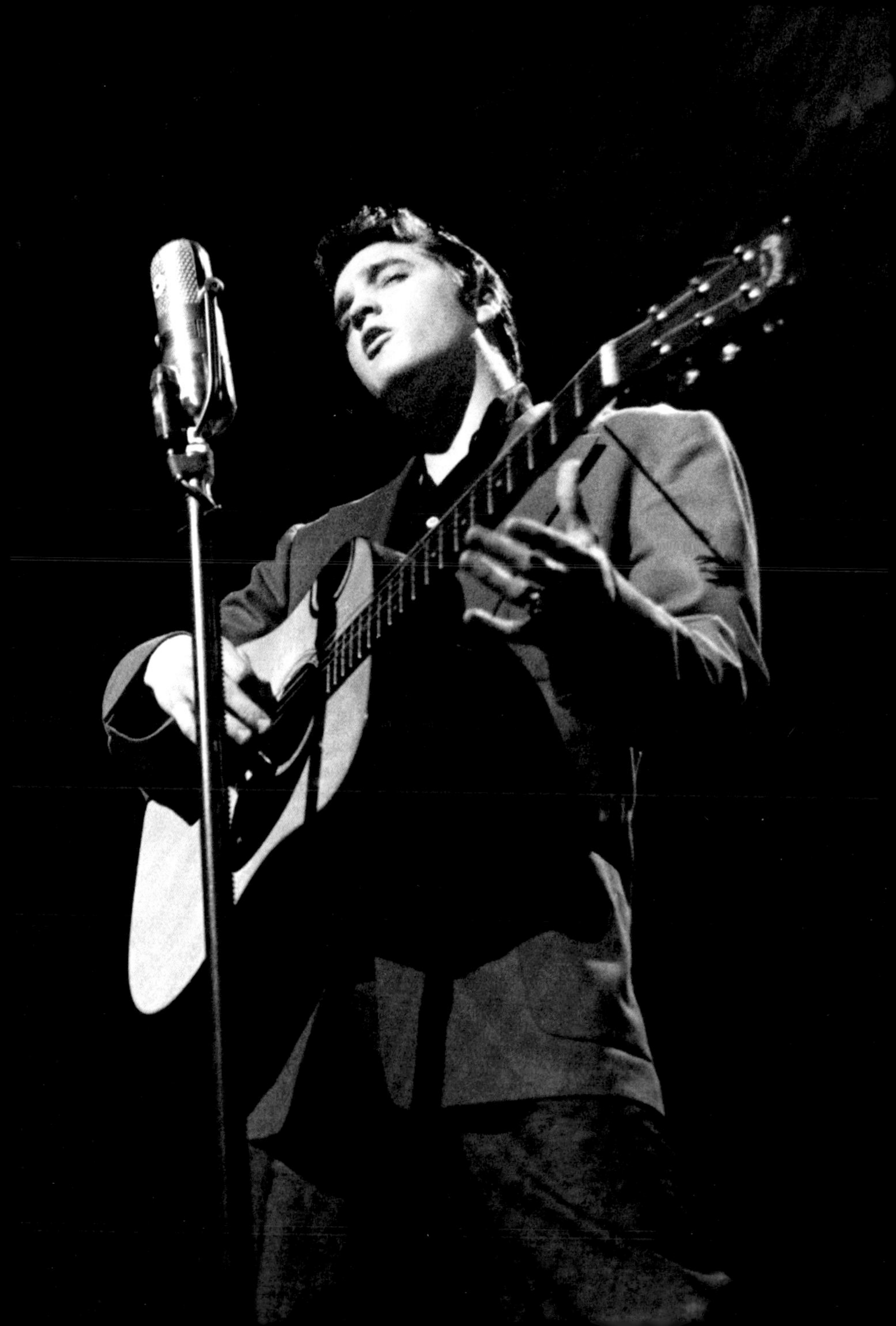

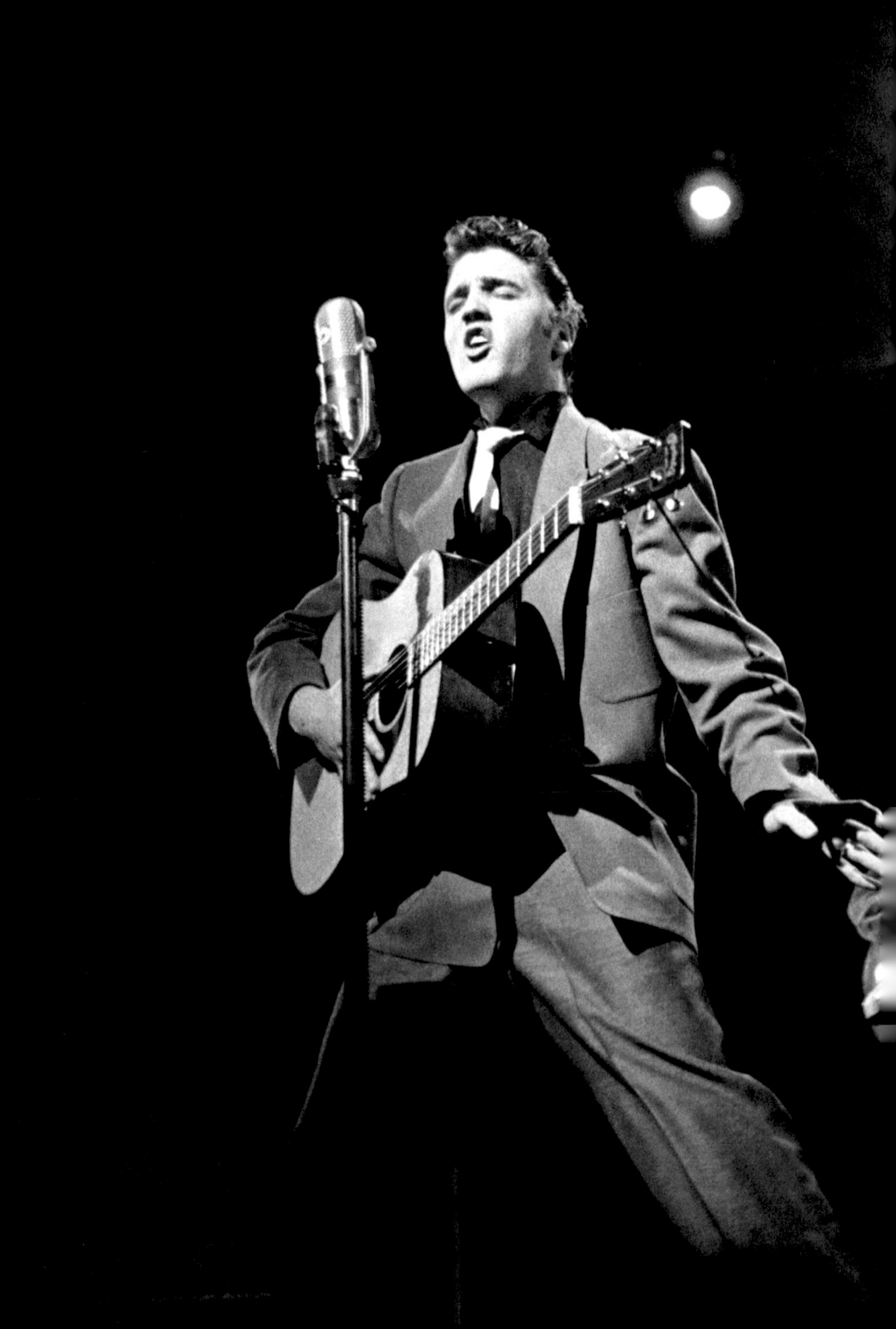

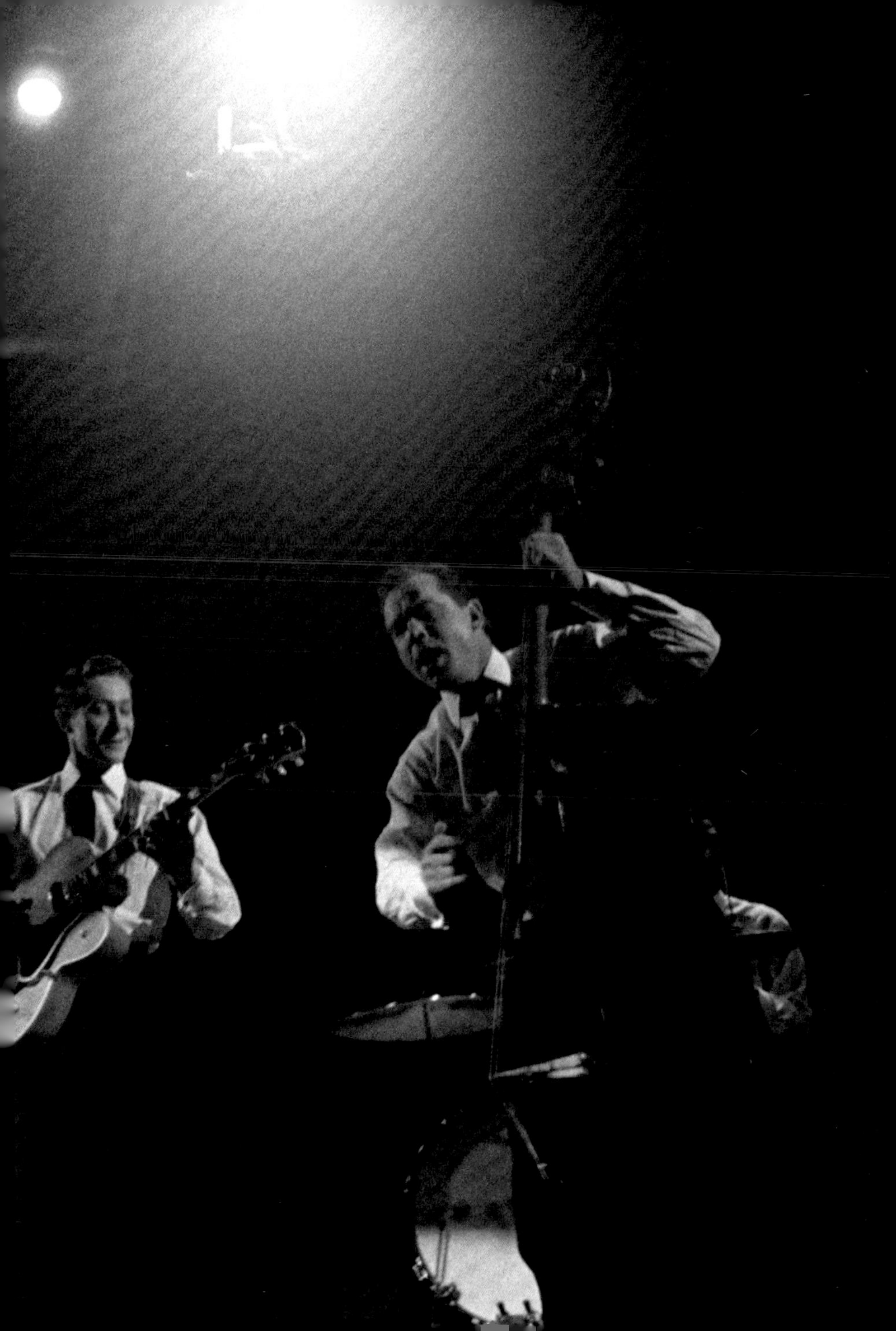

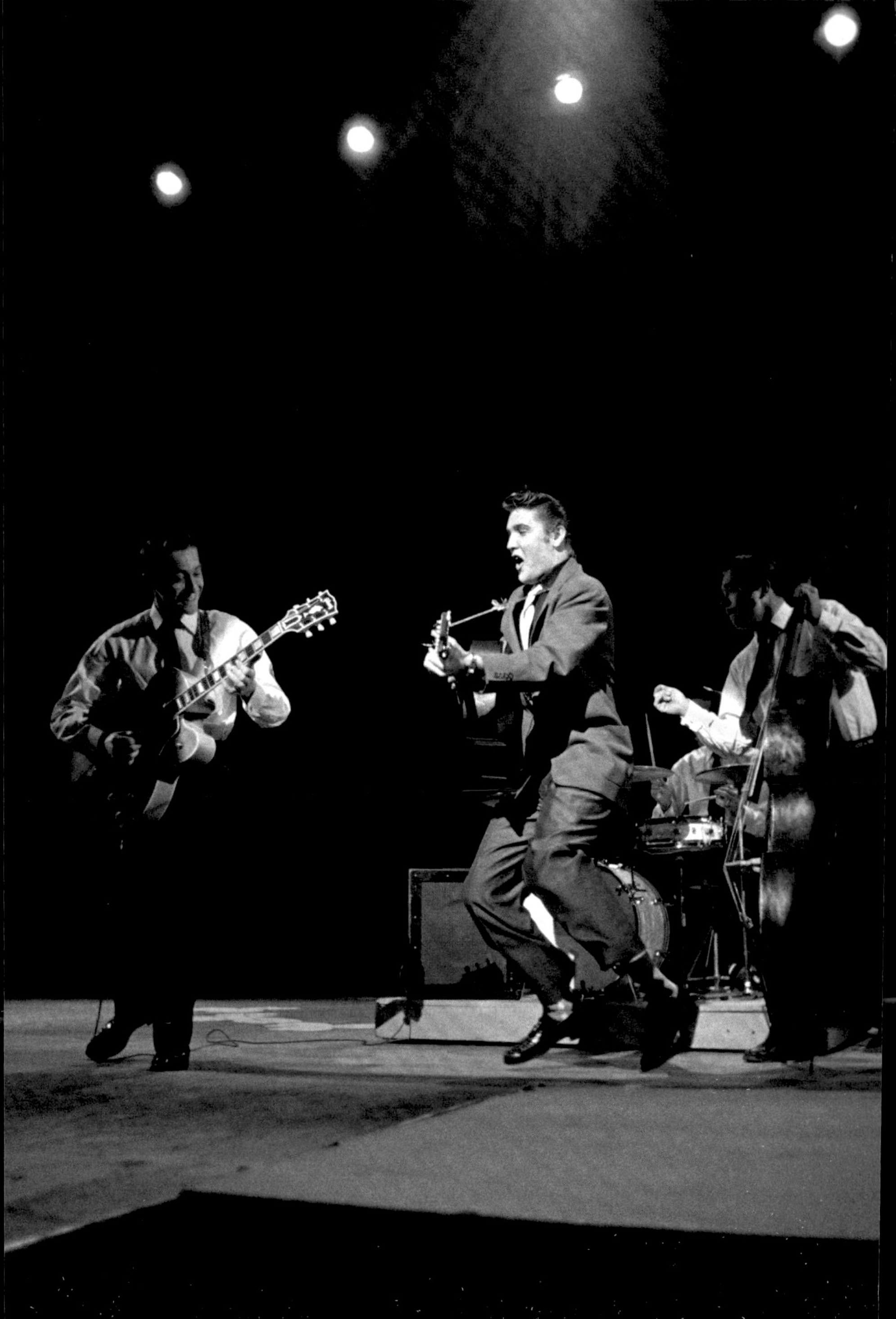

He is a rock-and-roll variation on one of the most standard acts in show business: the virtuoso of the hootchy-kootchy. His one specialty is an accented movement of the body that heretofore has been primarily identified with the repertoire of the blonde bombshells of the burlesque runway.

JACK GOULD
The New York Times,
June 6, 1956

Jump, live on *Stage Show*, March 17, 1956.

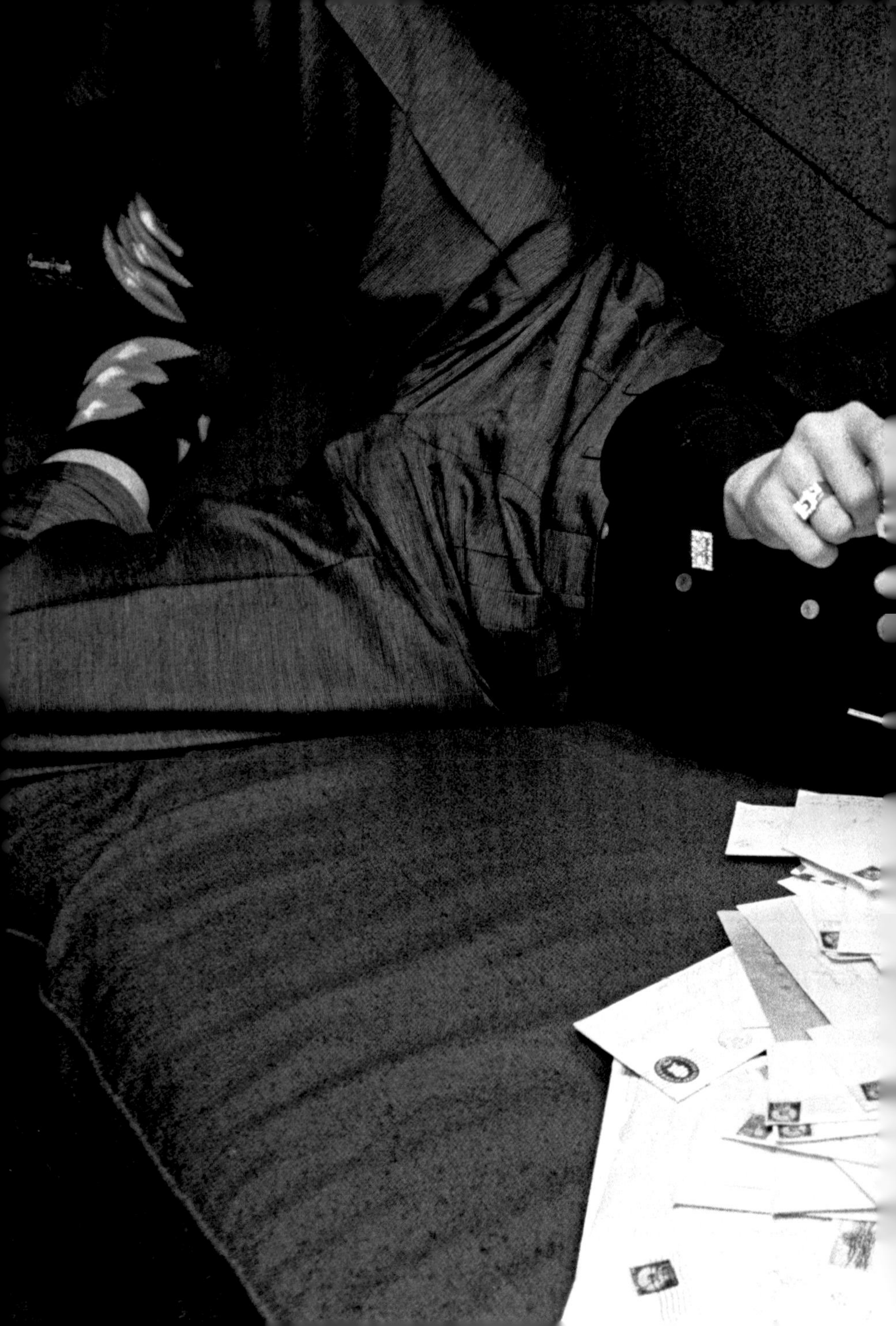

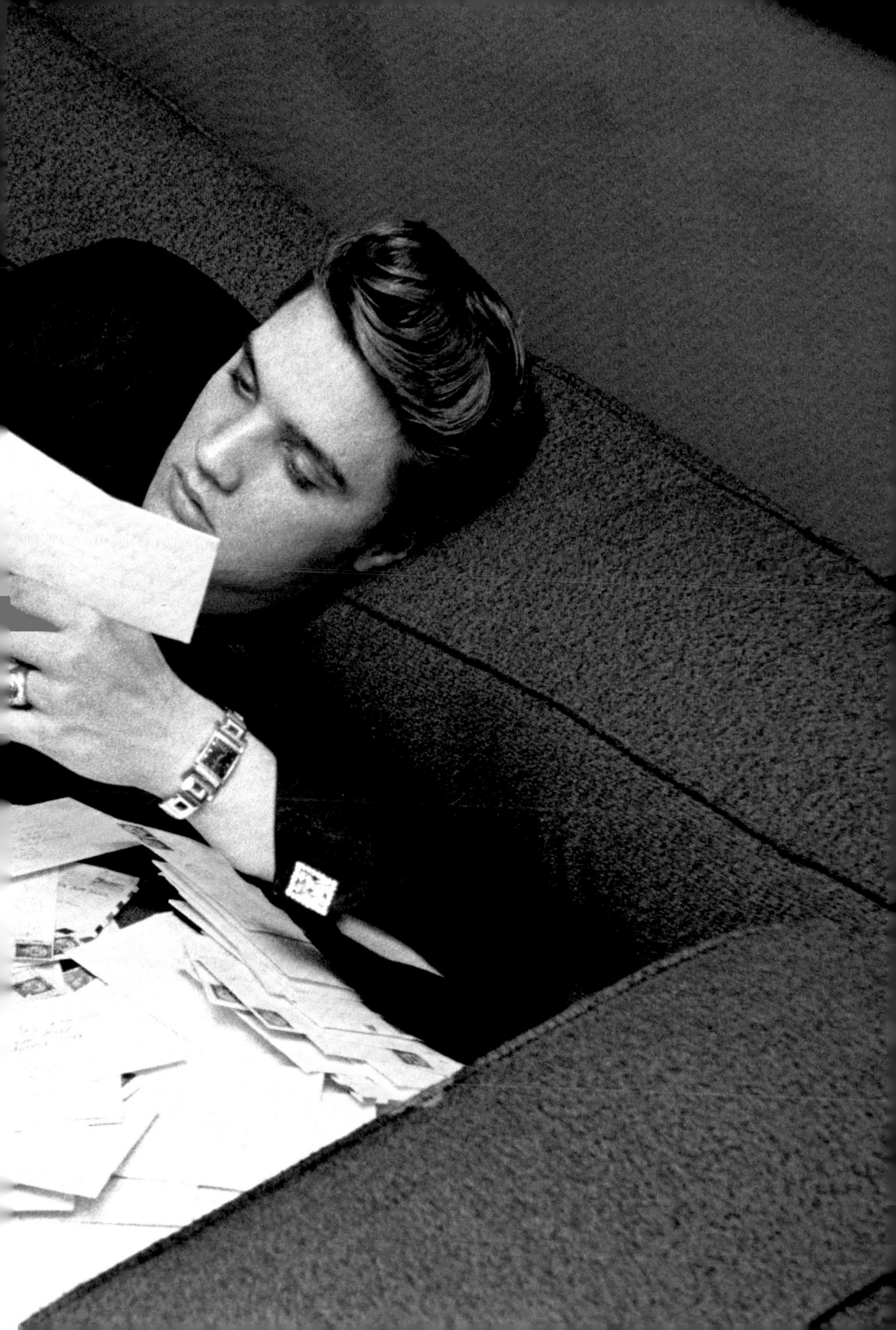

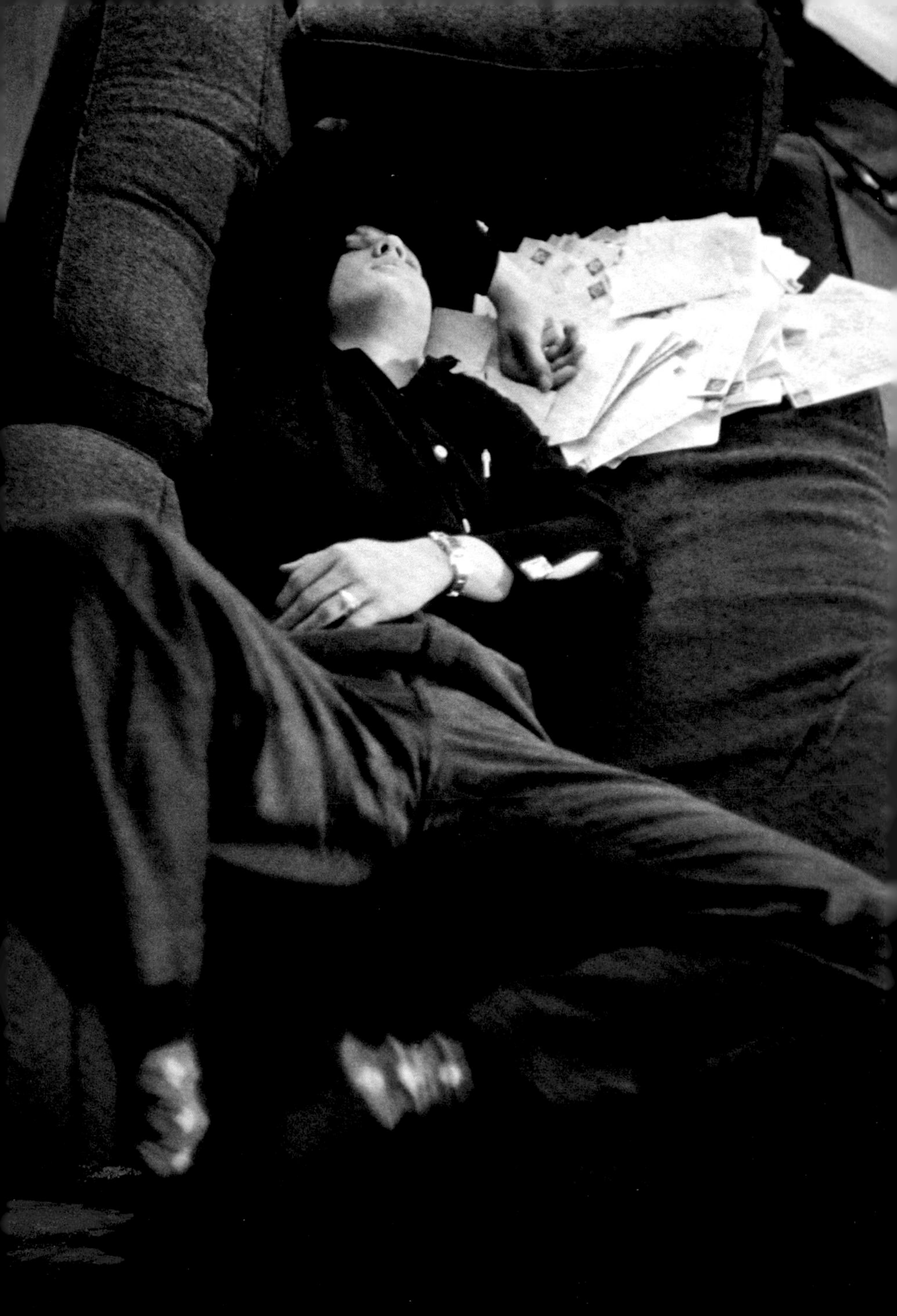

At the Warwick Hotel in New York City,
he falls asleep on the couch,
while reading—and on top of—his fan mail.
The whole time I'm hovering over
him—and he doesn't care that I'm three
feet away from his nose—it doesn't bother
him at all—he is the perfect subject.

ALFRED WERTHEIMER

PREVIOUS SPREAD
"Dear Elvis, I love you..." Back at the Warwick between the rehearsal and live taping of *Stage Show*, Elvis begins to read the dozens of fan letters delivered to the hotel.

OPPOSITE
A nap before the evening show.

THE NEW ELVIS PRESL

THE

STEVE ALL

SHOW

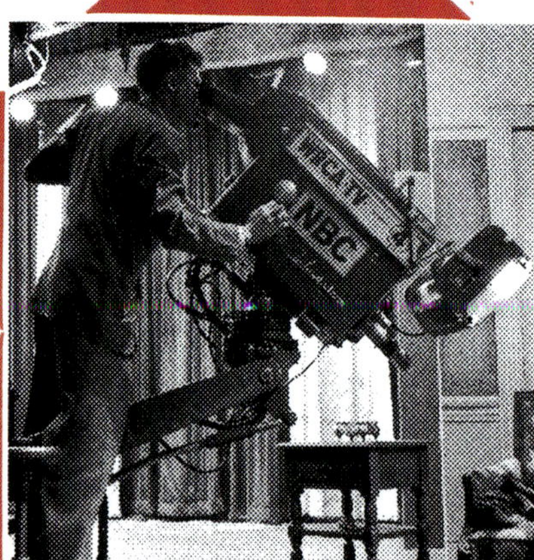

BI

HU

NE

Y ON

EN

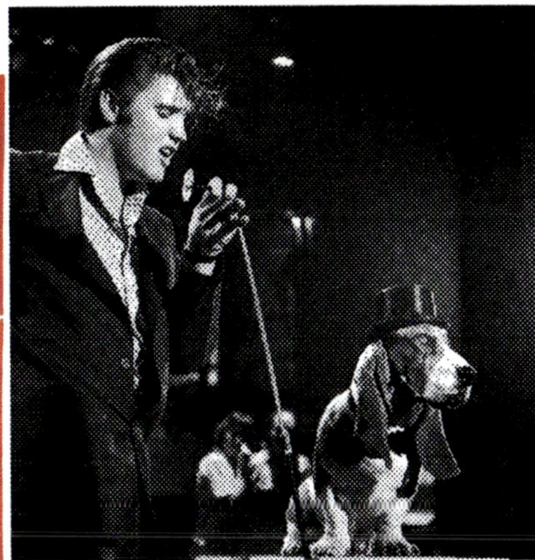

OADCAST

THE

SON THEATER

JULY 1, 1956

V YORK CITY

★ ★ ★

WHEN I ARRIVED IN THE MIDTOWN MANHATTAN LOFT to photograph Elvis's rehearsal for NBC's *The Steve Allen Show*, he was in the corner of the studio, playing and singing gospel music on an upright piano, as Junior Smith, his sidekick, gopher, and cousin, watched over dutifully. Elvis would rather play music, to get people to gather round quietly and not disrupt his focus or engage him in small talk. The next day we would be off for a night of concerts in Richmond, Virginia, then back to New York City for the television show the following day. Some conservative church groups were making a fuss about Elvis's free style of moving below the waist, so Steve Allen's script was written to curtail any possible gyrations: Dressed in a tux, Elvis would start singing "Hound Dog" to a live basset hound, and continue with a ballad. Finally, in a debut that would help lead him into a successful acting career, he changed into a cowboy outfit for a comedy skit, "Range Roundup," where he appeared as Tumbleweed Presley, with Imogene Coca, Andy Griffith, and Steve Allen. Well, the strategy worked and *The Steve Allen Show* was able to keep the family television night "clean" and beat the ratings for *The Ed Sullivan Show* on CBS.

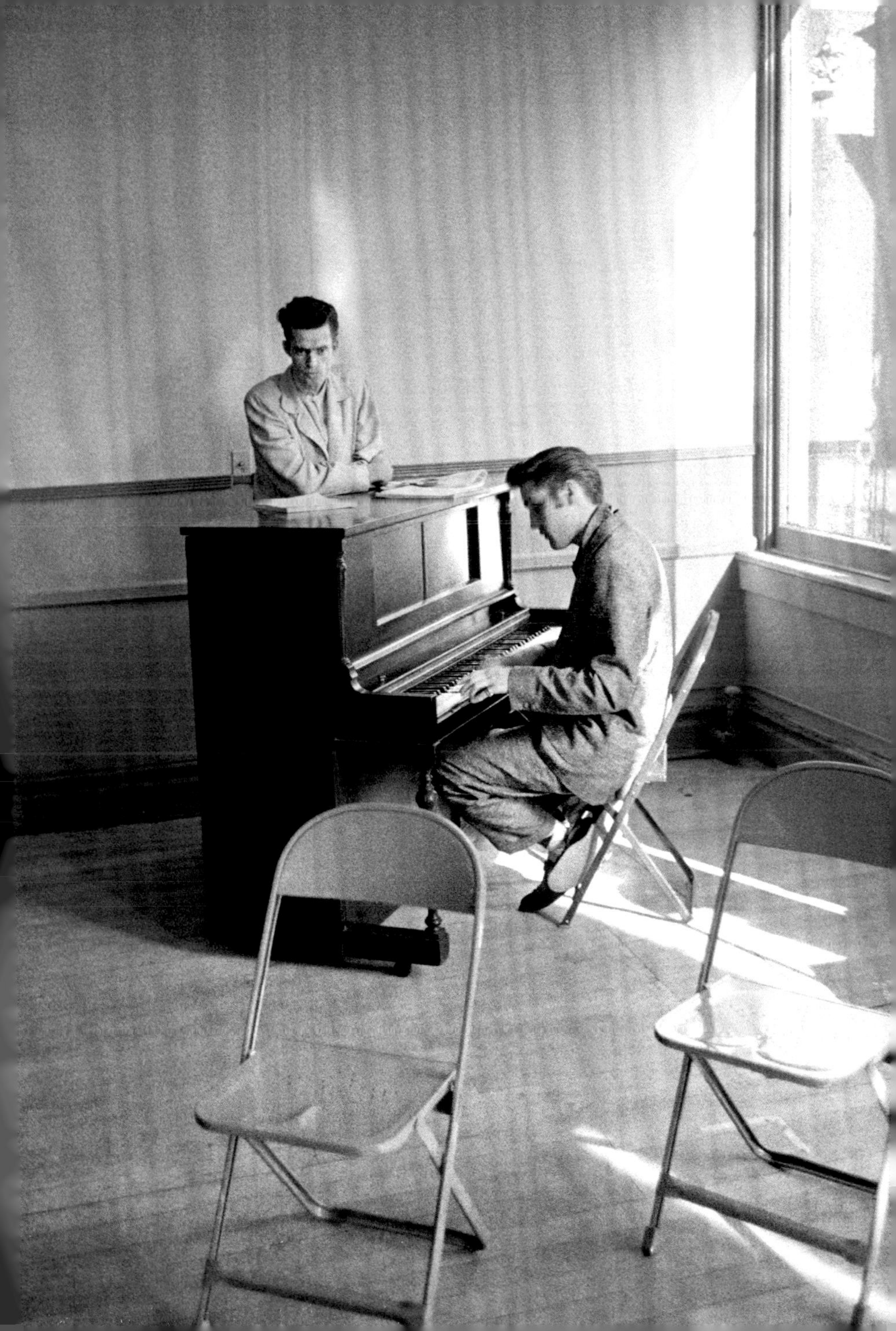

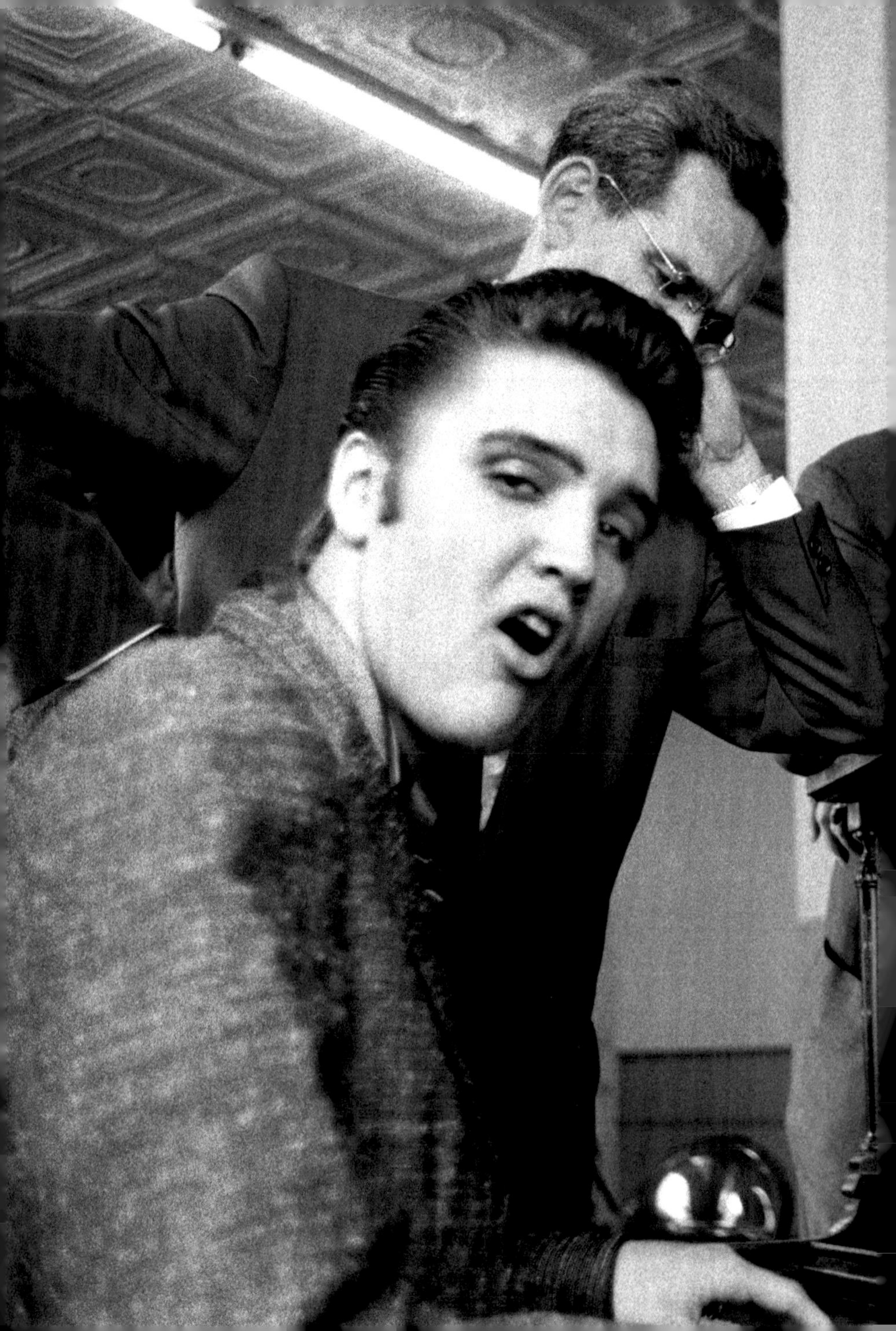

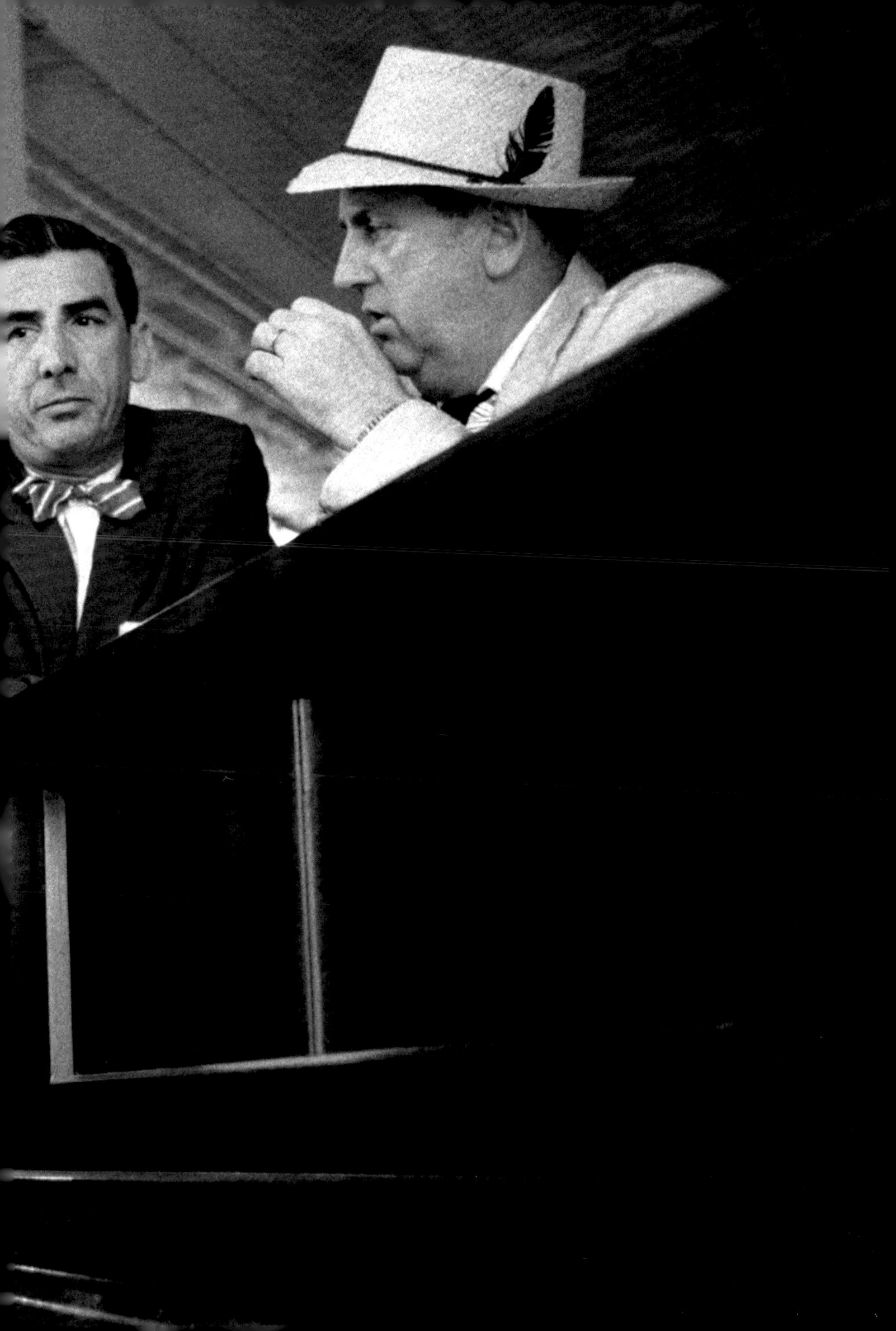

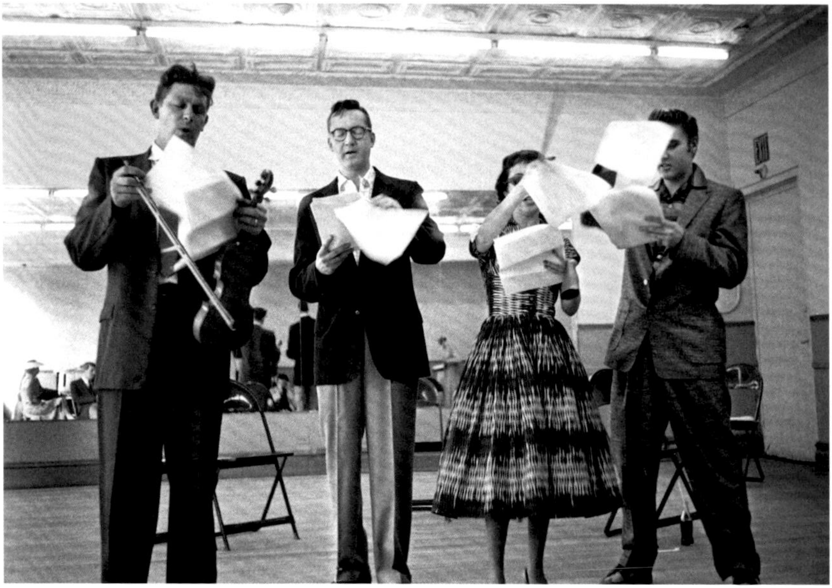

PAGE 53
At the piano at a mid-Manhattan loft studio,
Elvis waits for *The Steve Allen Show* script rehearsal to
start with his cousin Junior Smith, June 29, 1956.

PREVIOUS SPREAD
Playing piano with television agents and manager,
Colonel Tom Parker (in hat), standing by.

ABOVE
Rehearsals for the "Range Roundup" skit with host
Steve Allen (in glasses), Andy Griffith, and Imogene Coca on
June 29. Elvis and the band will leave New York that evening for
two shows at the Mosque Theater in Richmond, Virginia.

OPPOSITE
Elvis sings some gospel songs for
his own pleasure.

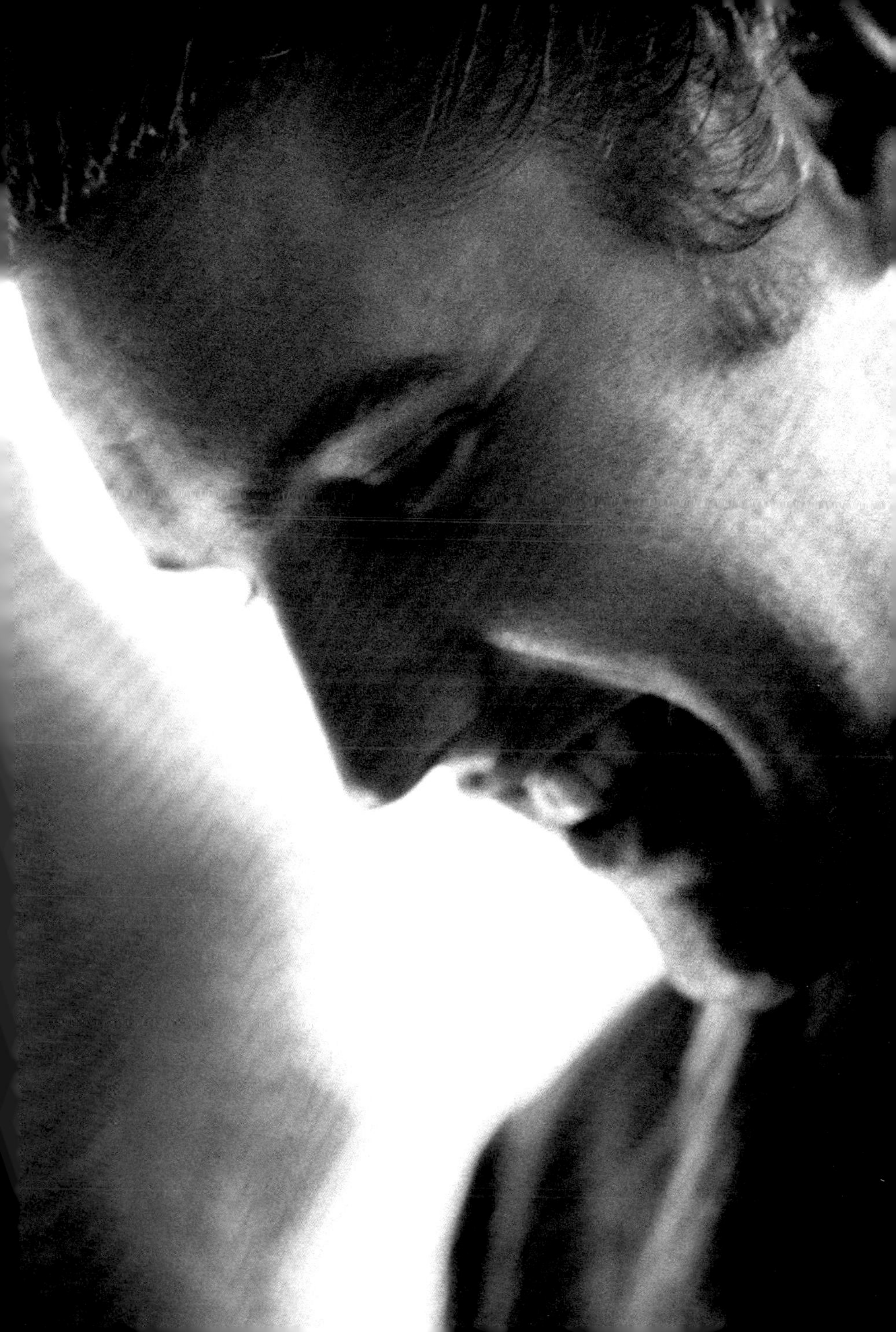

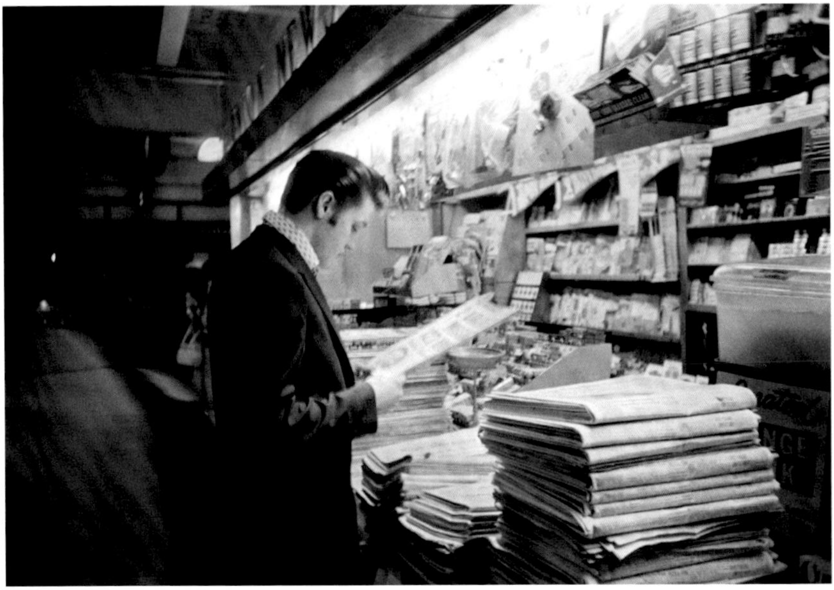

ABOVE
At a Penn Station newsstand, Elvis picks up a paper with a front page story about a mid-air collision of two planes over the Grand Canyon.

OPPOSITE
"Two Airliners Missing. 128 Aboard." Waiting for a cab, Elvis is absorbed by the story. Earlier that year, Elvis's own tour plane made a terrifying emergency landing between Amarillo, Texas, and Nashville, Tennessee.

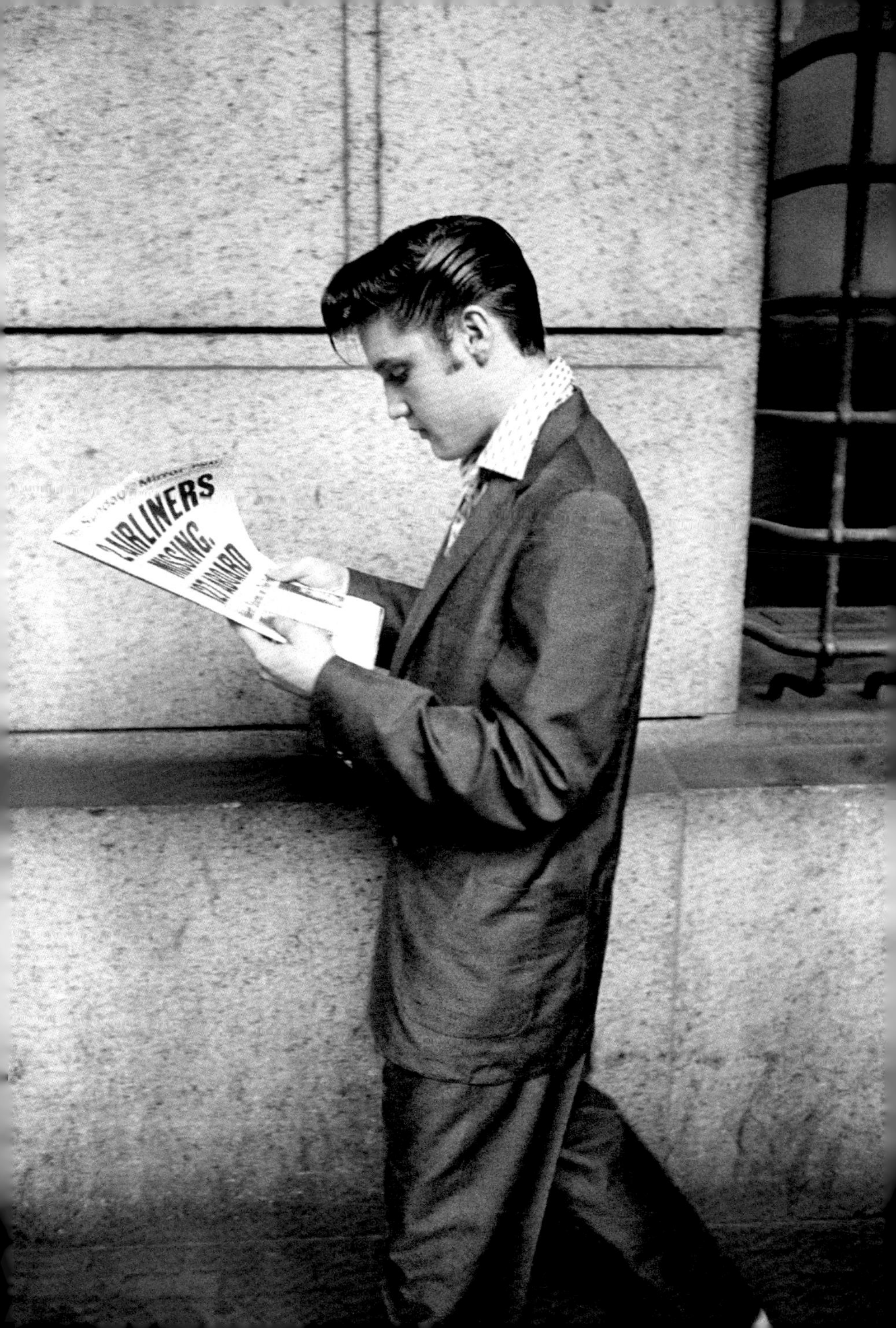
Mirror
AIRLINERS
MISSING,

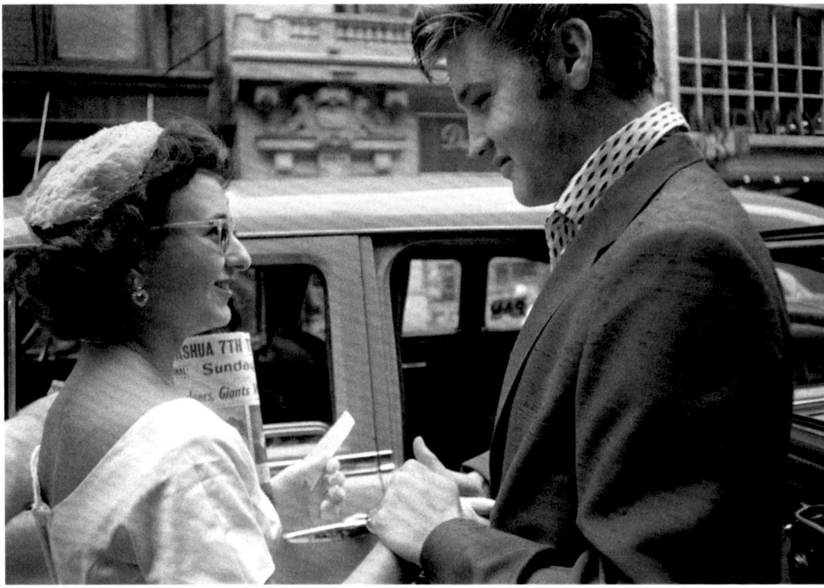

ABOVE & OPPOSITE
Elvis arrives at the Hudson Theatre, 141 West 44th Street in New York City on July 1, where *The Steve Allen Show* is to be broadcast that evening. Outside, he is greeted by a girl in white, whose father drove her in from Long Island. She breaks down in tears when Elvis slips into the theater.

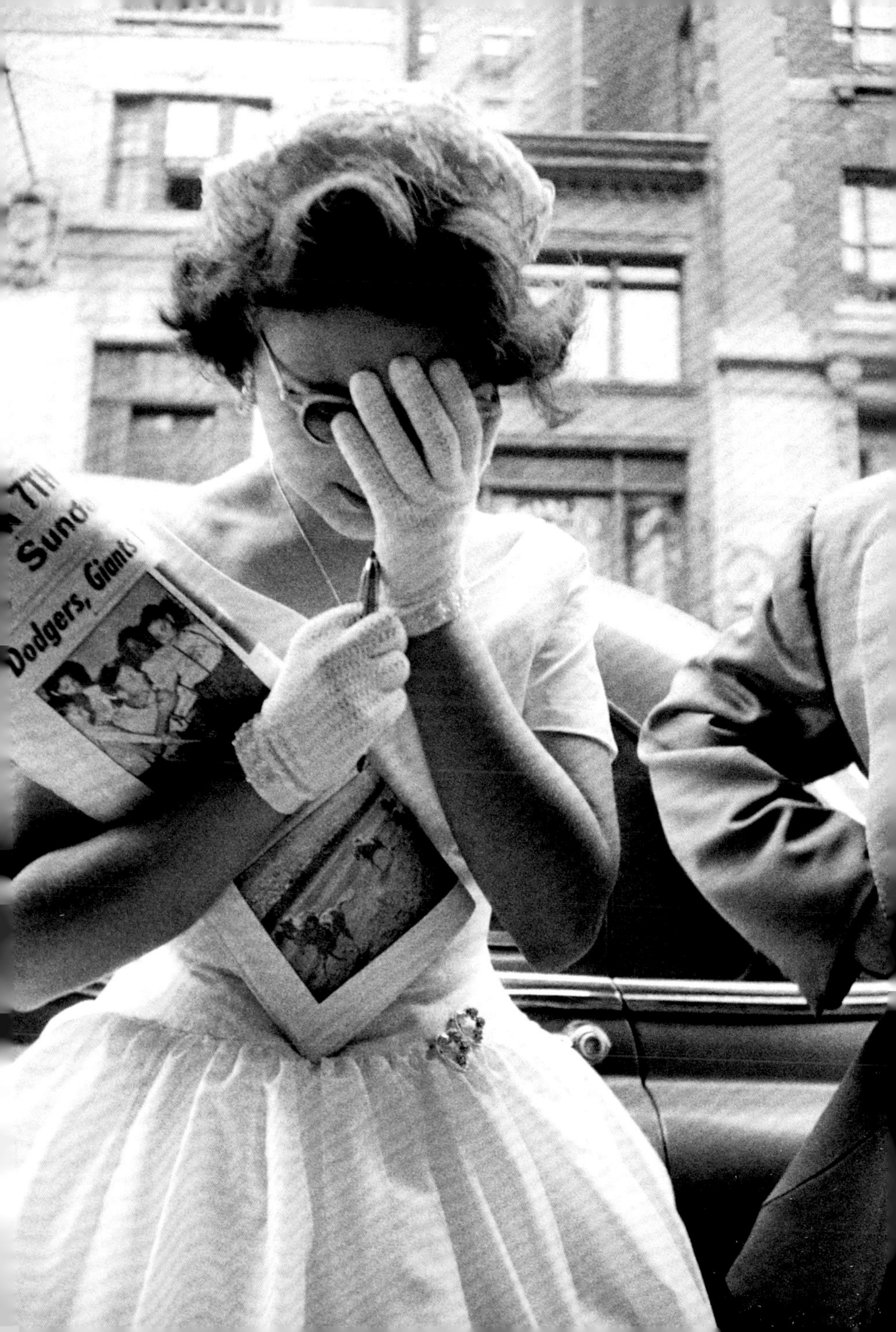
Dodgers, Giants

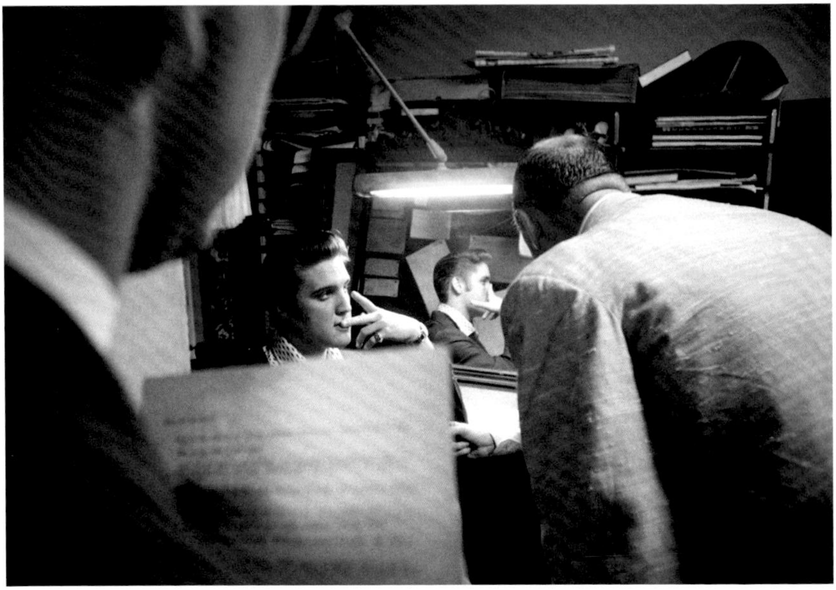

ABOVE
Backstage at the Hudson, awaiting a press conference.

OPPOSITE
NBC's boom man adjusts the microphone.

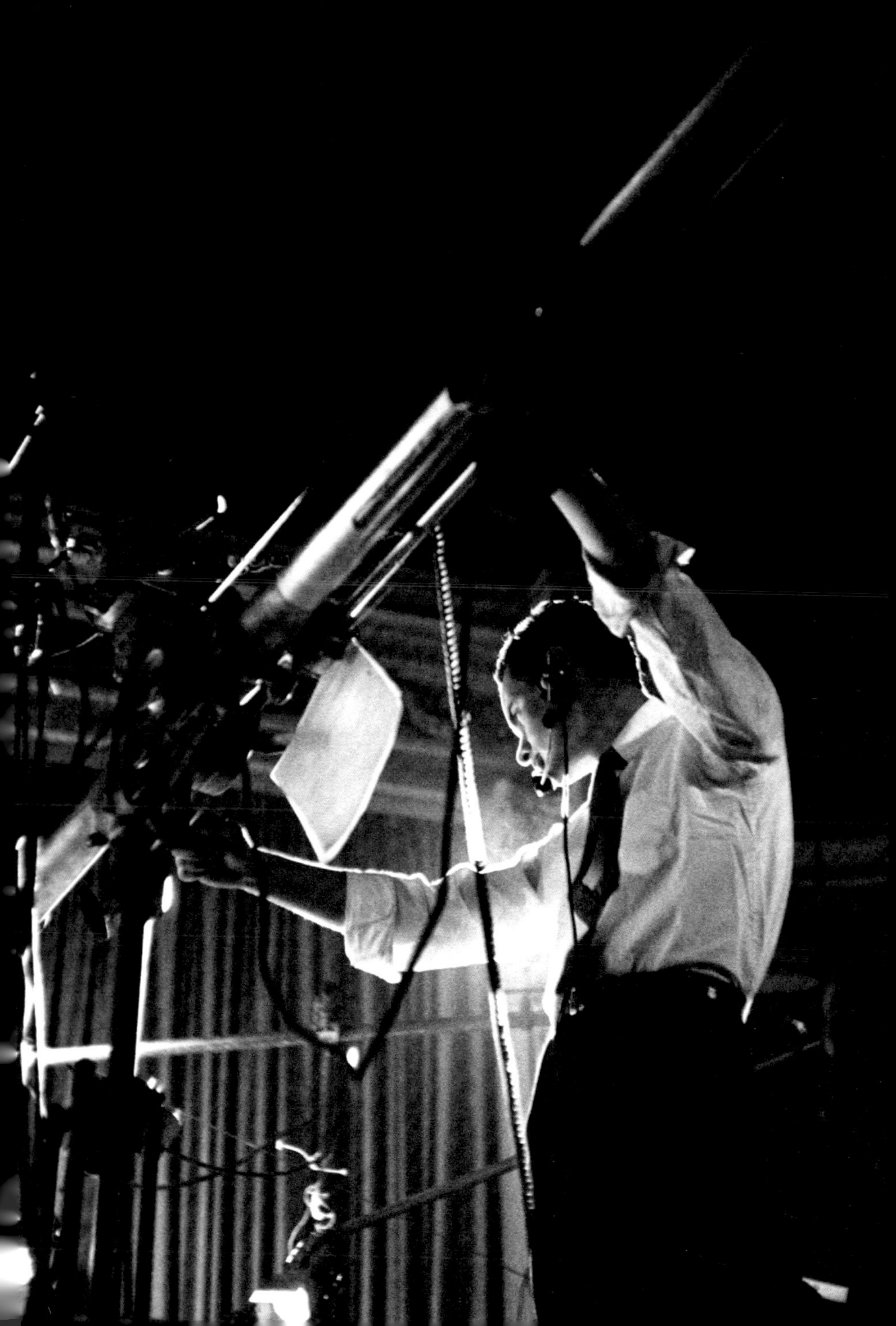

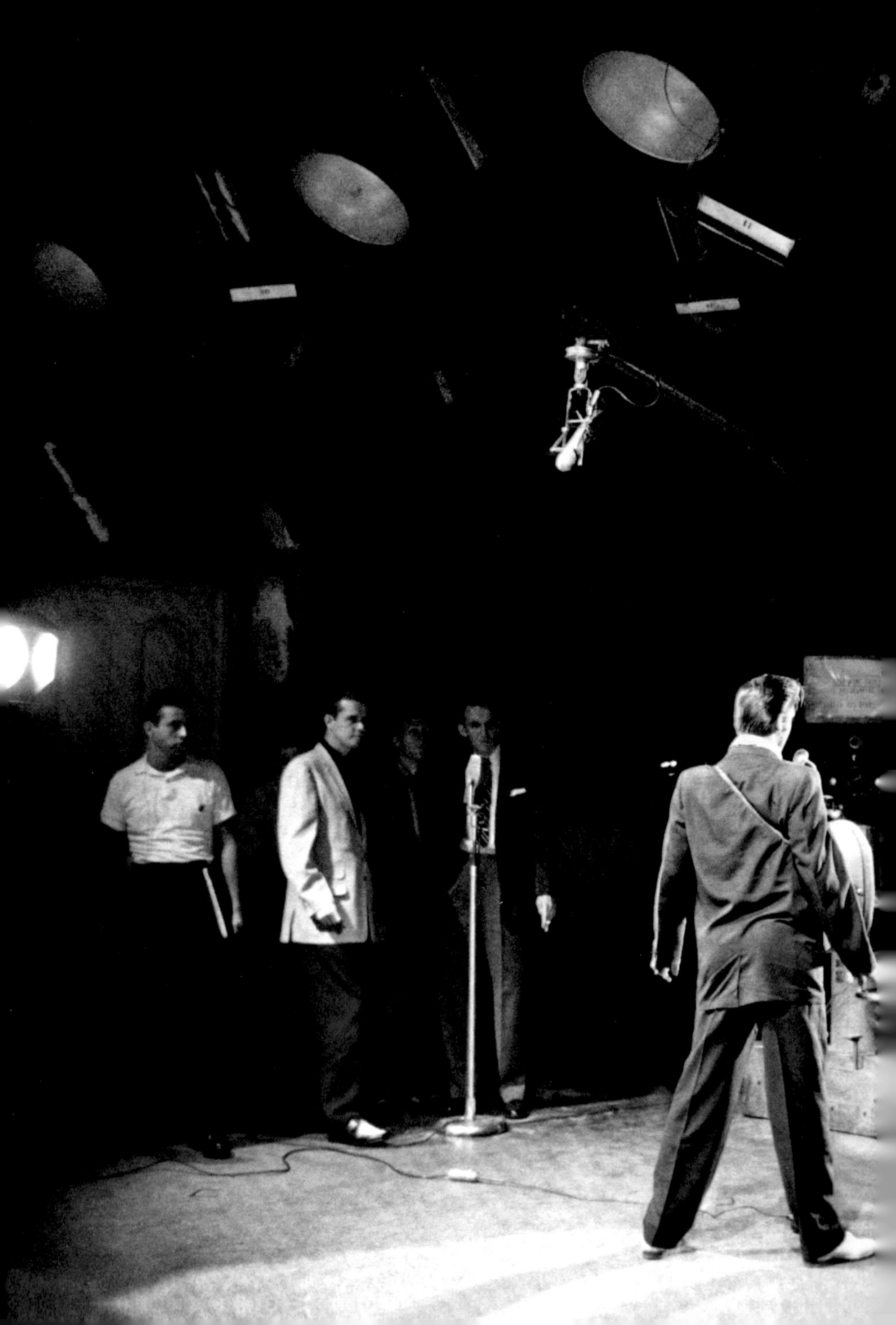

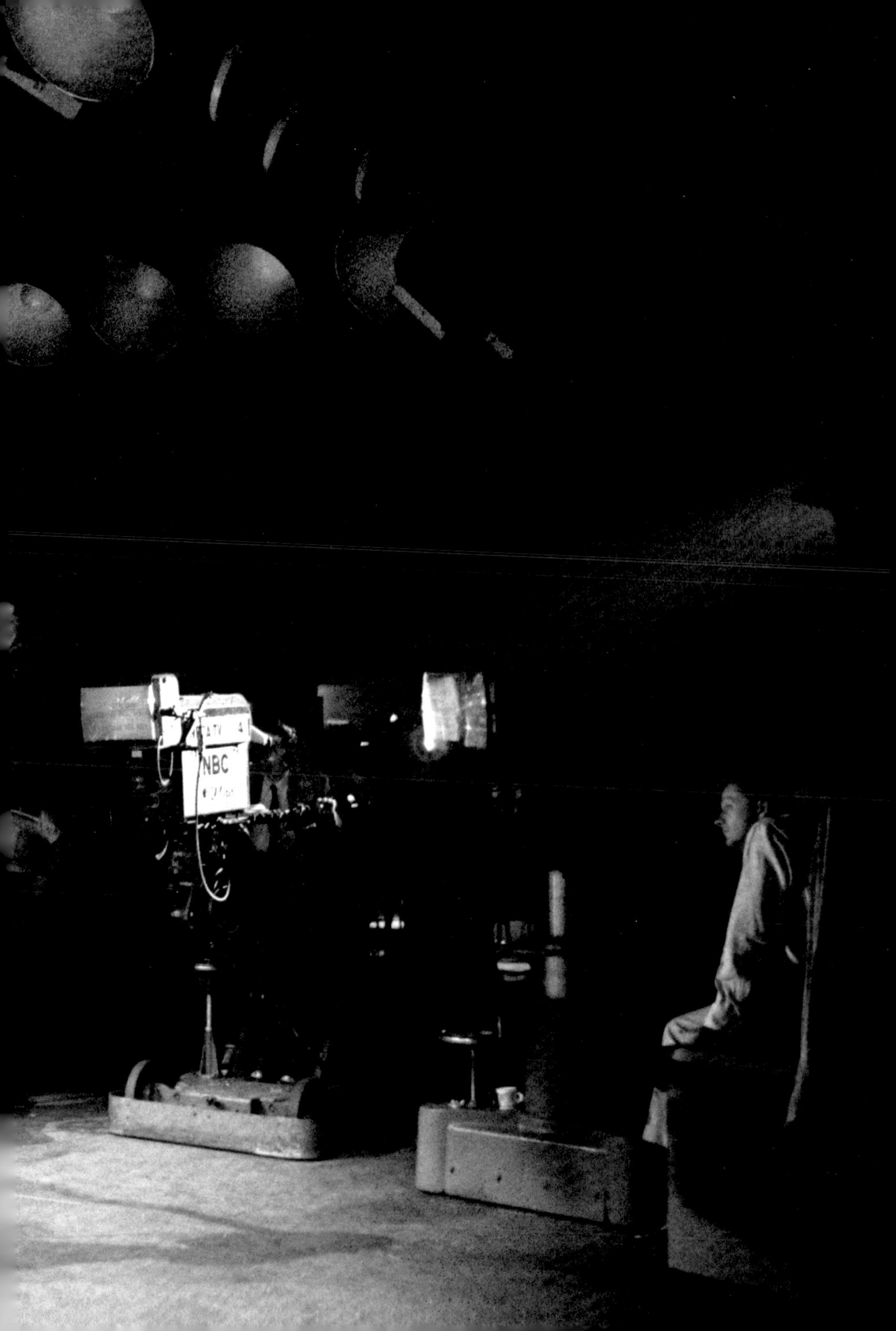
NBC

I don't feel I'm doing anything wrong...
I don't see how any type of music would have
any bad influence on people when it's only music.
I can't figure it out...How would rock and roll
music make anyone rebel against their parents?

ELVIS PRESLEY
The Hy Gardner Show,
July 1, 1956

PREVIOUS SPREAD
Rear view of the rehearsal; background singers
the Jordanaires stand by to the left.

OPPOSITE
Portrait backstage, *The Steve Allen Show.*

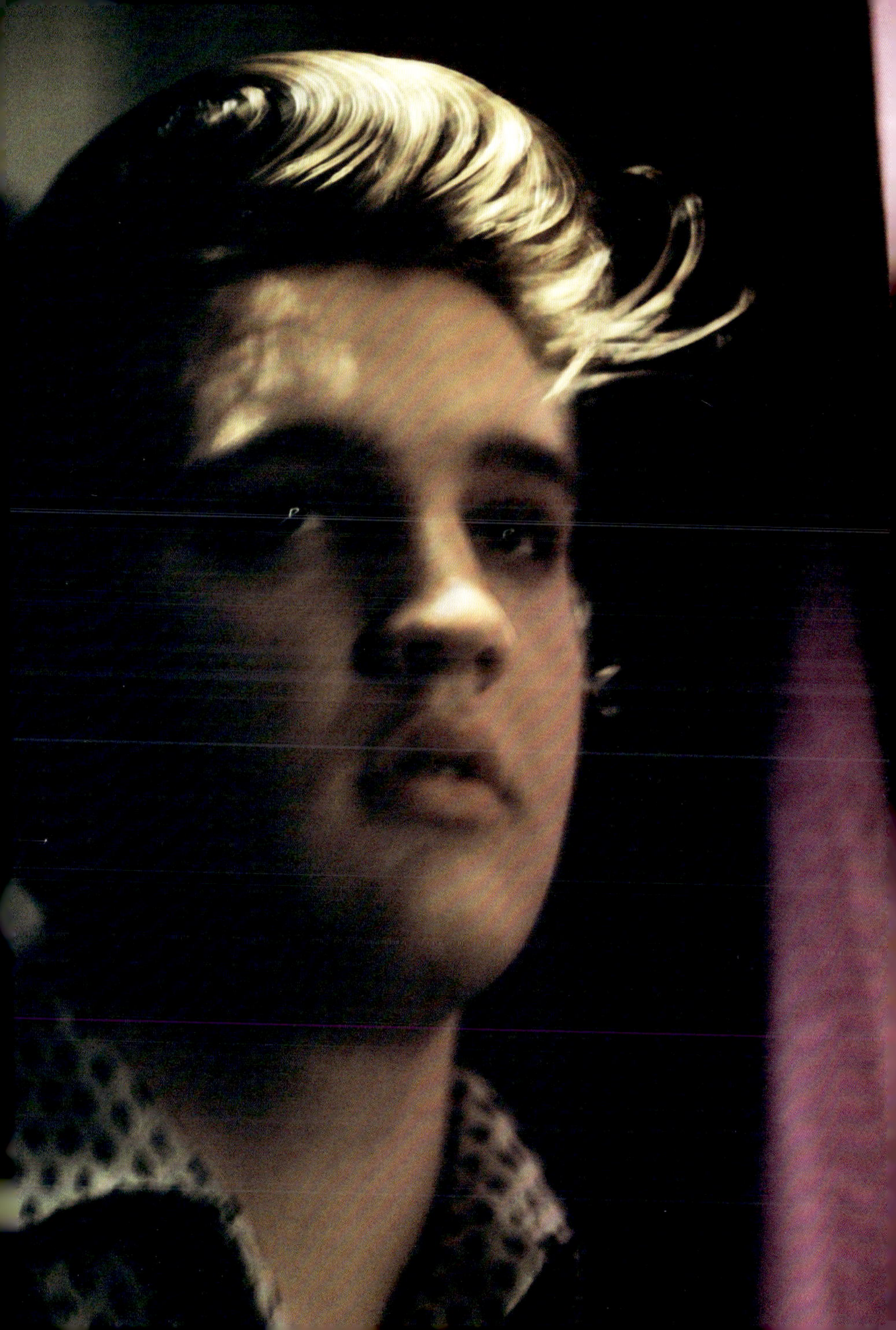

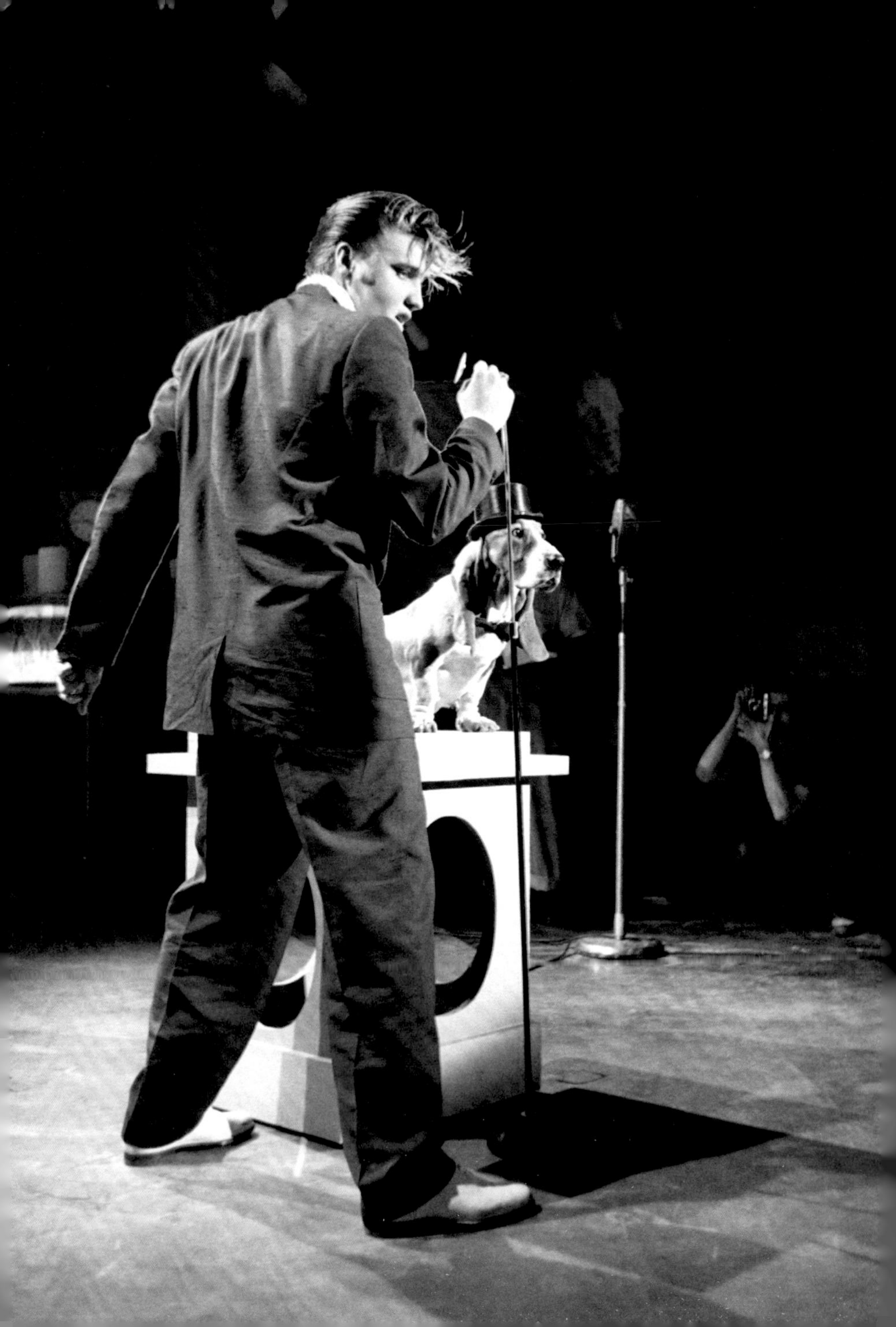

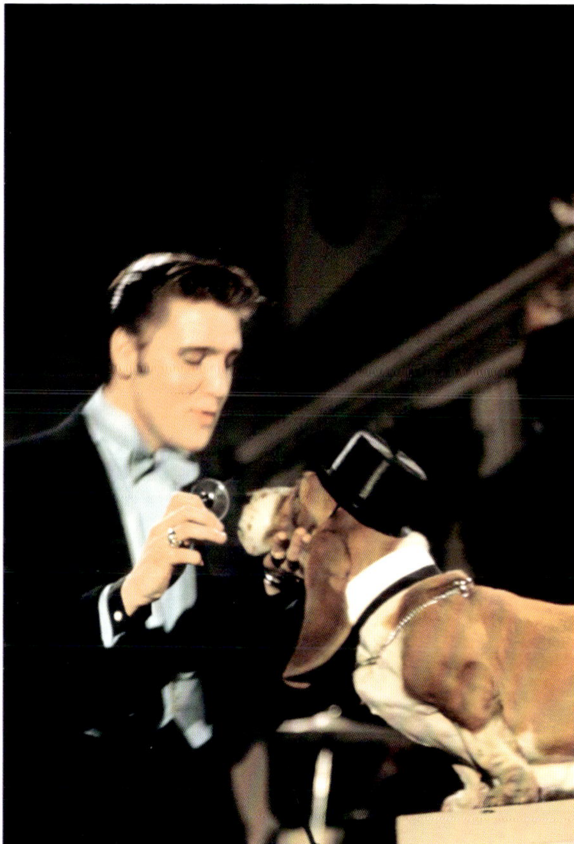

OPPOSITE & ABOVE
"It's showbiz time": Elvis tries out "Hound Dog" in two rehearsals.

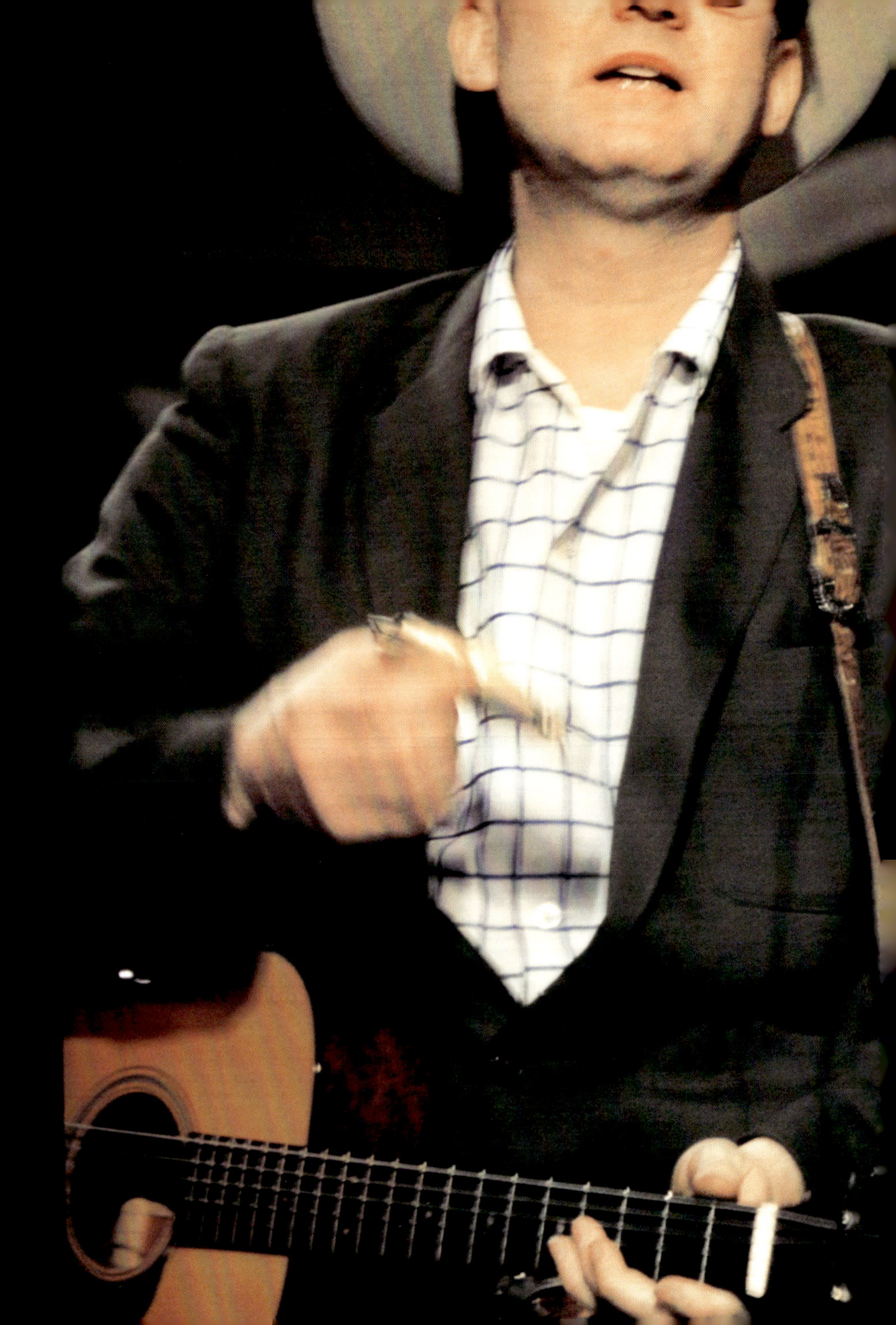

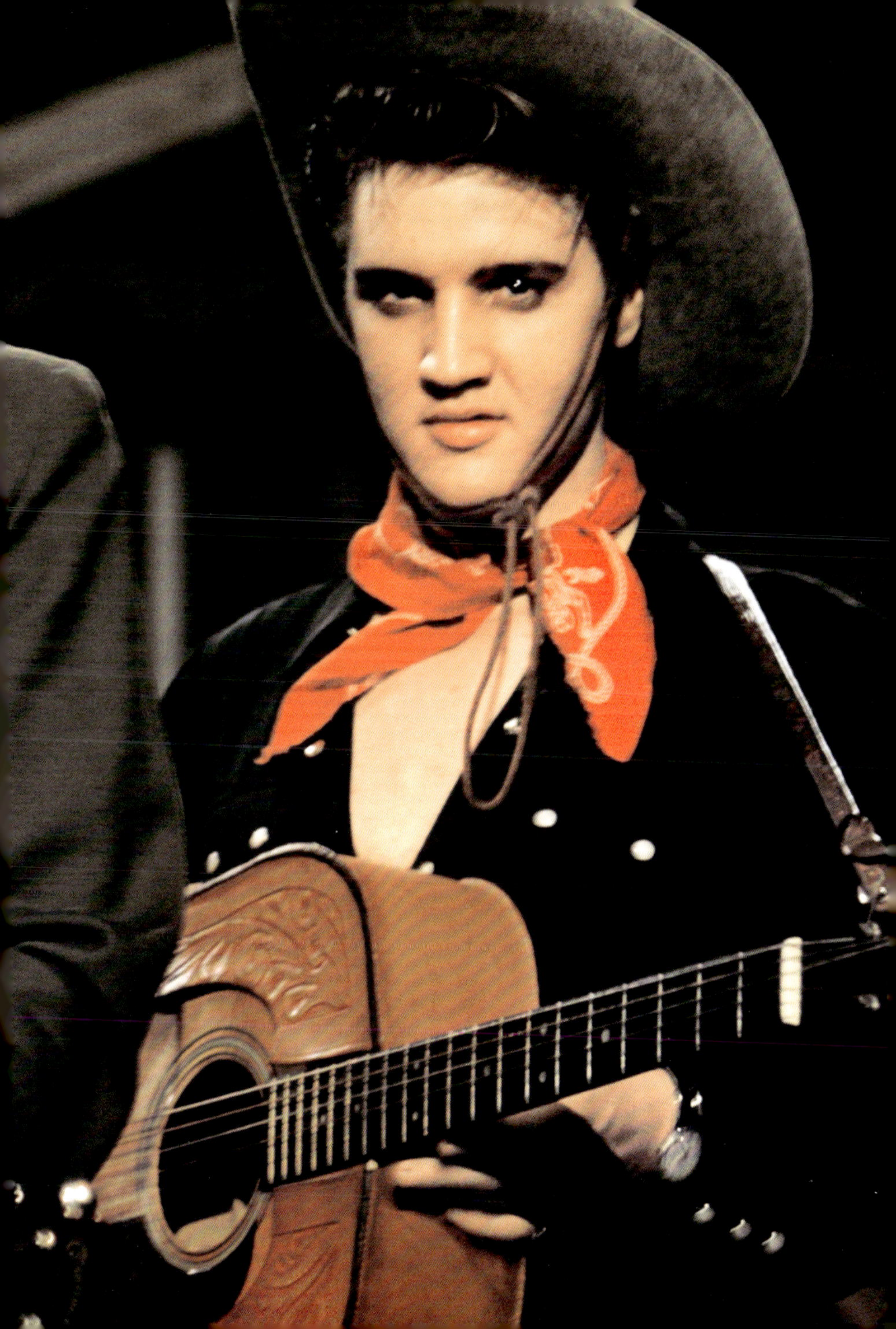

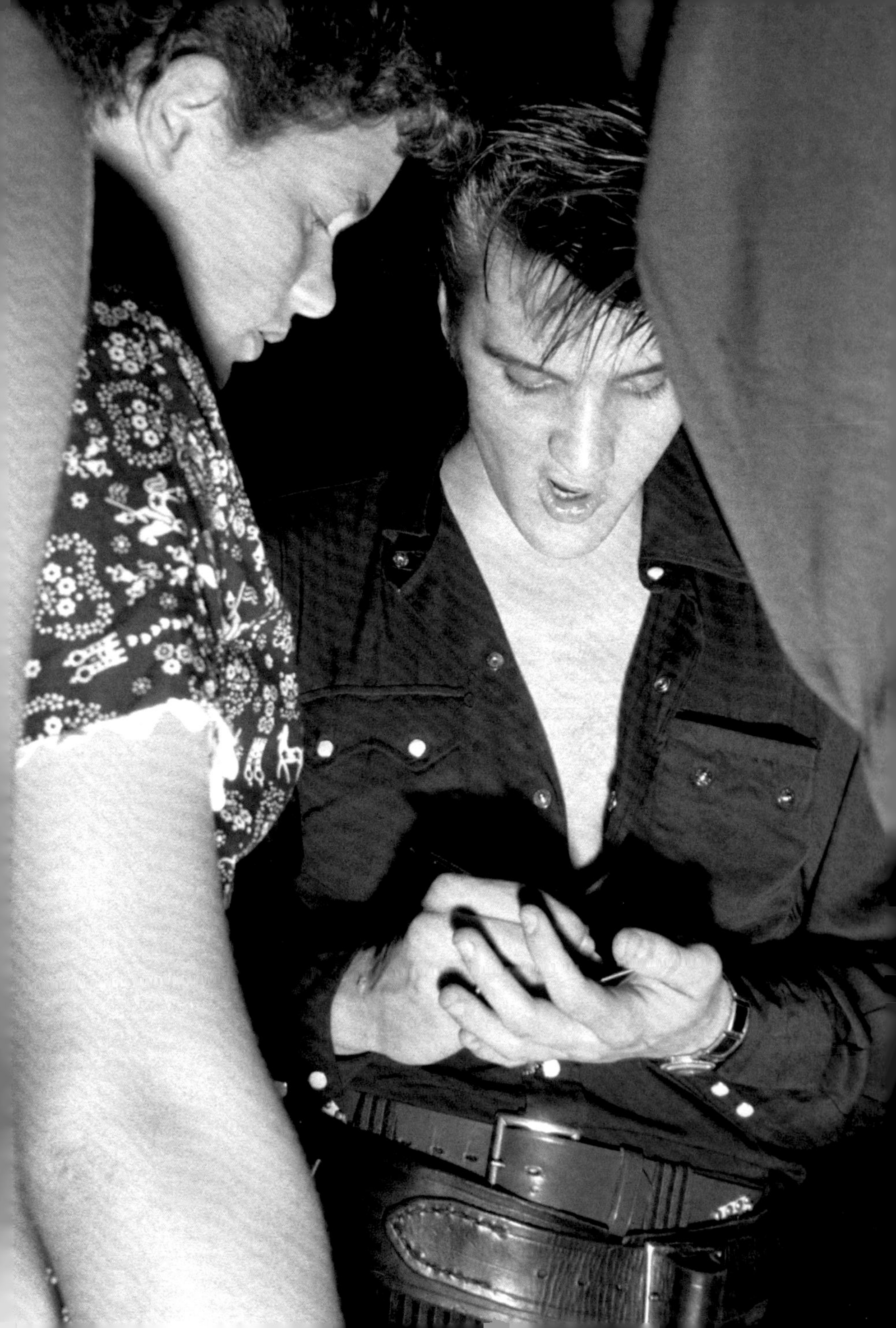

In his dressing room between shows, Presley still couldn't get away from his following. The fans, oblivious to the dressing and undressing members of the band, leaked through police at the doorway to get pictures, autographs or just to look. He signed autographs on pictures, notebooks, papers, legs, arms and foreheads.

KEN KENNAMER
Lubbock Avalanche Journal,
April 11, 1956

PREVIOUS SPREAD
Dress rehearsal for the "Range Roundup" skit with Steve Allen.

OPPOSITE
An autograph after the "Range Roundup" performance.

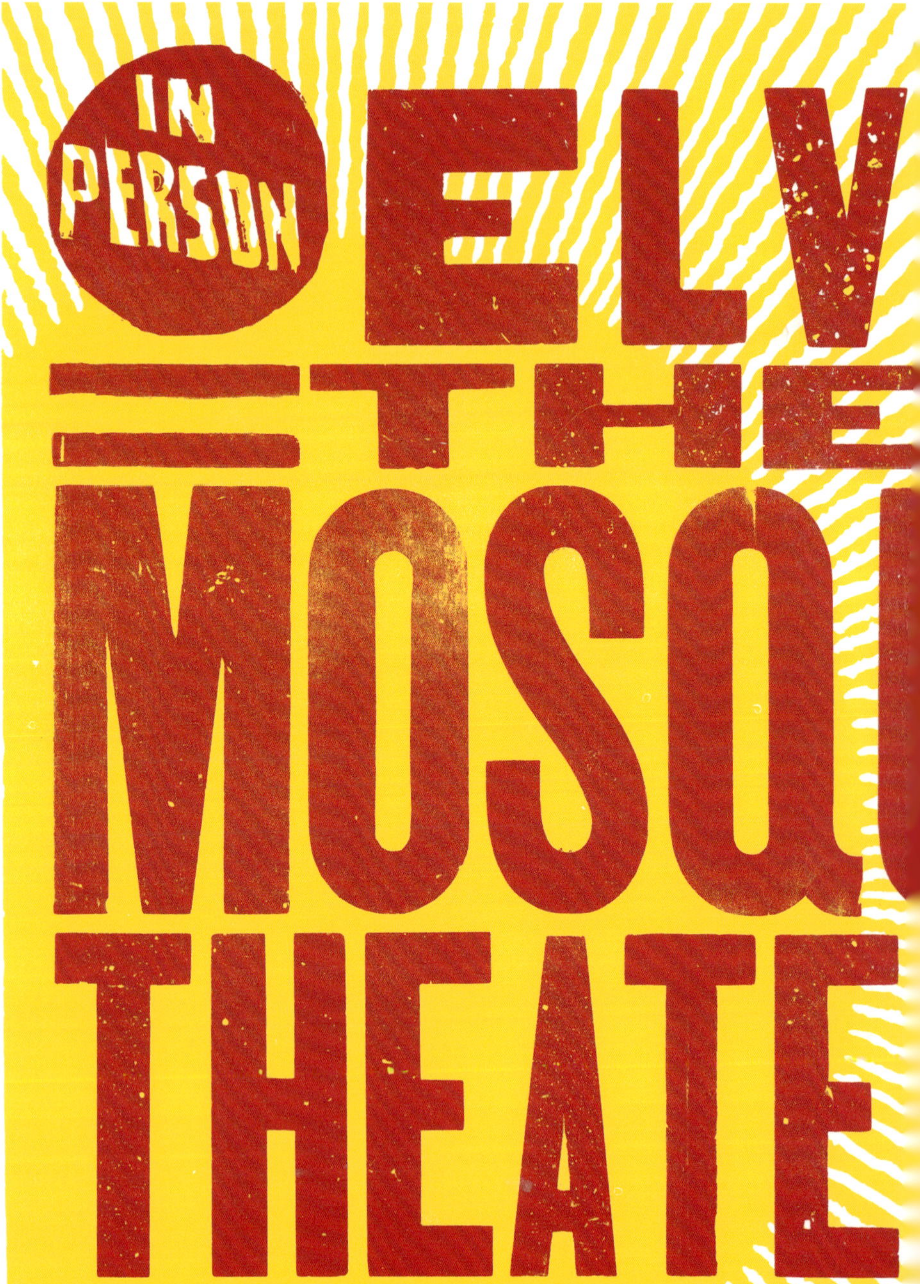
IN PERSON
ELV
THE
MOSQ
THEATE

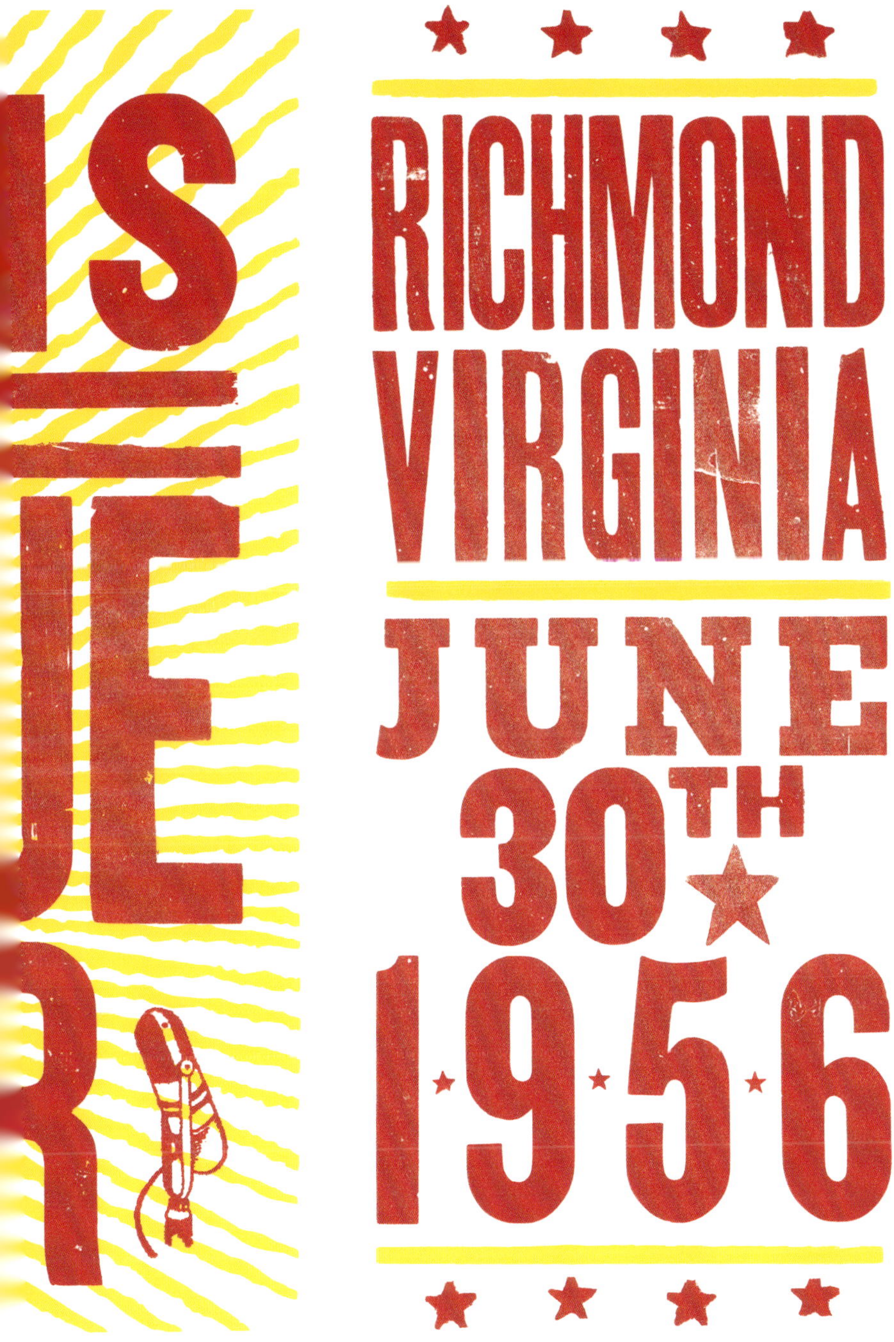
RICHMOND
VIRGINIA
JUNE
30TH
1956

BETWEEN THE REHEARSAL AND PERFORMANCE on *The Steve Allen Show*, Elvis took a train from New York to Richmond, Virginia, where he was to play two concerts of *The Elvis Presley Show*. My camera and I tagged along. When we arrived at the Jefferson Hotel, I watched him charm the ladies, from the elevator operator to the waitress to the mystery date who accompanied him, his cousins Junior and Bobby Smith, and myself in a cab to the Mosque Theater. During the first concert, while other acts were onstage, I briefly lost track of the singer, only to find him and his date at the end of a dark passageway. They were so intimately involved that I was invisible to them…but my camera froze the memory in a photograph known today as *The Kiss*. Elvis's electrifying performances that night ended with a flurry of screaming, crying fans and the final announcement: "Ladies and gentlemen, Elvis has left the building." It was the night of June 30, 1956, as Elvis headed back to New York to perform live on the nationally televised *Steve Allen Show*.

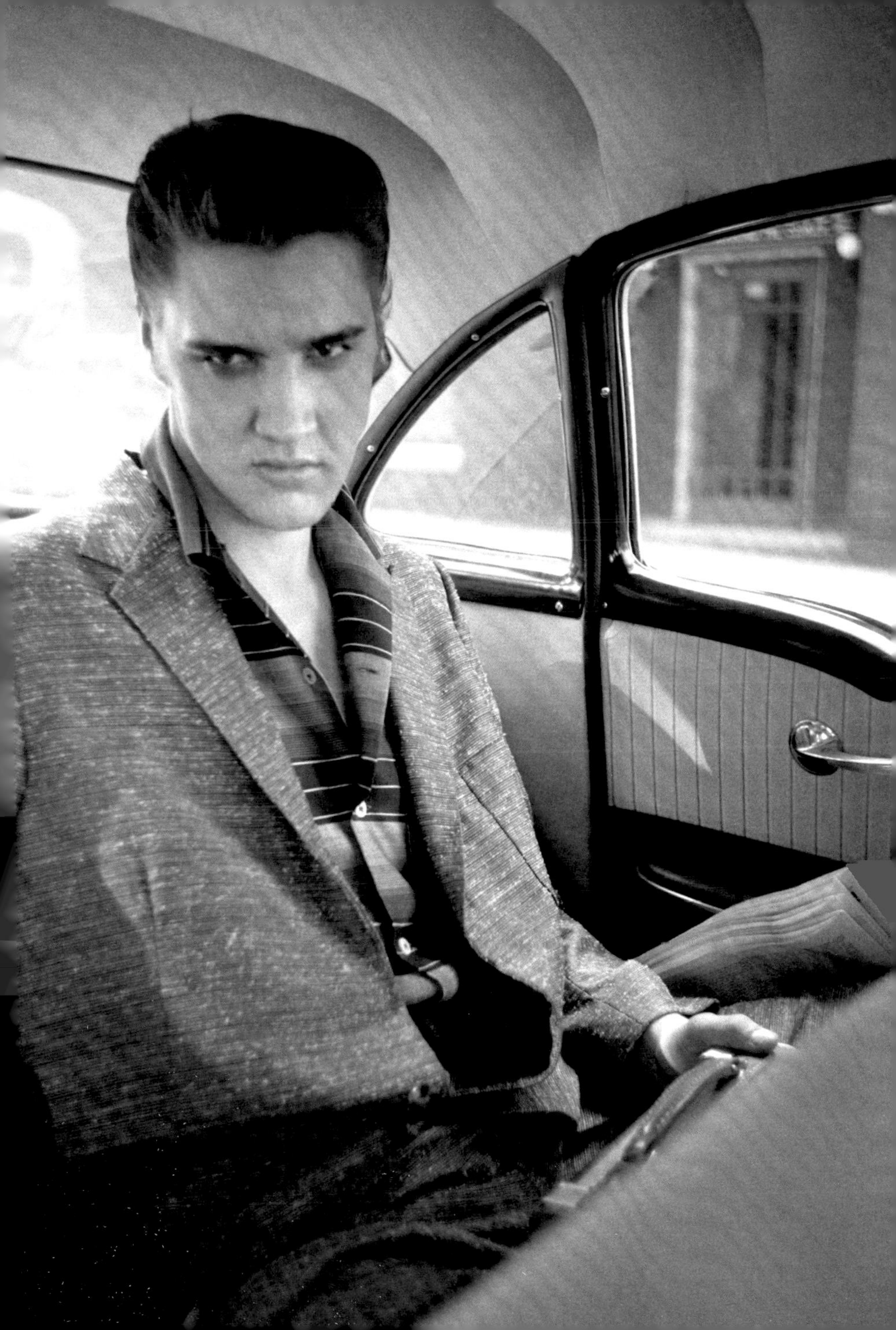

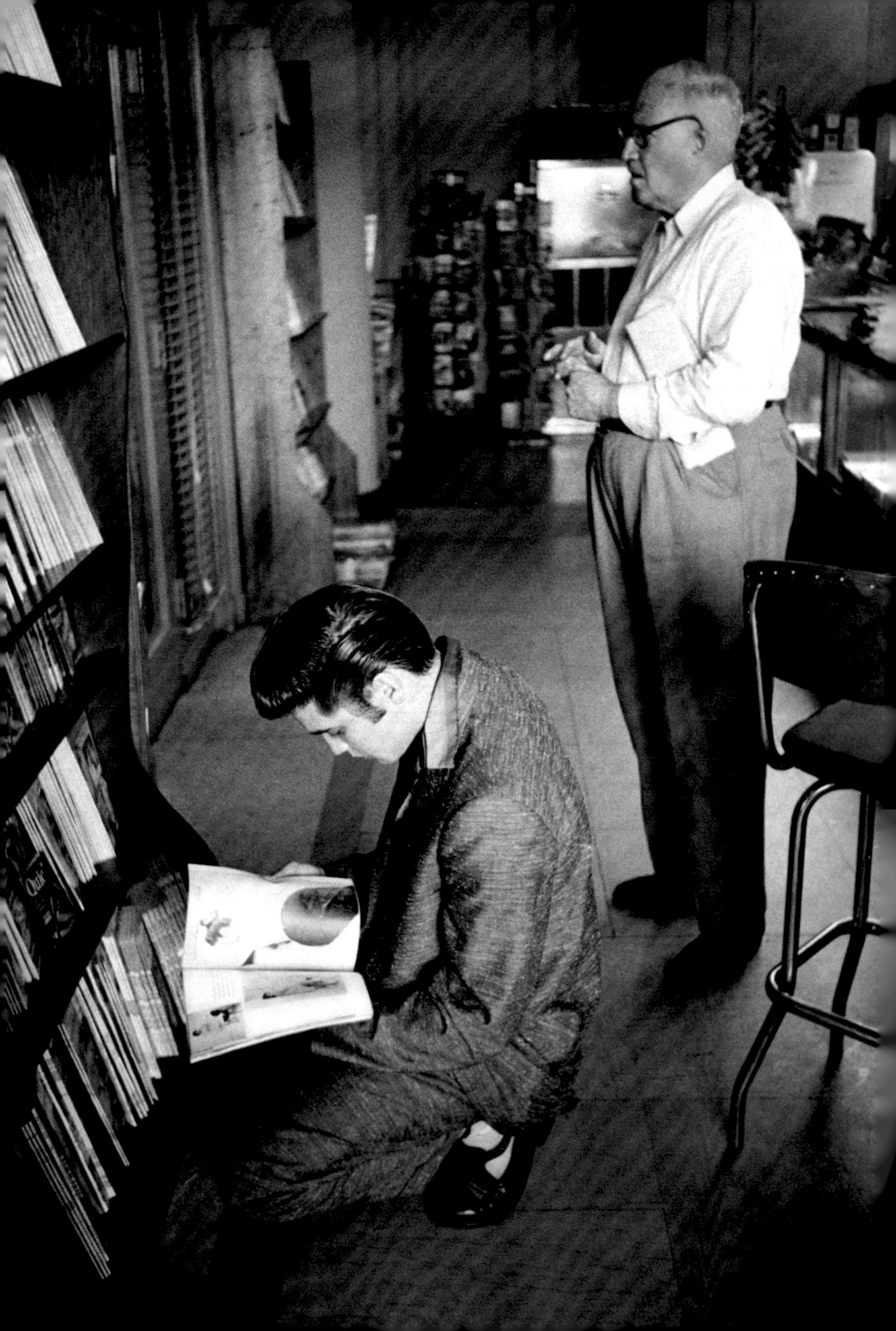

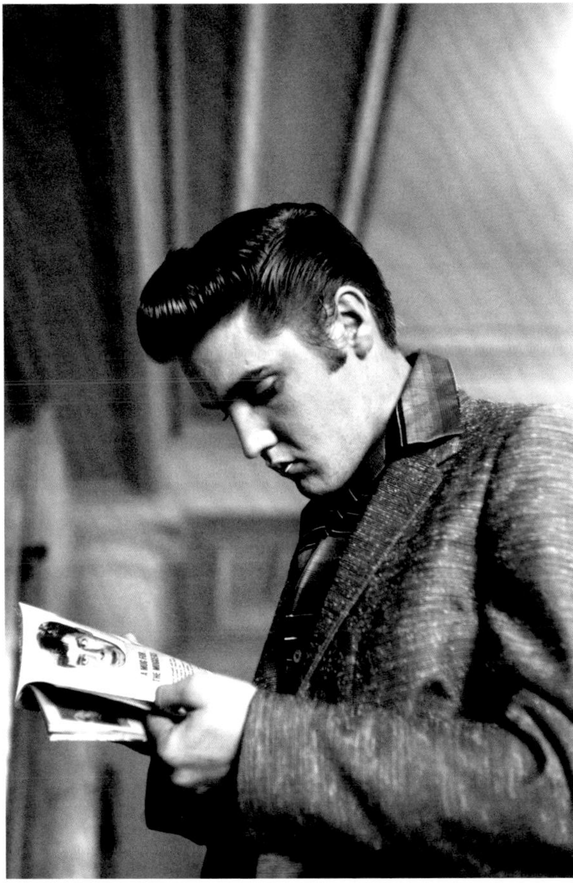

PAGE 77
The Elvis stare, captured in the backseat of a taxi, Richmond, Virginia.

OPPOSITE & ABOVE
Elvis peruses the Jefferson Hotel coffee shop's magazine rack upon arrival.

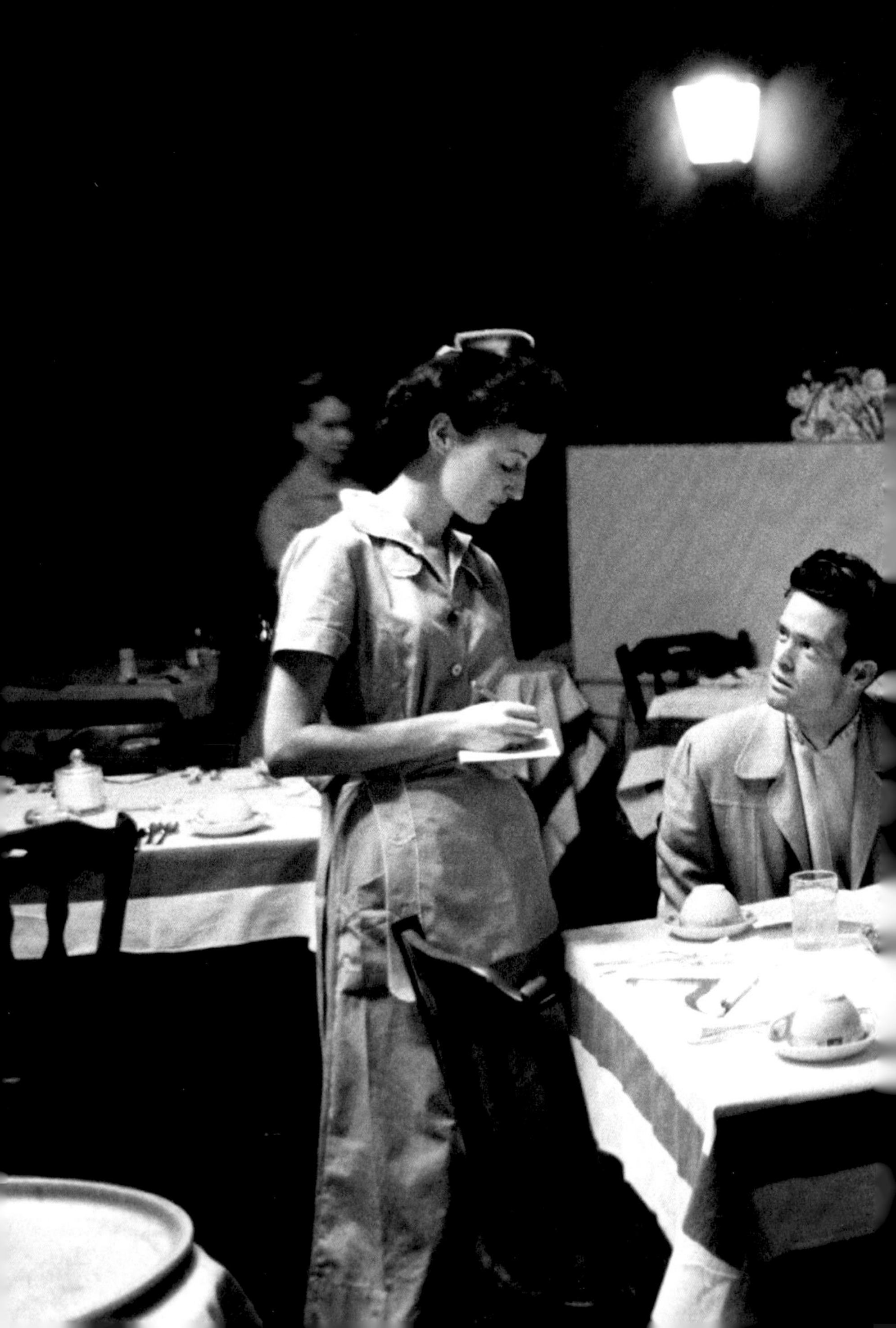

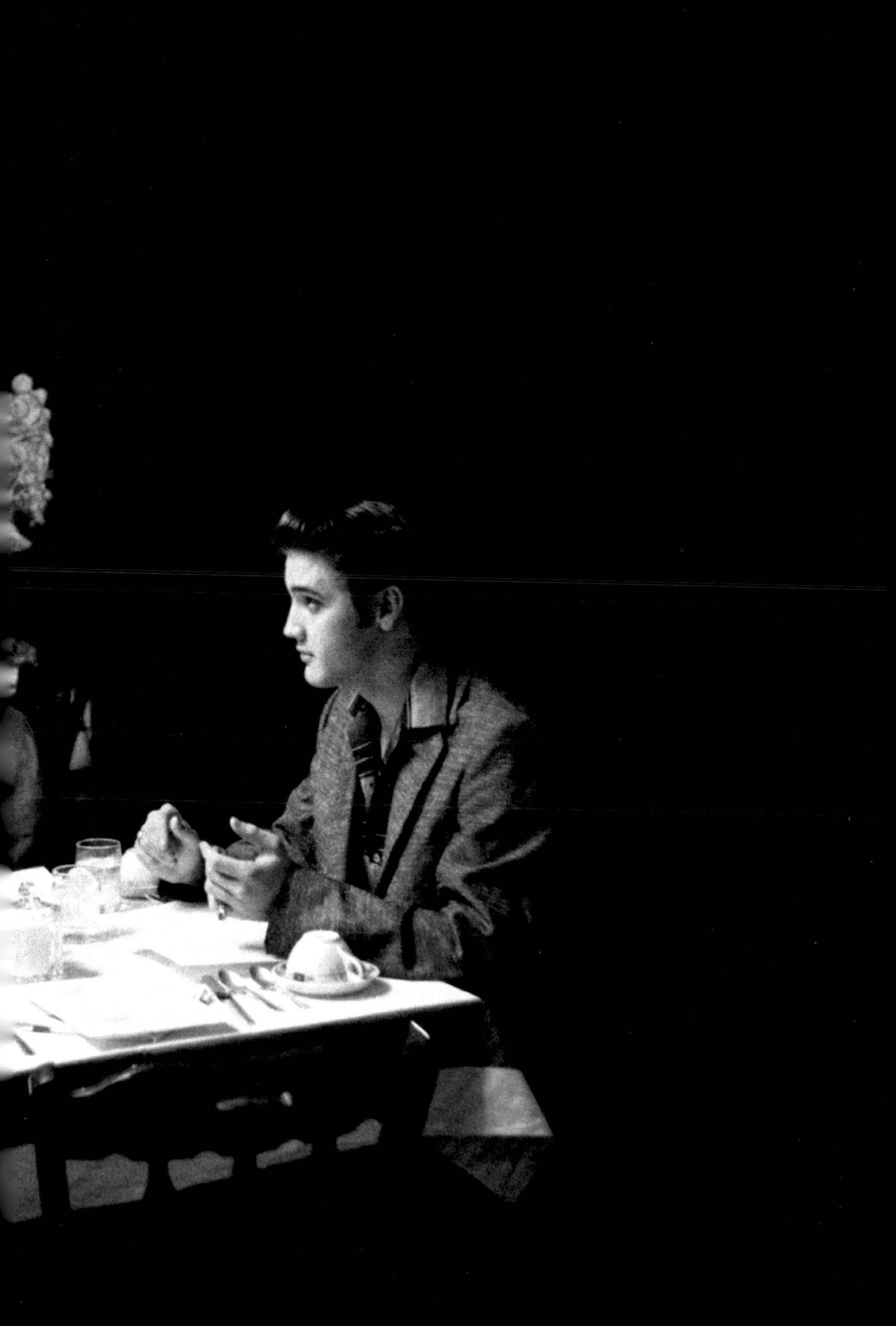

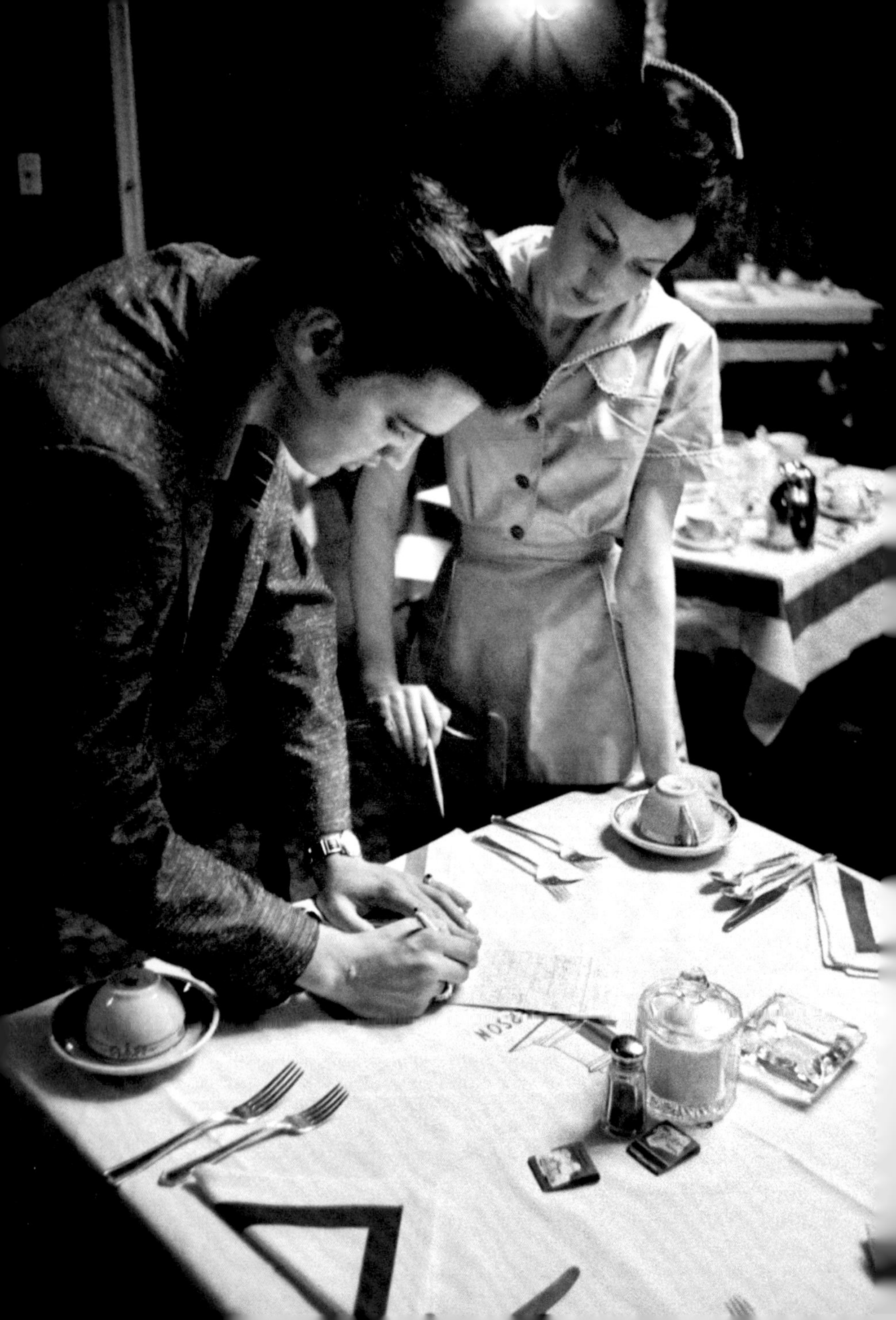

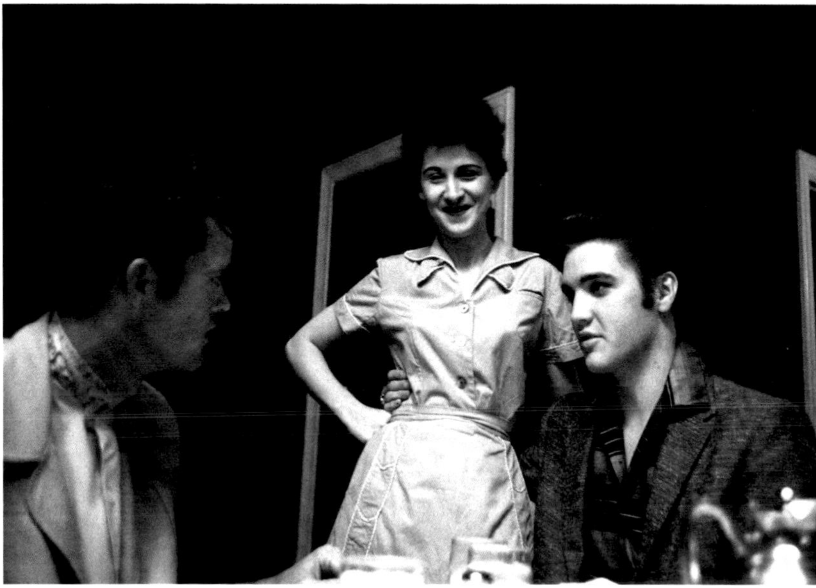

PREVIOUS SPREAD
"Gentlemen, what would you like?" Junior Smith places his order while his cousin prepares to turn on the charm with a waitress at the hotel restaurant.

OPPOSITE
Elvis charges the bill to his room at the Jefferson.

ABOVE
Within 15 minutes of ordering his breakfast, Elvis has his arm around the waist of the delighted waitress.

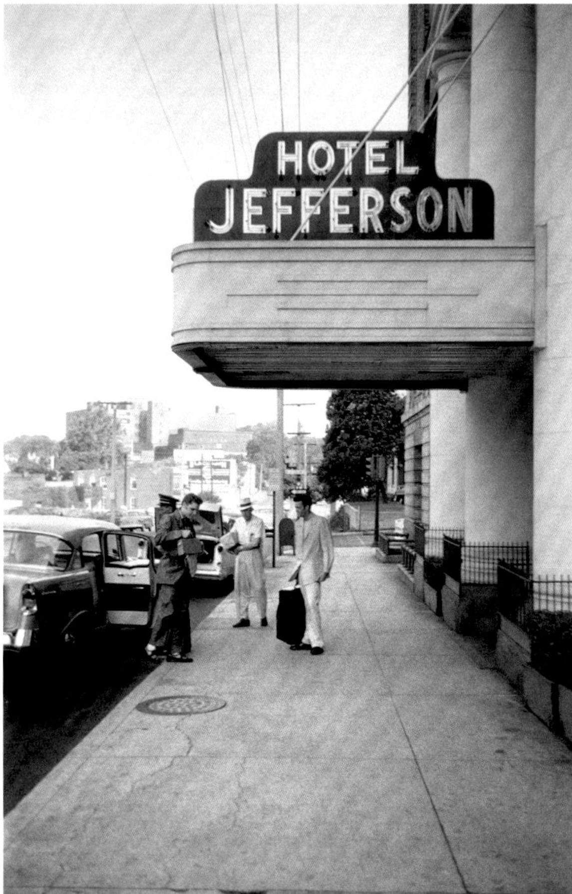

ABOVE & OPPOSITE
Check-in at the Jefferson Hotel with Junior Smith. Right, another of Elvis's cousins, Gene Smith, carries the green jacket the singer will wear for his second performance that night. His date, Barbara Gray (formerly Bobbi Owens), has also arrived from Charleston, South Carolina.

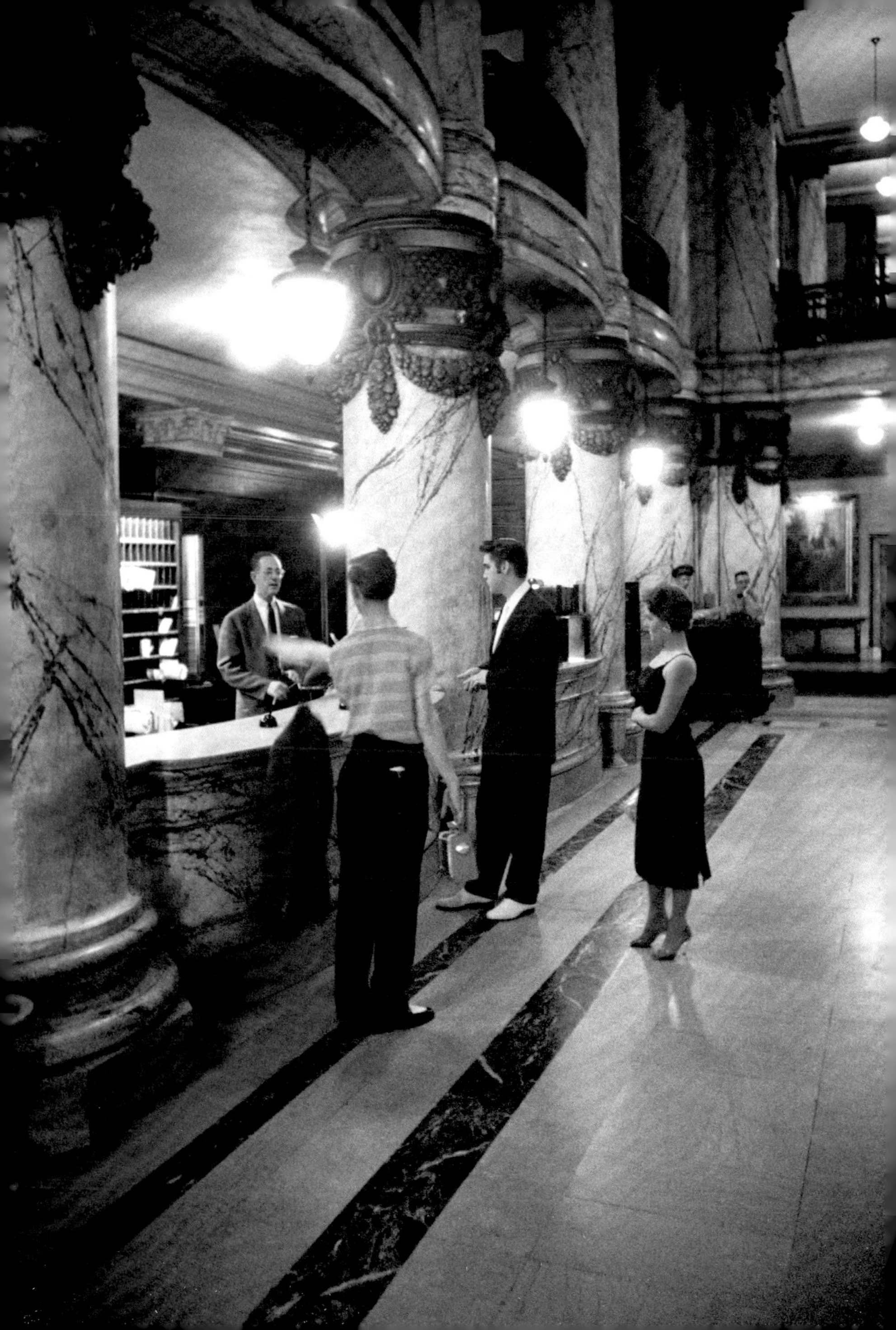

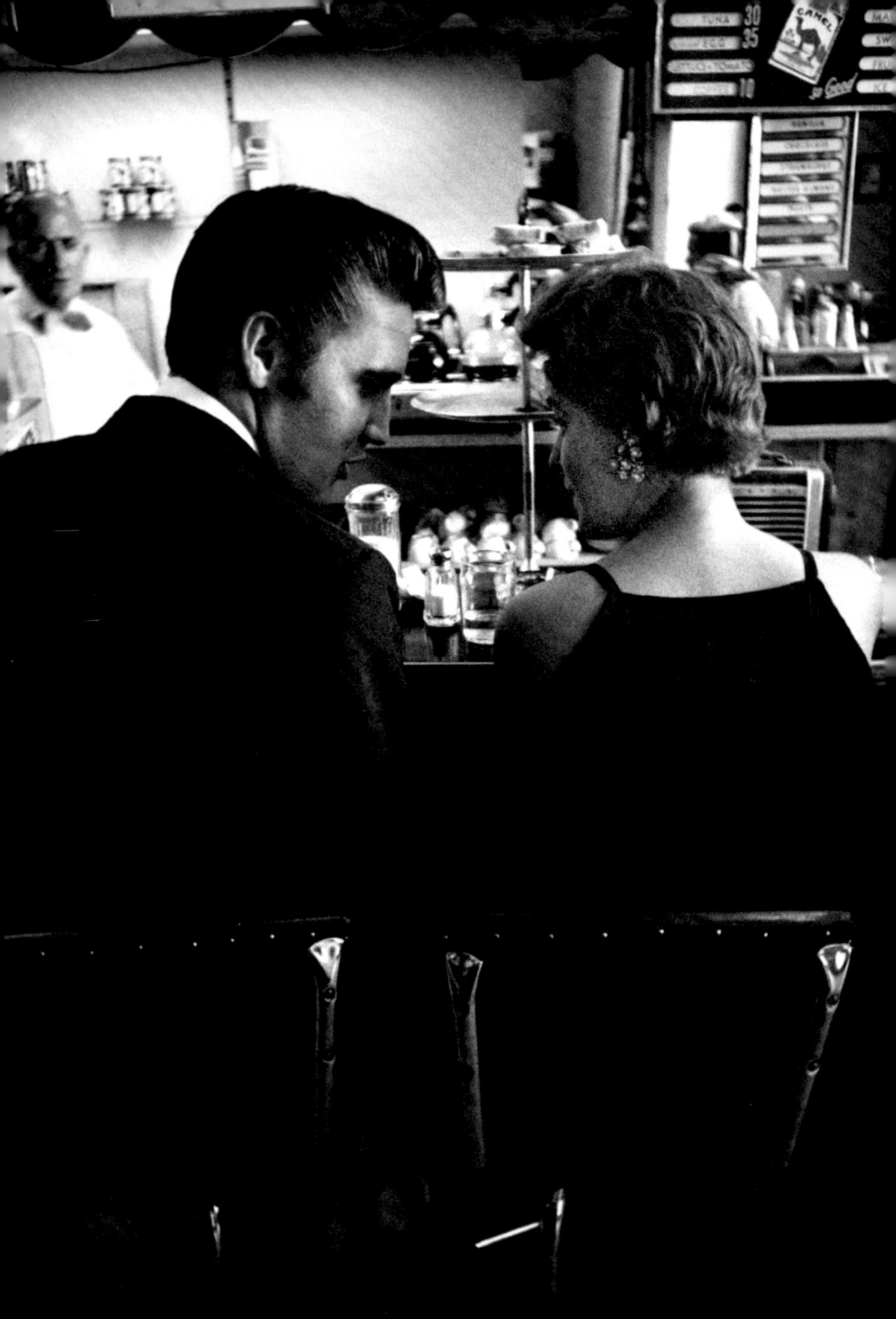
TUNA 30
EGG 35
10
CAMEL

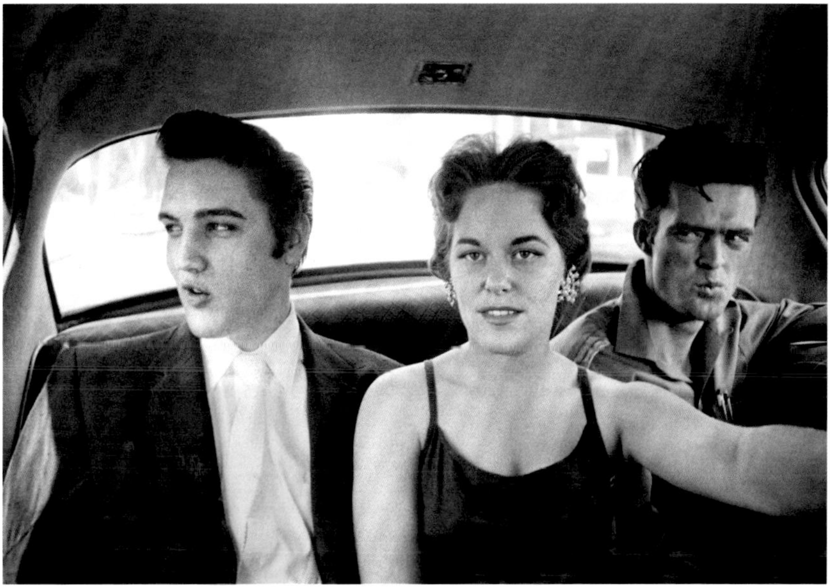

OPPOSITE
Flirting with Barbara Gray at the Jefferson Hotel coffee shop.

ABOVE
Elvis gets close to his date in the back of a Richmond cab.

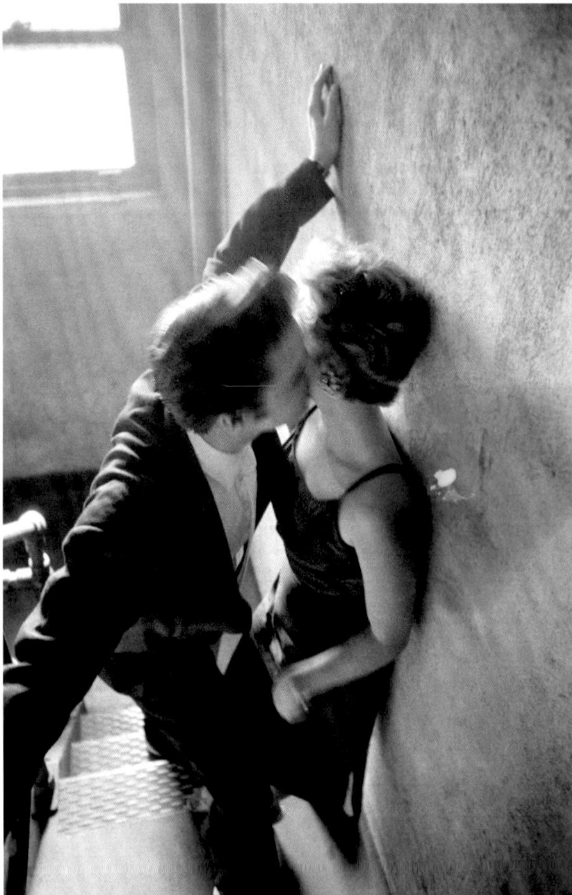

ABOVE
The photographer finds his subject in the stairwell, making his move.

OPPOSITE
Hold Me Tight, the Mosque Theater, June 30, 1956.
Elvis performs with Barbara Gray while another act performs onstage. In order to capture the closeness between the couple, Wertheimer had to get close.

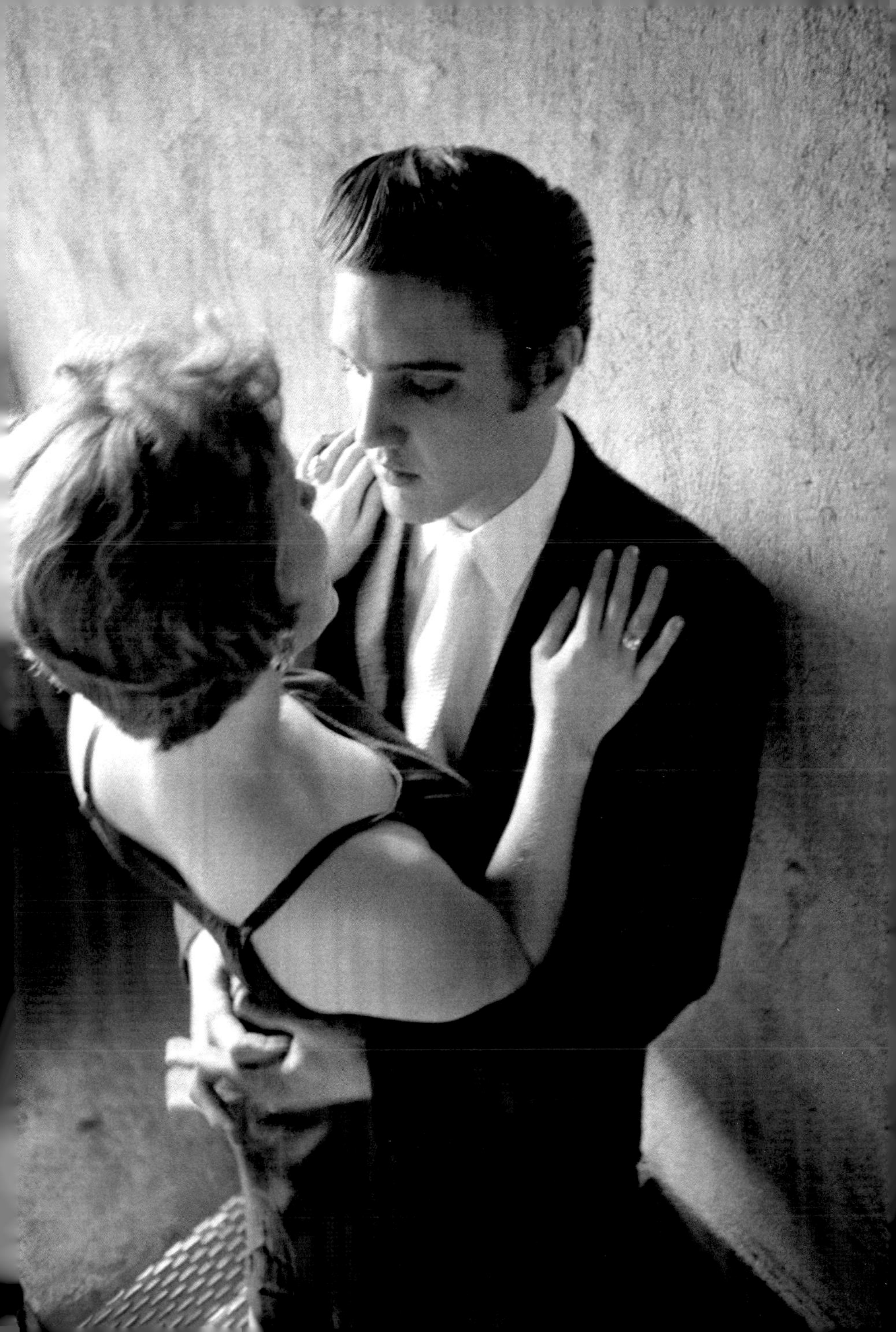

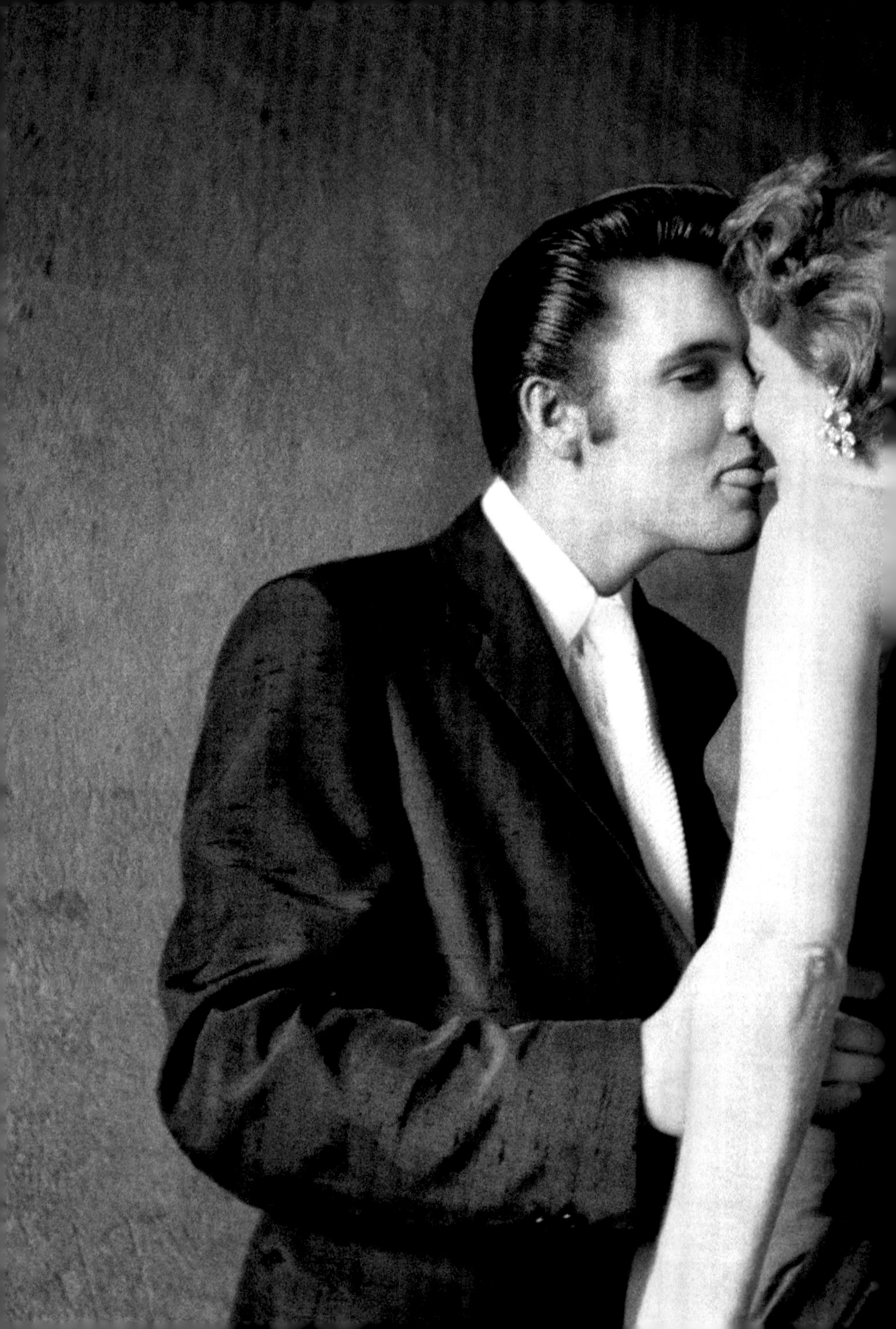

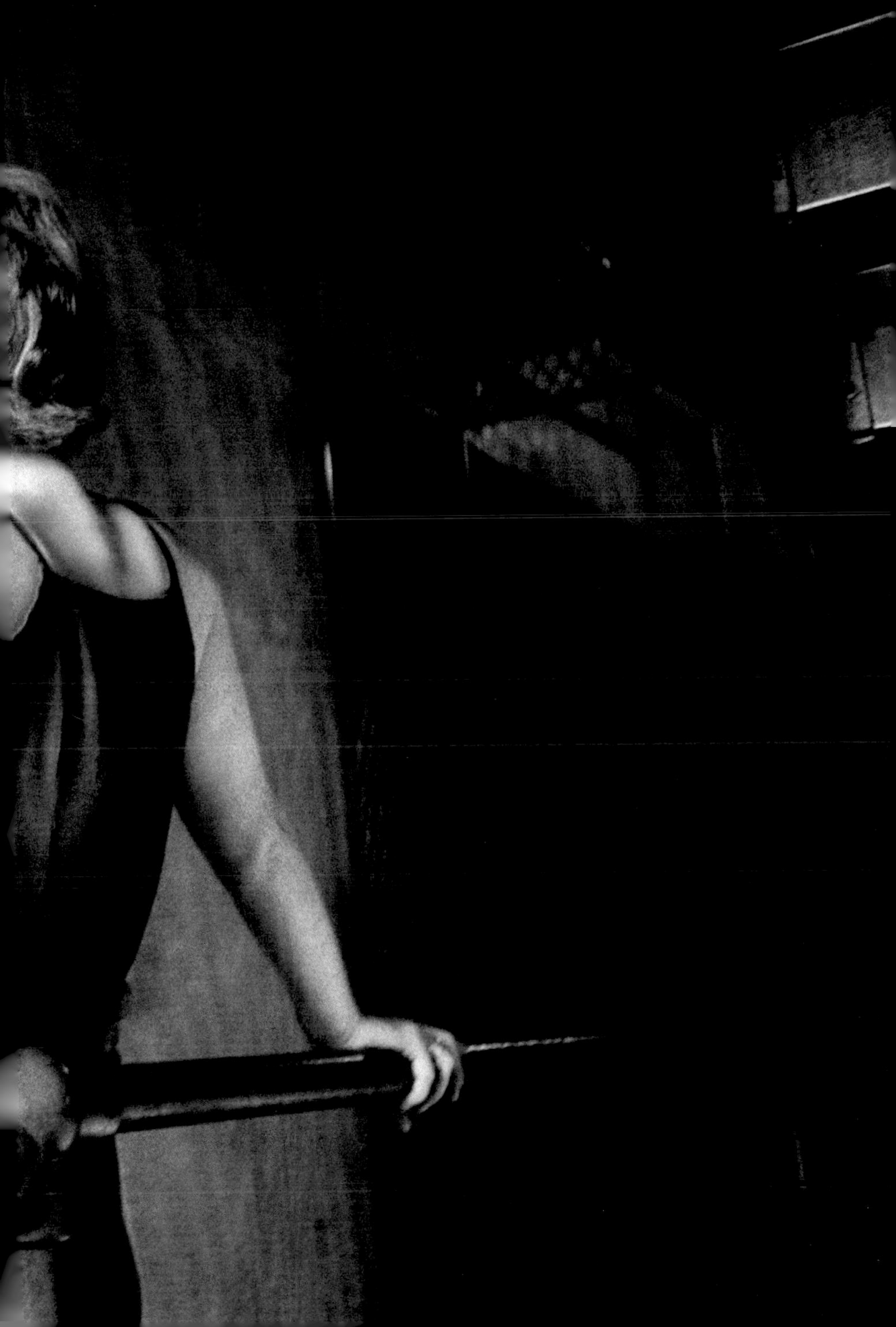

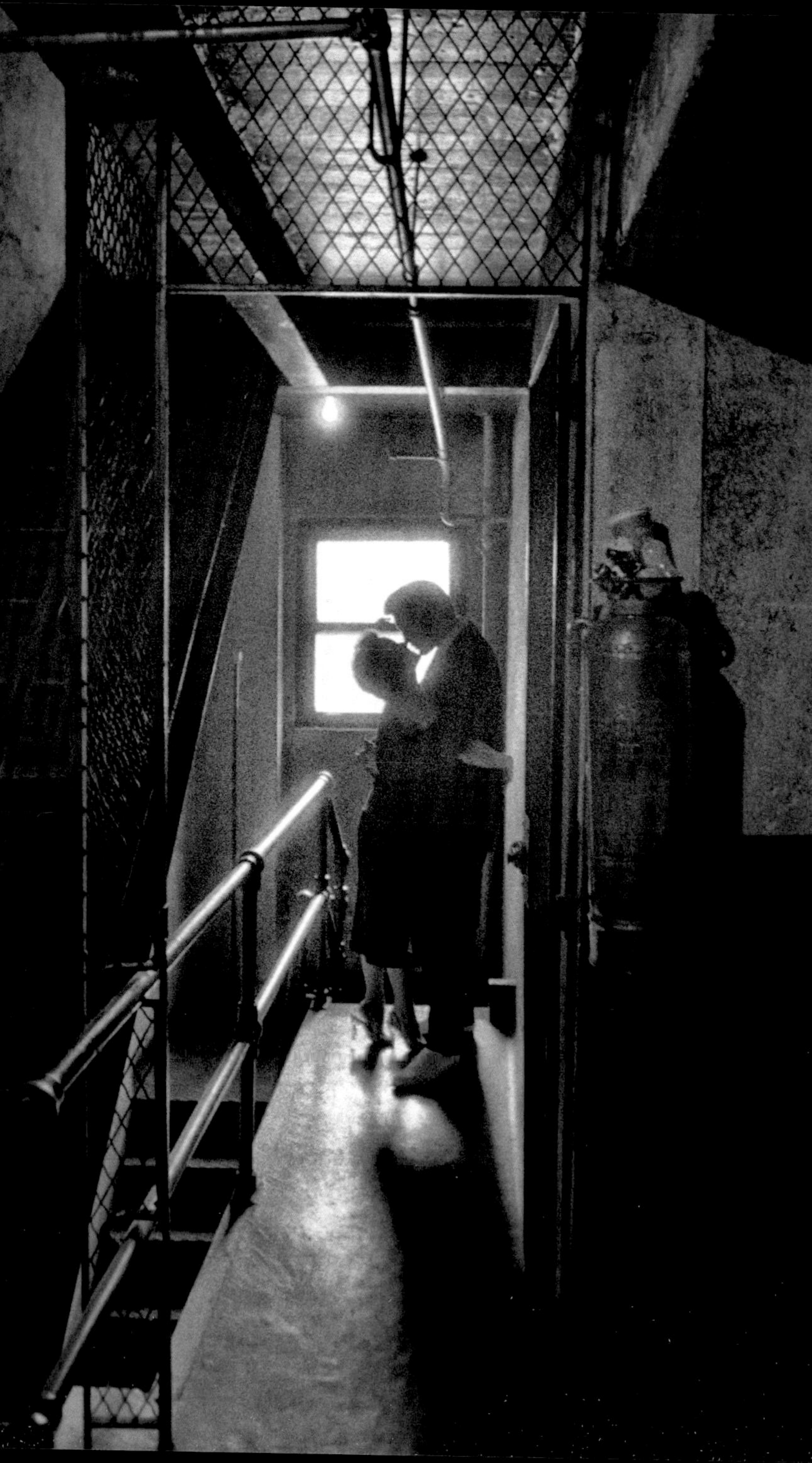

Maybe we had sparks…but
I didn't know who he was. He was very silly.
We were running around chasing
each other and just being young.

BARBARA GRAY
"The Kiss Lady" on The Today Show,
August 8, 2011

PREVIOUS SPREAD
The Kiss, the Mosque Theater, June 30, 1956.
Though perhaps Wertheimer's most iconic photograph, the identity of the woman remained unknown until she came forward in 2011, 55 years after the photo was taken.

OPPOSITE
A last embrace before Elvis prepares to go onstage.

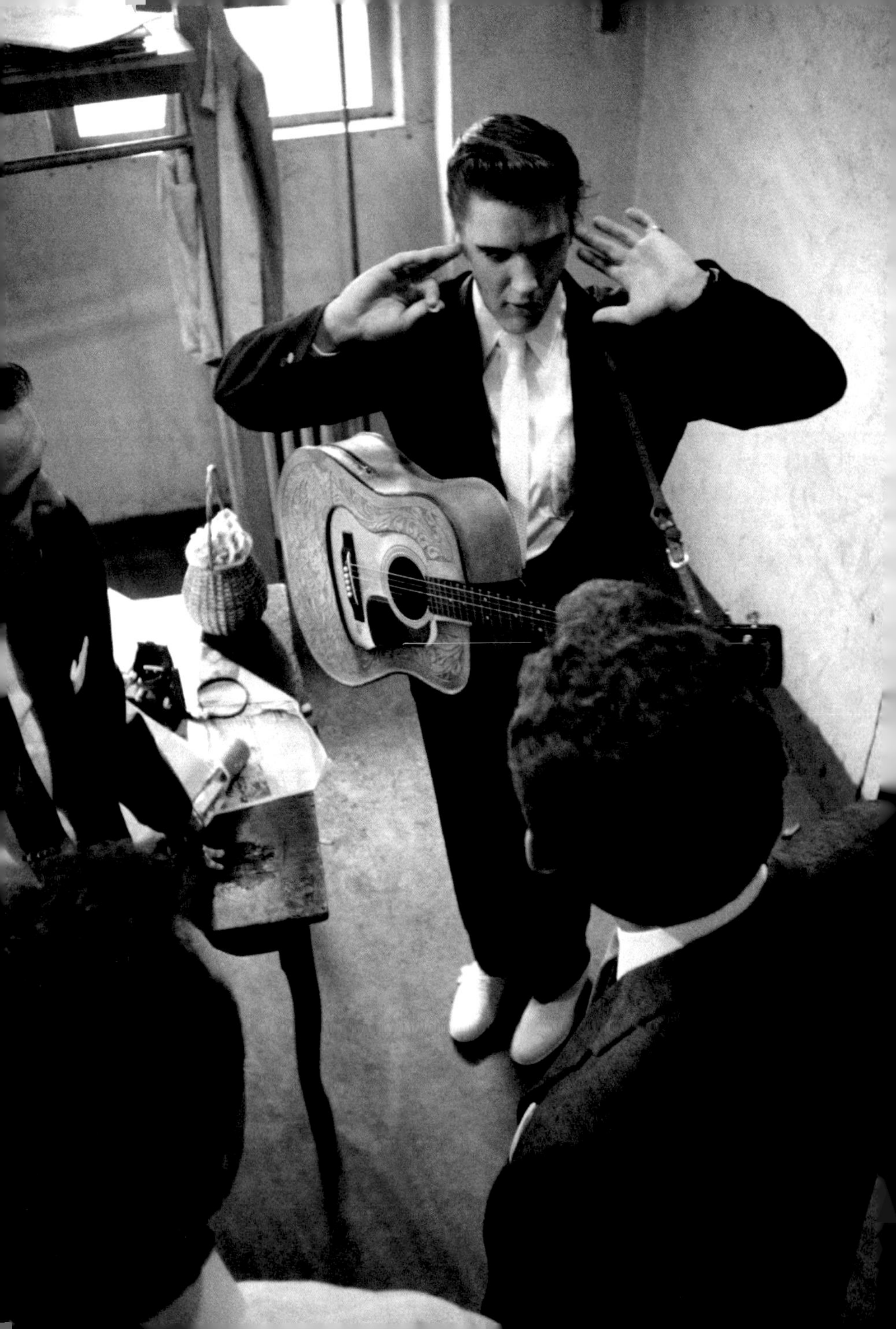

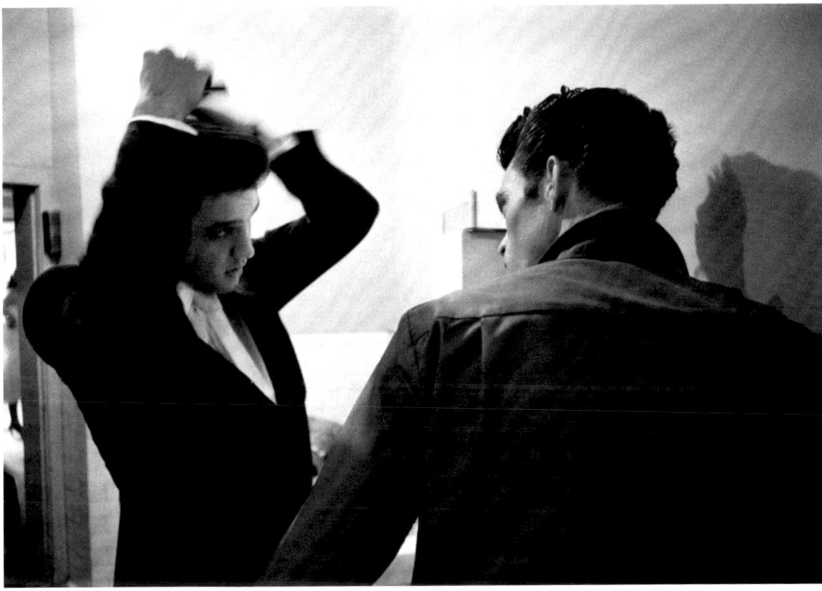

OPPOSITE
Rehearsal is interrupted by the high-pitched screams of fans outside. When Elvis opens the window and asks them to quiet down so he can concentrate, they comply.

ABOVE
Junior Smith gives encouragement while Elvis combs his hair in the men's room of the Mosque.

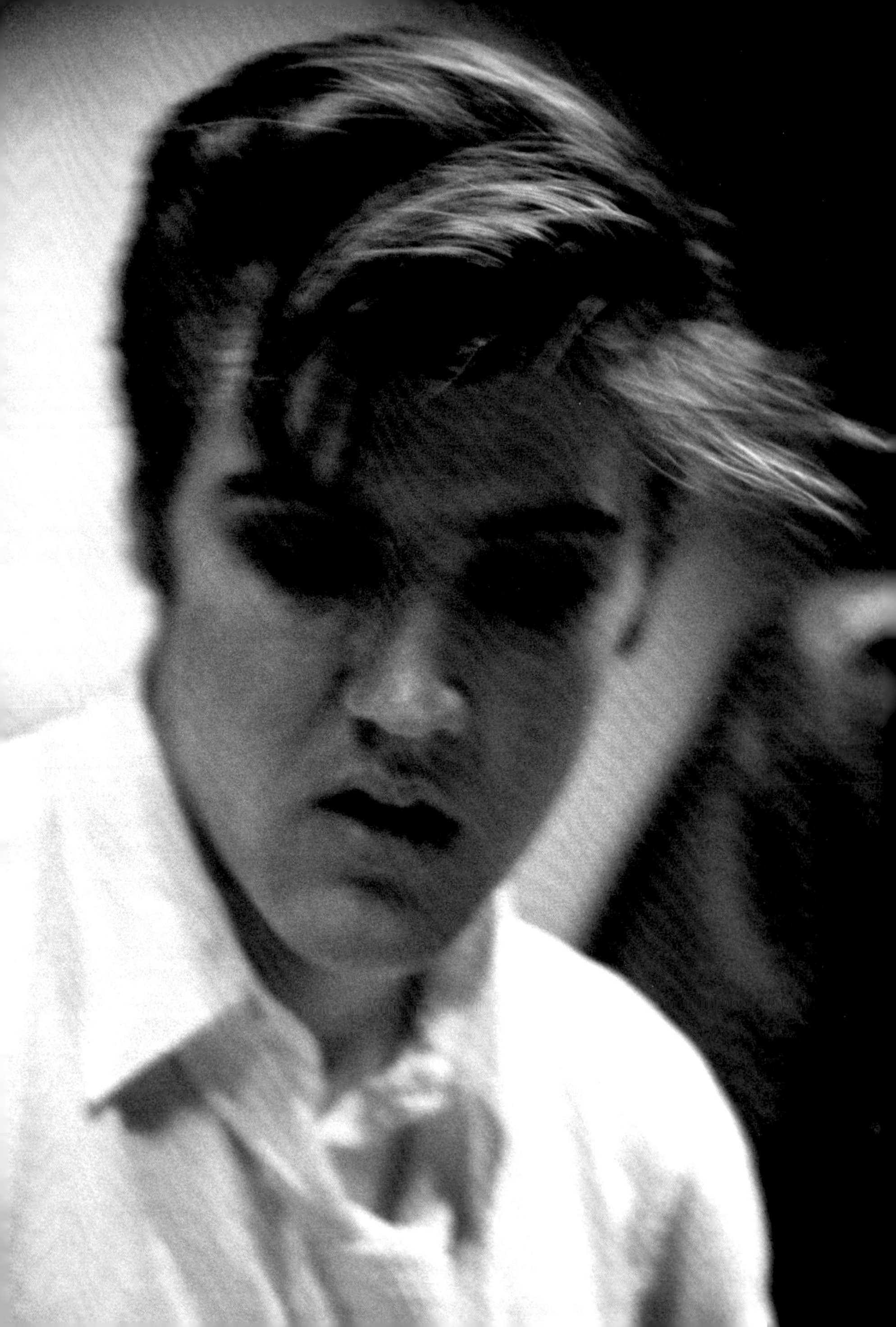

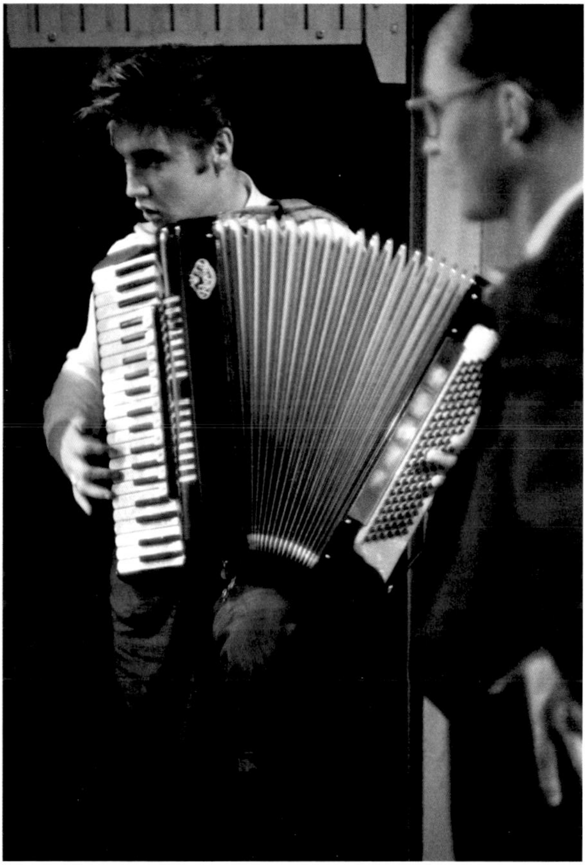

OPPOSITE
Portrait in motion.

ABOVE
Between shows, Elvis relaxes by playing an accordion. He found that when he had an instrument in his hands people left him alone.

FOLLOWING SPREAD
Portrait studies in color: the 8 P.M. show at the Mosque Theater.

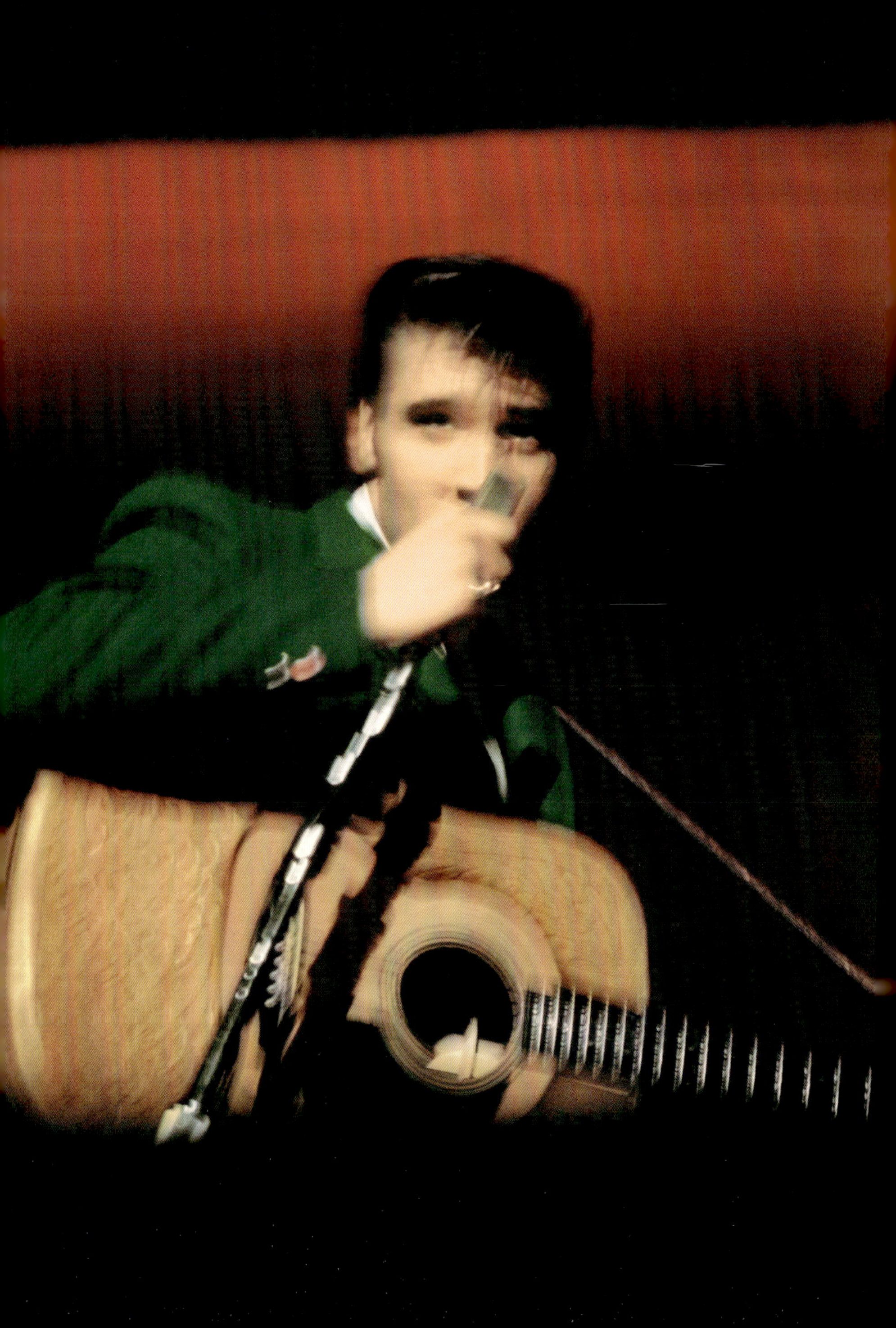

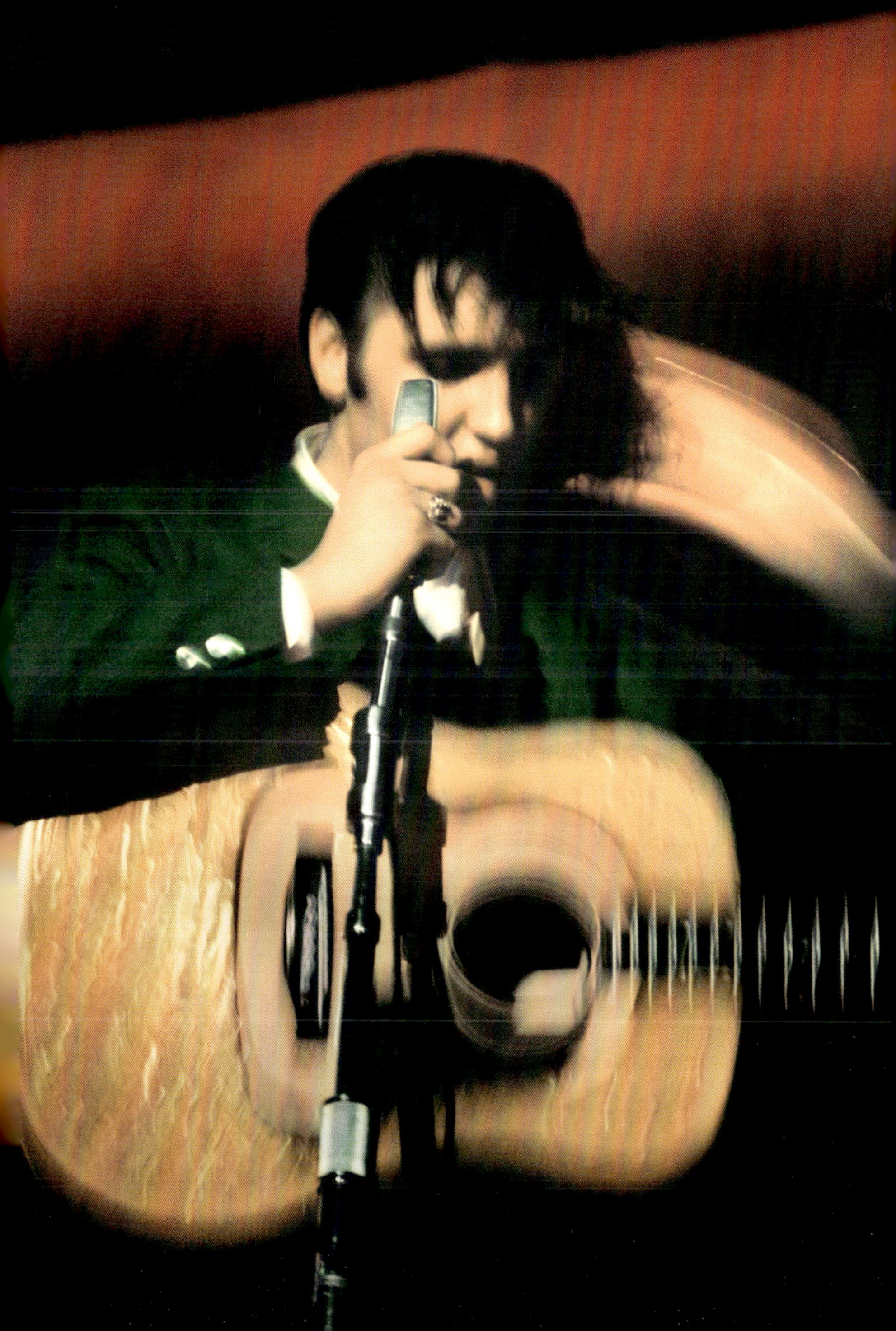

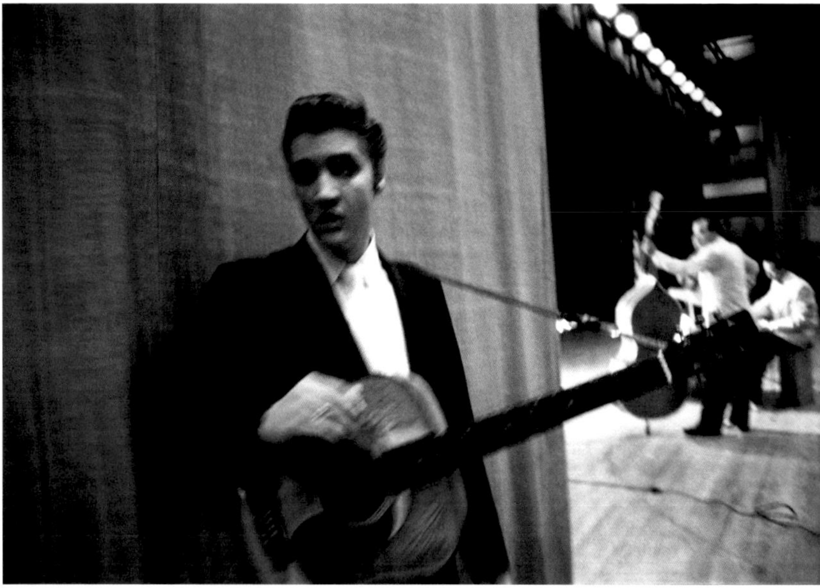

ABOVE
His tooled-leather Martin strapped on, Elvis waits in the wings for the curtains to part.

OPPOSITE
Kneeling at the Mosque,
Richmond, Virginia, June 30, 1956.

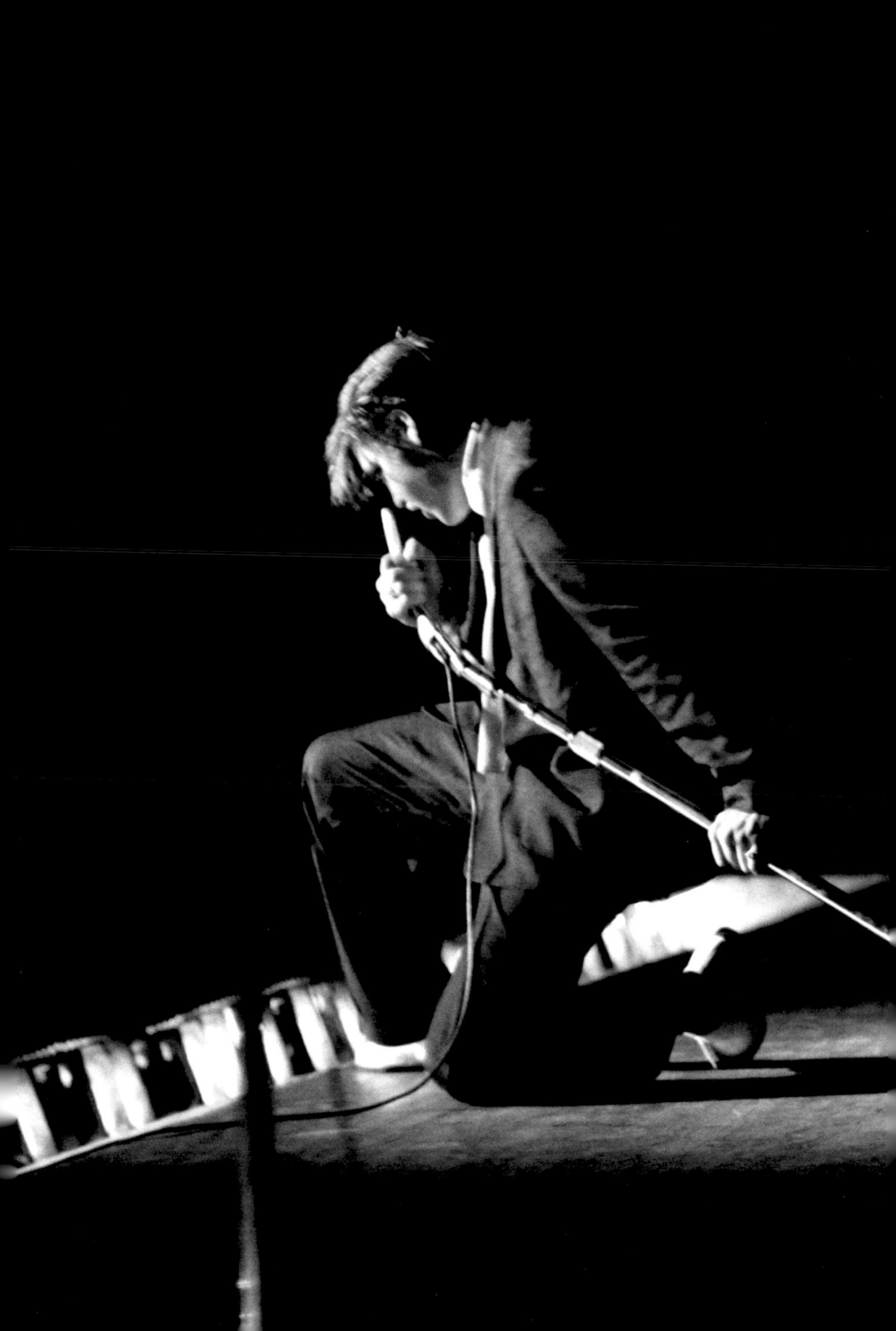

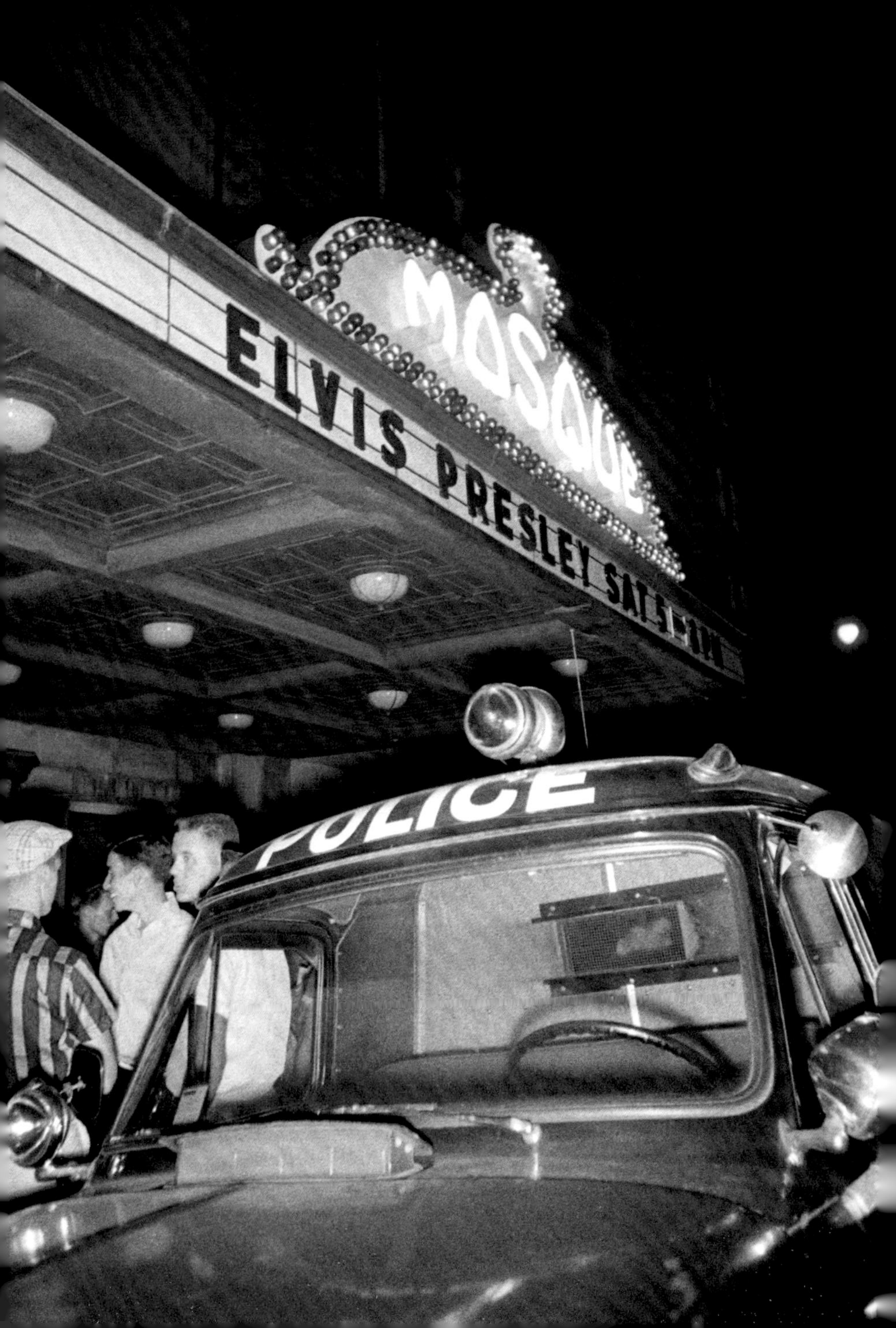
MOSQUE
ELVIS PRESLEY SAT
POLICE

My pelvis had nothin' to do with what I do. I just get kinda in rhythm with the music. I jump around to it because I enjoy what I'm doin'—I'm not tryin' to be vulgar, I'm not tryin' to sell any sex, I'm not tryin' to look vulgar and nasty. I just enjoy what I'm doin' and tryin' to make the best of it.

ELVIS PRESLEY
TV Guide interview,
August 6, 1956

OPPOSITE
"Elvis has left the building":
the Mosque marquee after the show.

ELVIS P

RCA V

STUD

RECO

SES

NEW YORK

RESLEY

ICTOR

IO 1

RDING

ION

ITY-JULY 2, 1956

★ ★ ★

RCA VICTOR STUDIOS ON 24TH STREET in Manhattan was the site of Elvis's legendary recording session of "Hound Dog" and "Don't Be Cruel," which became his third and fourth gold records, along with "Any Way You Want Me." Junior Smith, the Jordanaires, Scotty Moore, D.J. Fontana, Bill Black, Shorty Long (an additional piano player), and Steve Sholes, the artist and repertoire man who had signed Elvis to RCA Victor—they were all there. At first Elvis had difficulty recording "Hound Dog." He just kept on moving off the fixed microphone, his voice fading in and out, until he ultimately adjusted to the studio's limitations. It still took about 20 takes for him to achieve his perfection. He was very absorbed in the process, choosing which songs to sing, how the arrangement for the band would go, and deciding which takes would stay and which would go. After a long day, Elvis and the group left the studio. This time there were no young girls; gathered on the sidewalk were a few blue-collar postal workers waiting for an autograph and small talk. His entourage then drove away in a white convertible into the darkness of the night.

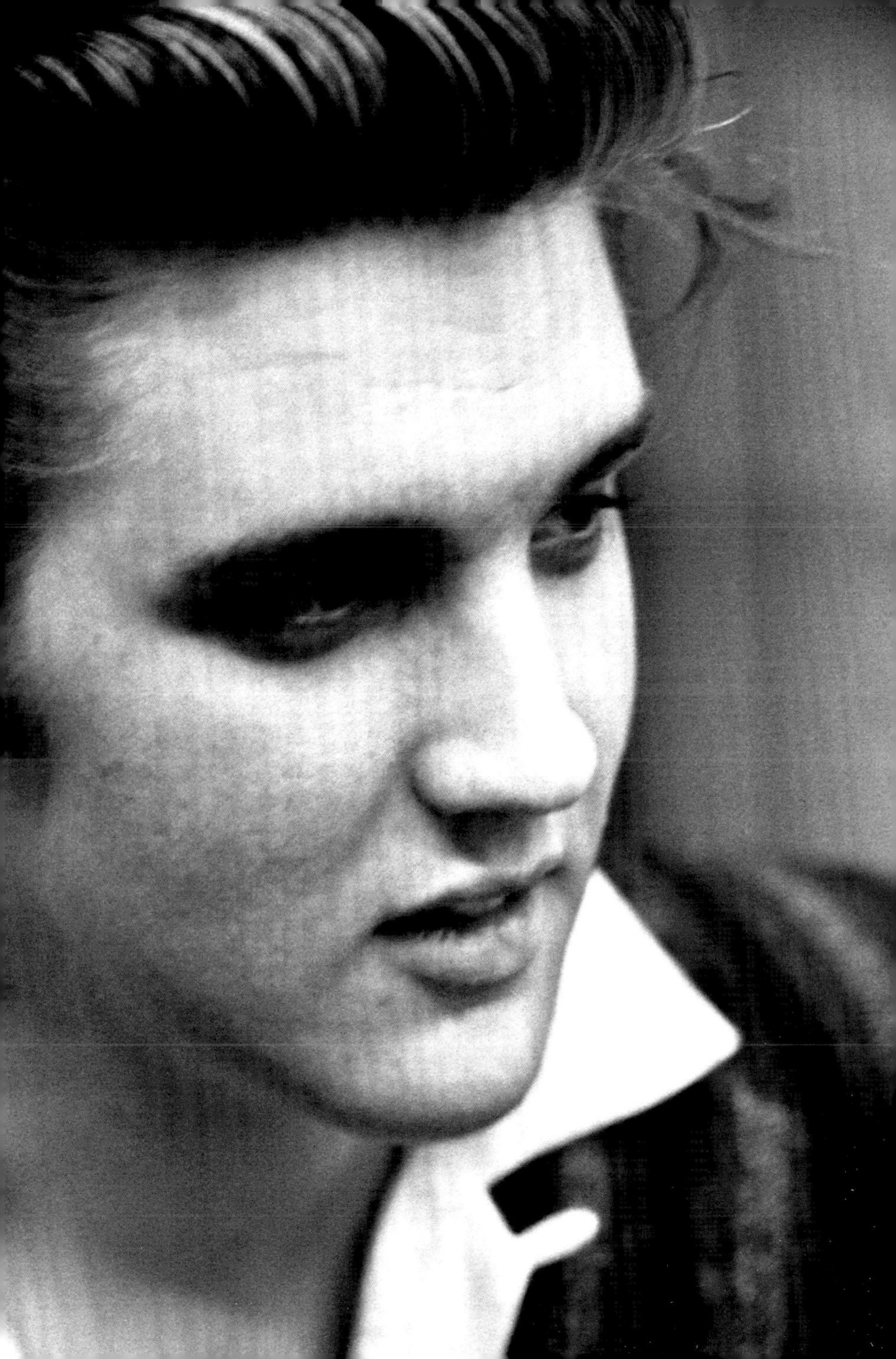

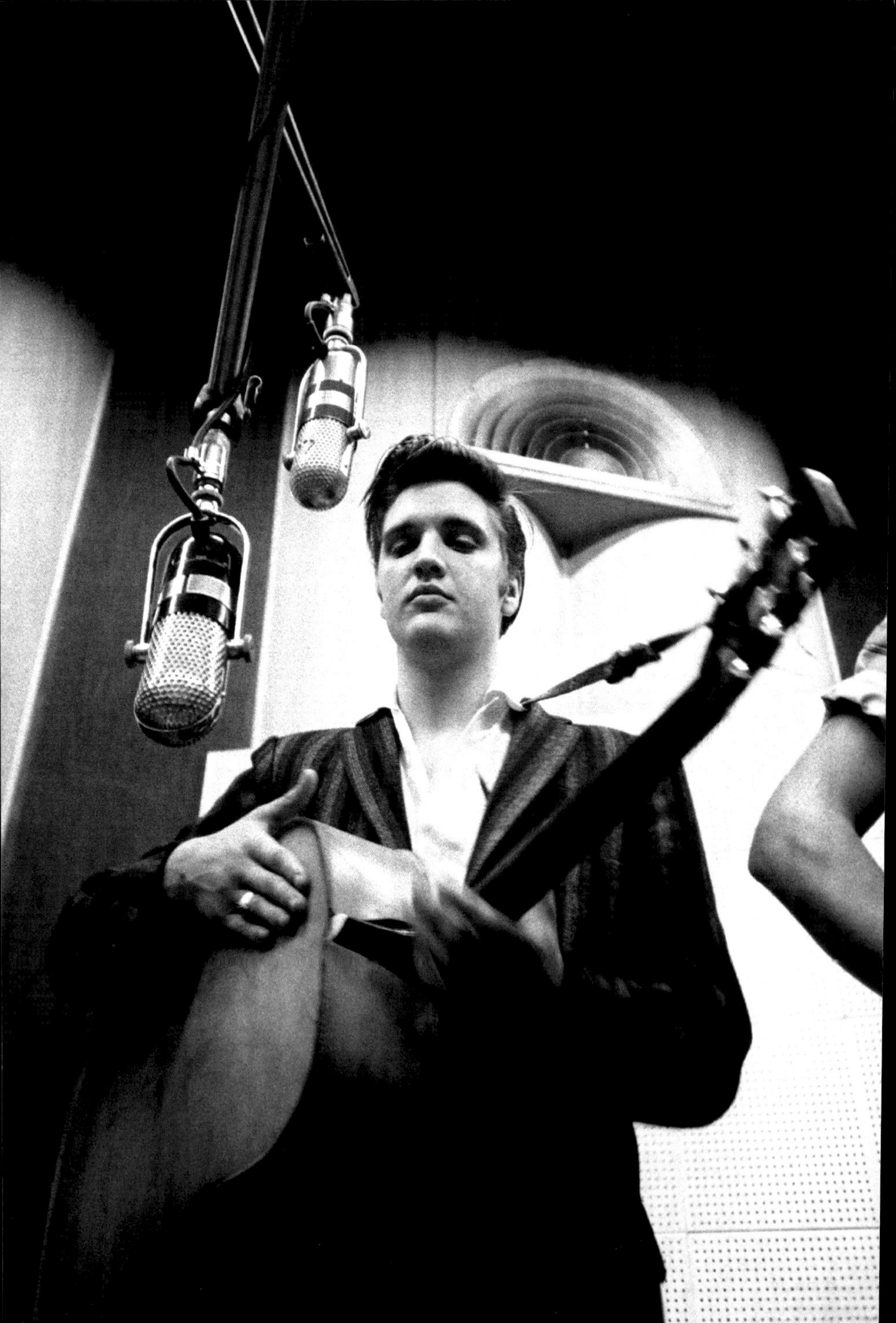

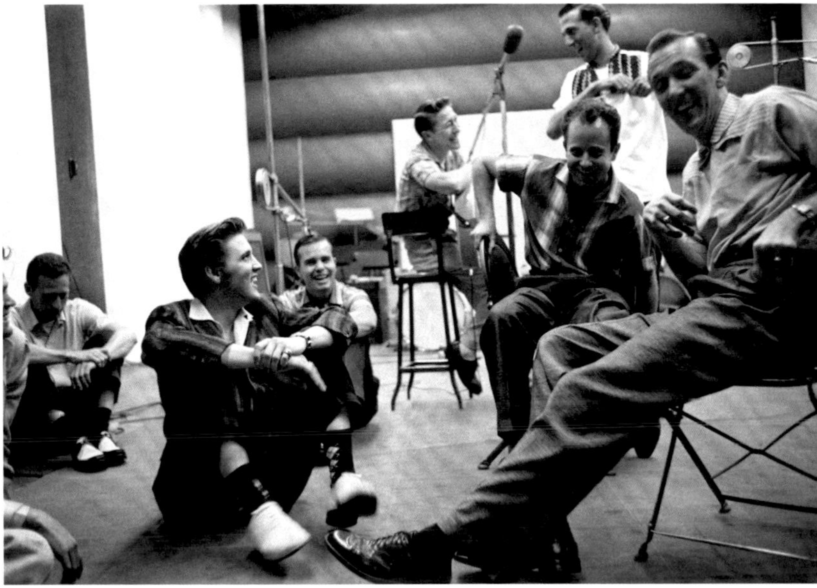

PAGE 107
Portrait at the RCA Victor recording studio on East 24th Street, New York City, July 2, 1956. The session will begin with recording the A-side song, "Hound Dog."

OPPOSITE
Twin microphones: the top one is for his voice, the bottom for his slap against the leather covering the guitar, and the song is "Don't Be Cruel."

ABOVE
Between songs, Elvis relaxes and cracks a joke.

Elvis was one of those artists, when he sang a song, he just seemed to live every word of it. There's other people that have a voice that's maybe as great or greater than Presley's, but he had that certain something that everybody searches for all during their lifetime.

JAKE HESS
Lead singer, the Statesmen Quartet

OPPOSITE
Don't Be Cruel, RCA Victor Studio 1, July 2, 1956.

FOLLOWING SPREAD
One of several takes of "Hound Dog."

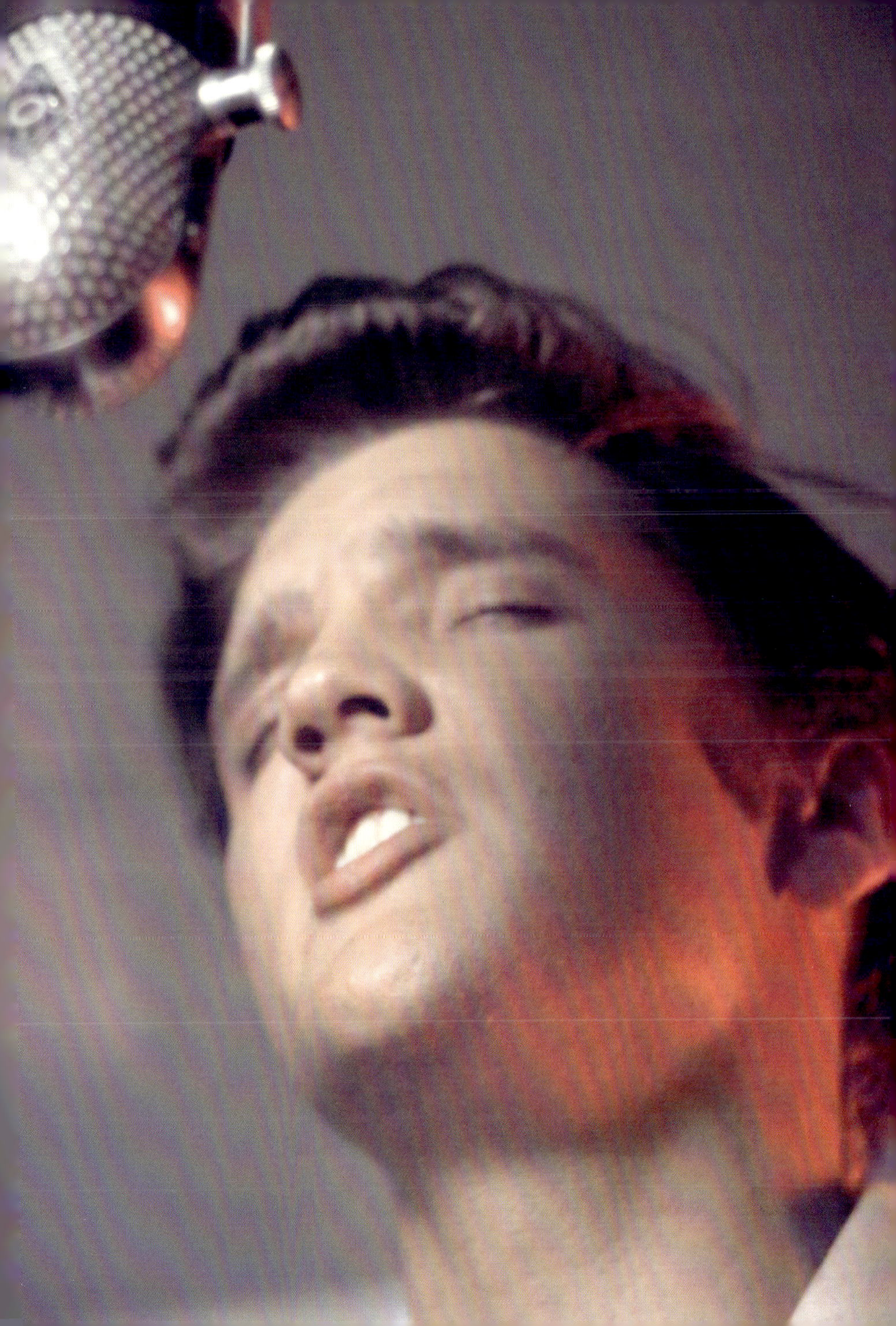

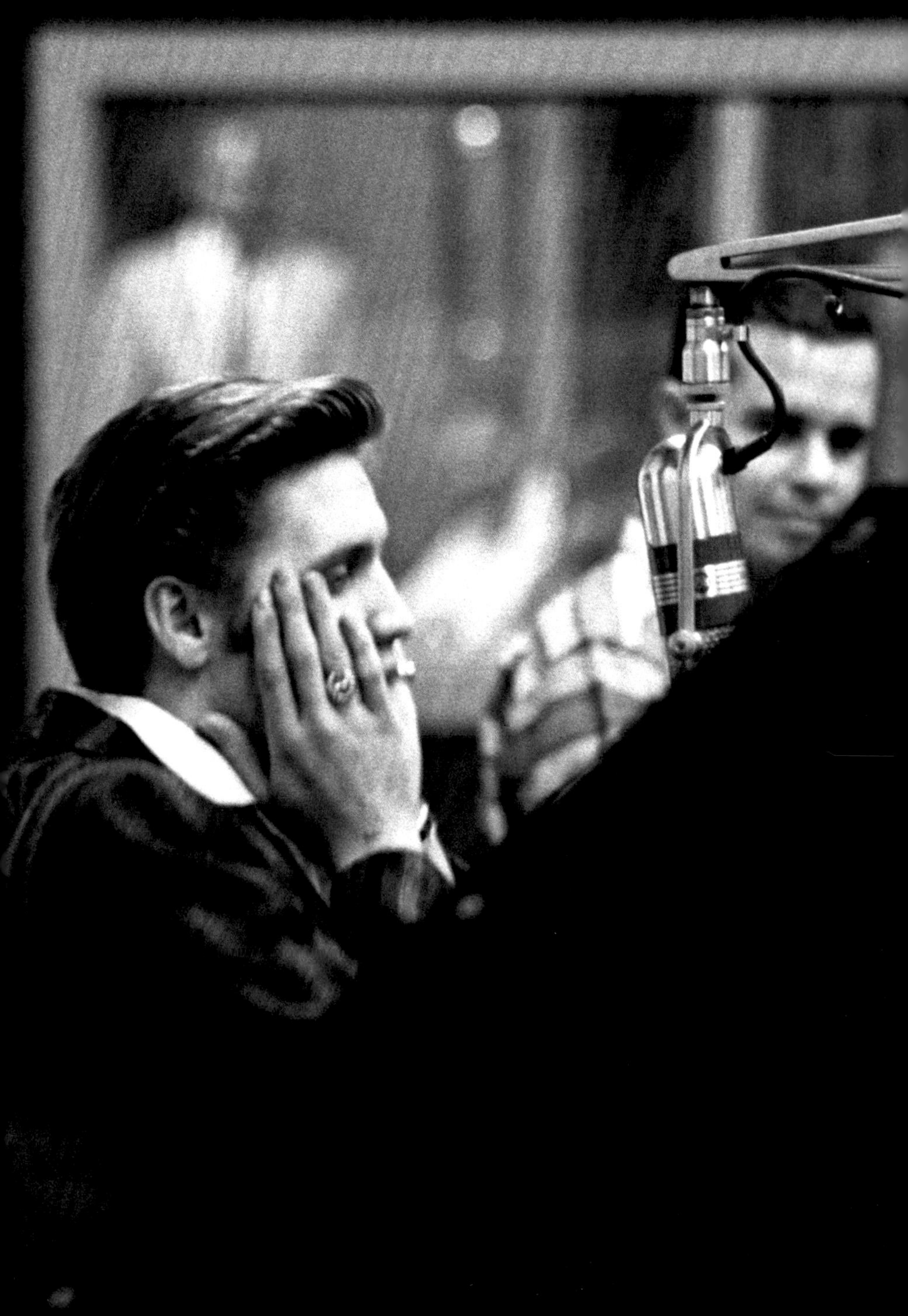

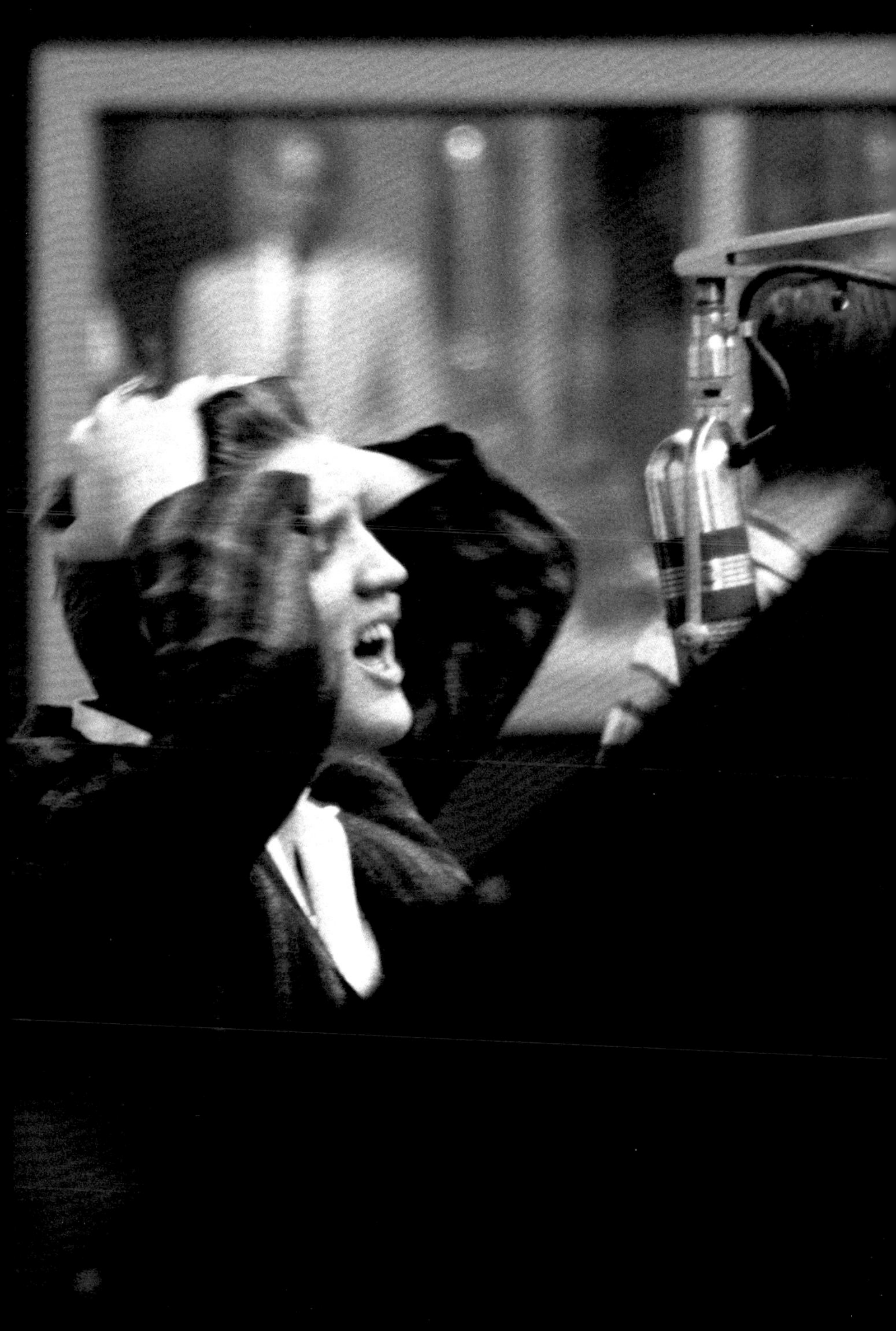

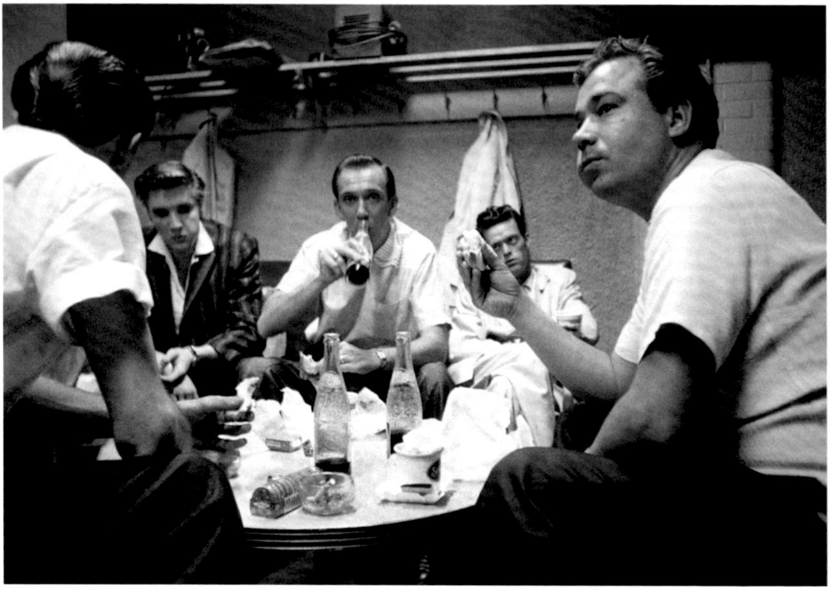

ABOVE
Lunch break with Hugh Jarrett,
Junior Smith, Bill Black, and others.

OPPOSITE
Elvis listens intently to each playback, waiting to hear the perfect take. "Hound Dog" and "Don't Be Cruel" will hit #1 on the charts—the first and only time both sides of a single record will do so.

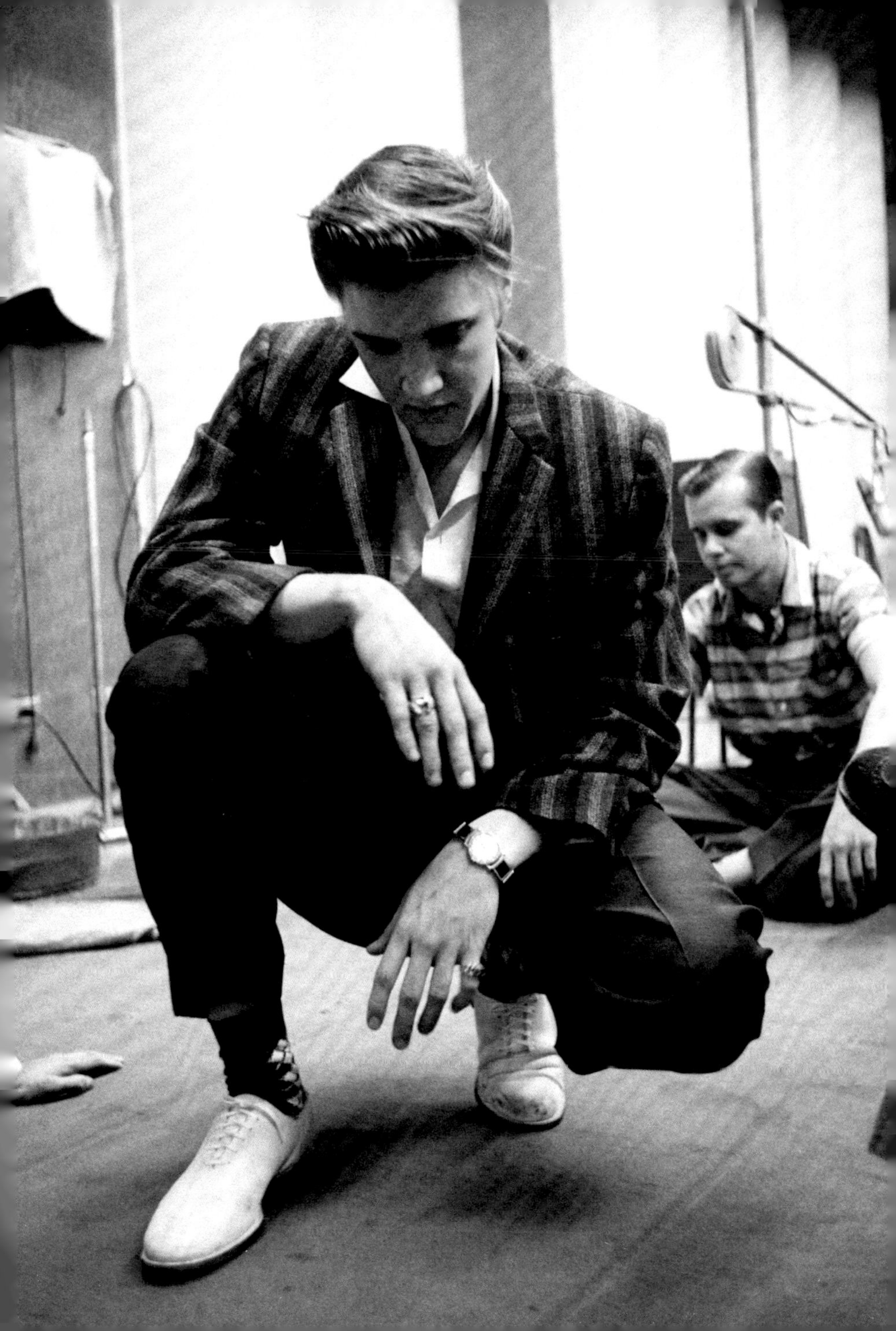

ELVIS P

RETU

MEM

ABOARD THE

SOUTHERN RAILW

JULY 3-4, 1956

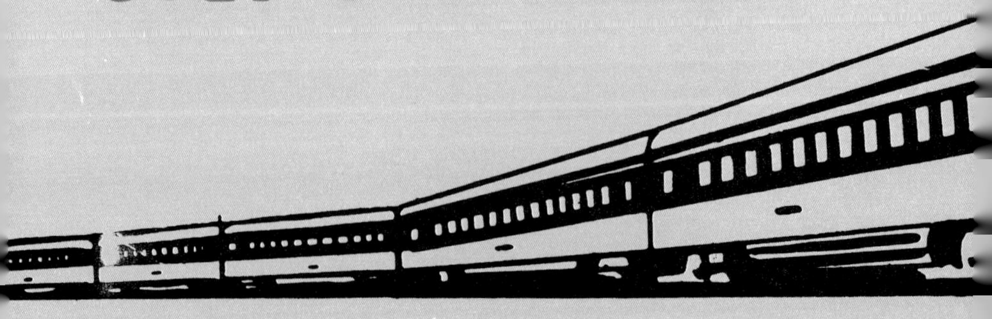

RESLEY'S

RN TO

PHIS

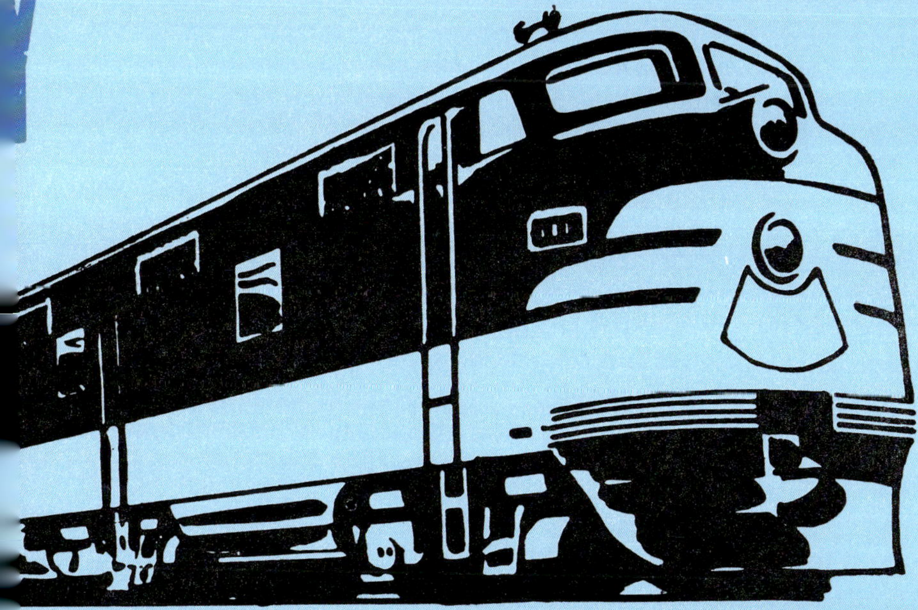

★ ★ ★

ON THE 27-HOUR TRAIN RIDE HOME from New York to Memphis, Elvis spent several hours repeatedly listening to quick acetate discs of the three final versions of his freshly recorded songs. When asked why he did not purchase a higher-quality record player, he remarked that he wanted to hear the songs the way his fans would. We transferred trains going west in Chattanooga, Tennessee, where Elvis flirted with girls and then had breakfast. Back on the train, I think Colonel Parker planted a giant stuffed panda bear knowing Elvis would find something to do with it to stir up some attention. Elvis in his boredom decided to pick up the panda, put it on his left hip, and proceeded to walk down the aisle to the other end of the car. I followed him discreetly with my camera. After drinking a cup of water, he asked some young girls if they were coming to his concert and they replied, "Who are you?" He said, "Elvis Presley." "How do we know that?" "You see that photographer over there? If I wasn't him do you think he would be taking my picture?" was his reply.

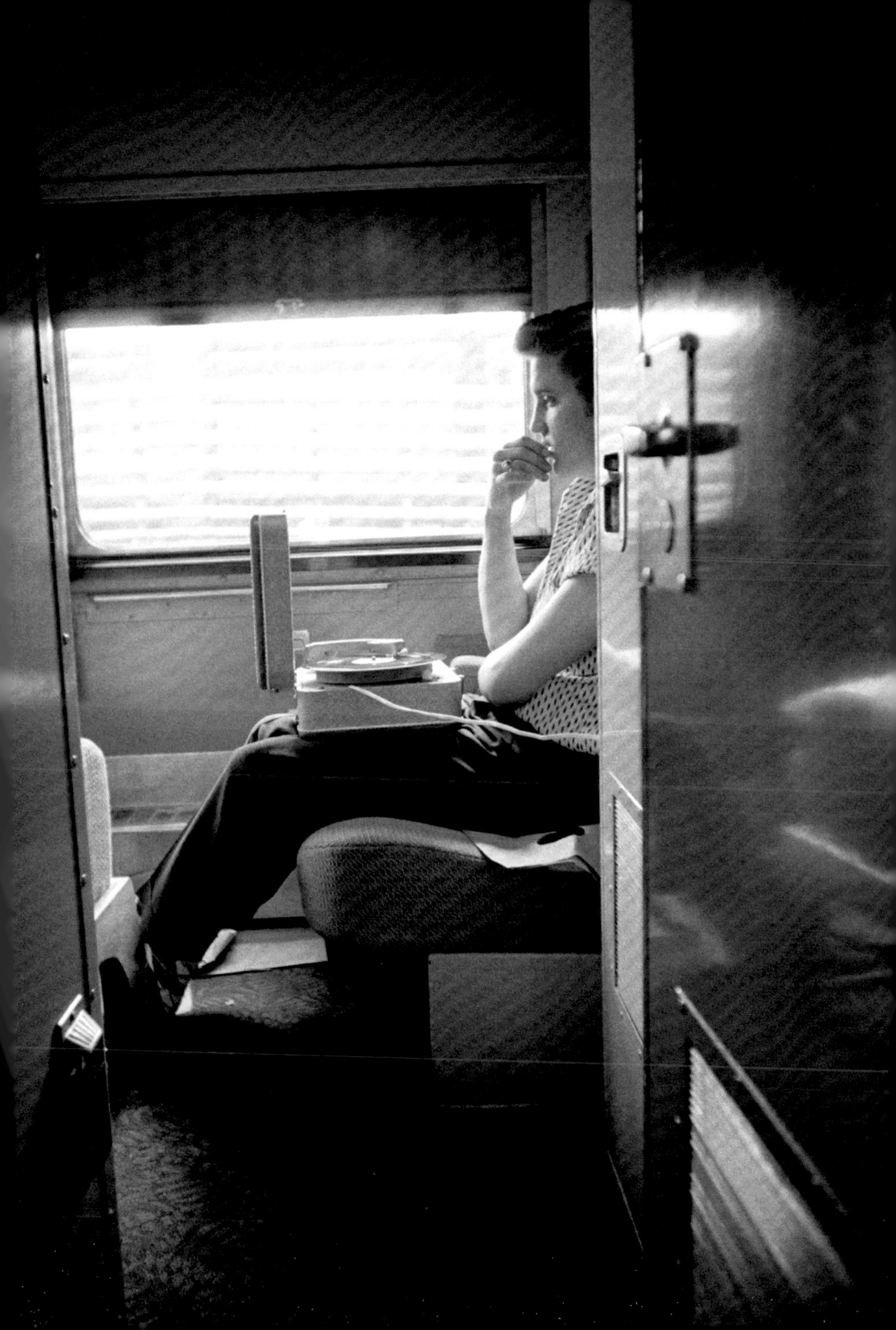

Elvis is a clean-cut, sincere, honest youngster who knows he is in the limelight but as yet is unspoiled. This six foot, blue eyed kid has his brown hair cut in a style that is his trade mark—a heavy mop over his forehead, a ducktail in the back, and sideburns. His nose is straight, a set jaw, and has a strong mouth. Yes, Madam, he is brutish and handsome.

RUBY WOODS
Detroit Tribune, March 23, 1957

PAGE 119
Aboard the train to Memphis, Elvis plays recordings from the RCA Victor session on an inexpensive portable record player to get a feeling for how his fans will hear the songs.

OPPOSITE
Even with his distinctive looks and recent shot to national fame over months of televised appearances, Elvis is still able to travel from New York to Memphis largely unrecognized.

FOLLOWING SPREAD
Wertheimer has complete access to his subject, even in the washroom, where the photographer will make one of his favorite Elvis images (right): *No More Paper Towels*, the Southern Railway local train, New York to Memphis, July 4, 1956.

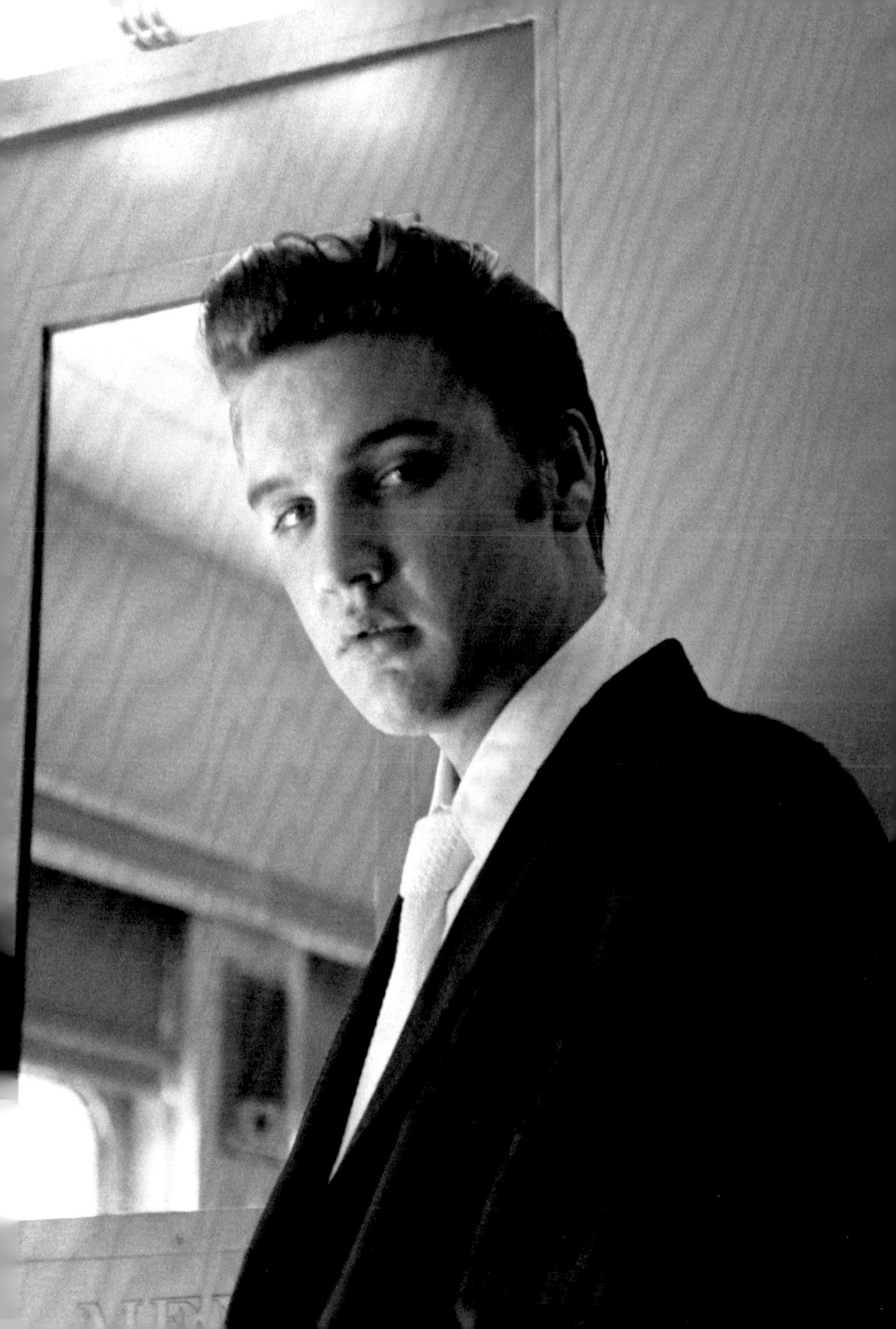

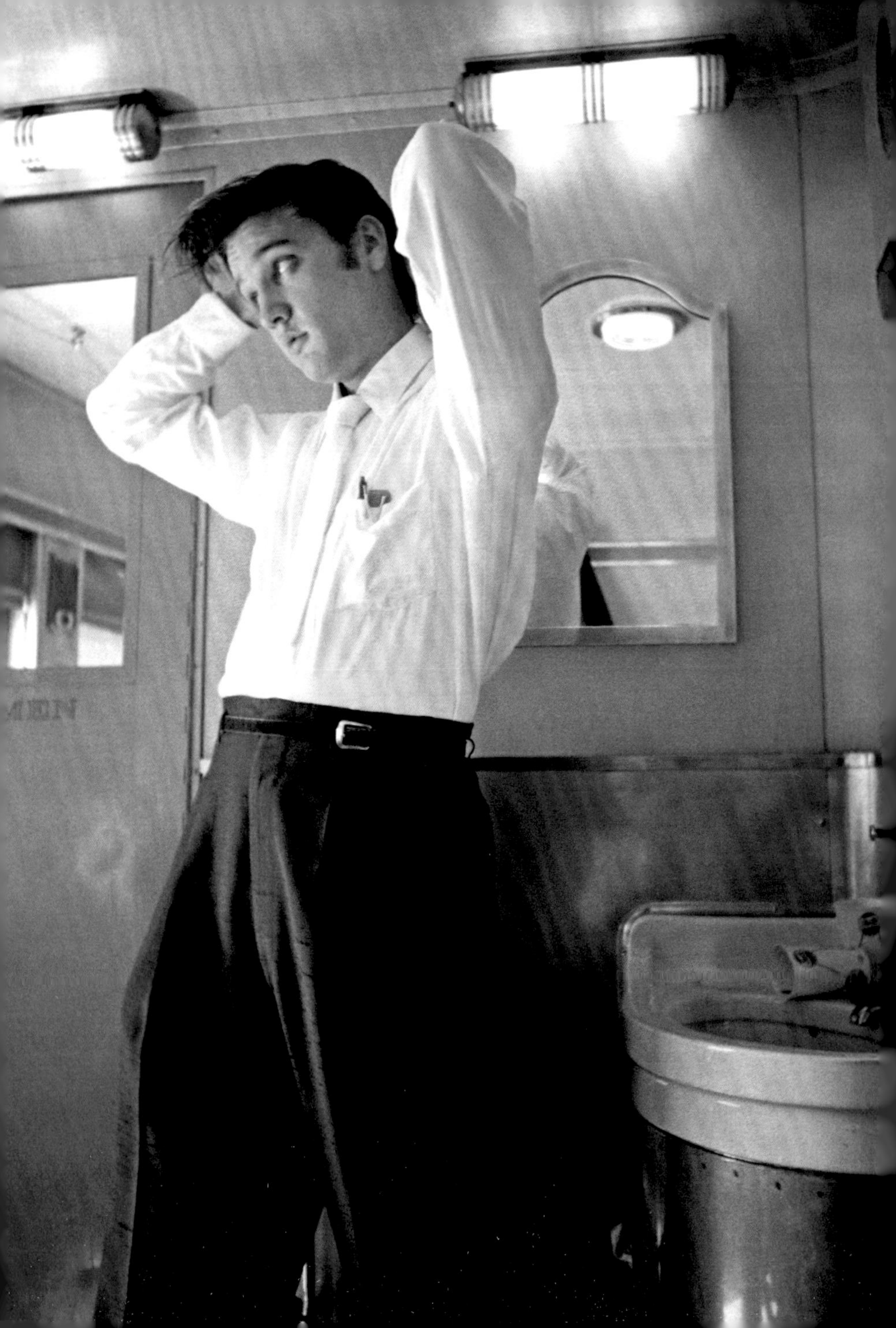

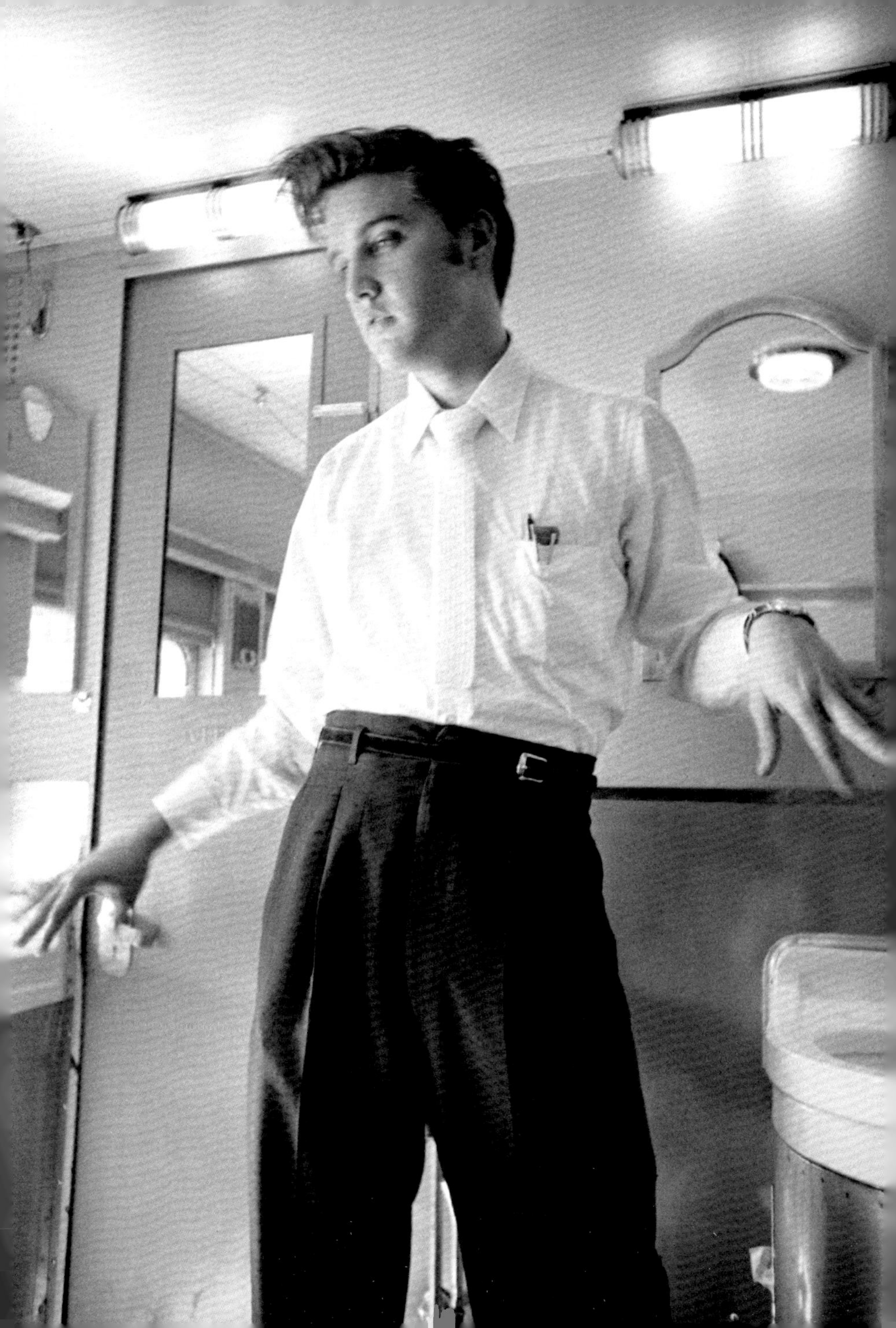

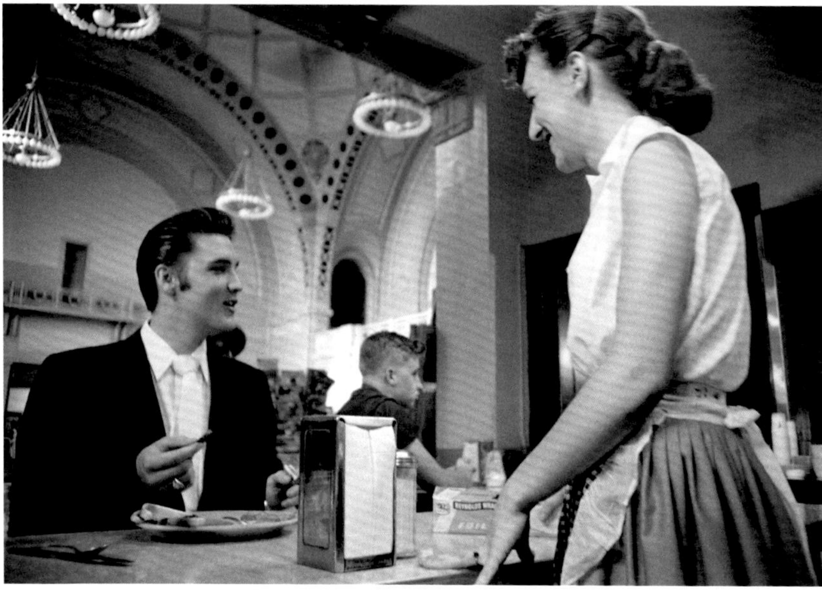

ABOVE
A stop for breakfast while changing trains in Chattanooga, Tennessee.

OPPOSITE
Segregated Lunch Counter, Chattanooga Terminal Station, July 4, 1956. While Elvis awaits his food, a woman orders a tuna fish sandwich but cannot sit down.

FOLLOWING SPREAD
Lunchtime, Sheffield, Alabama, en route to Memphis, July 4, 1956.

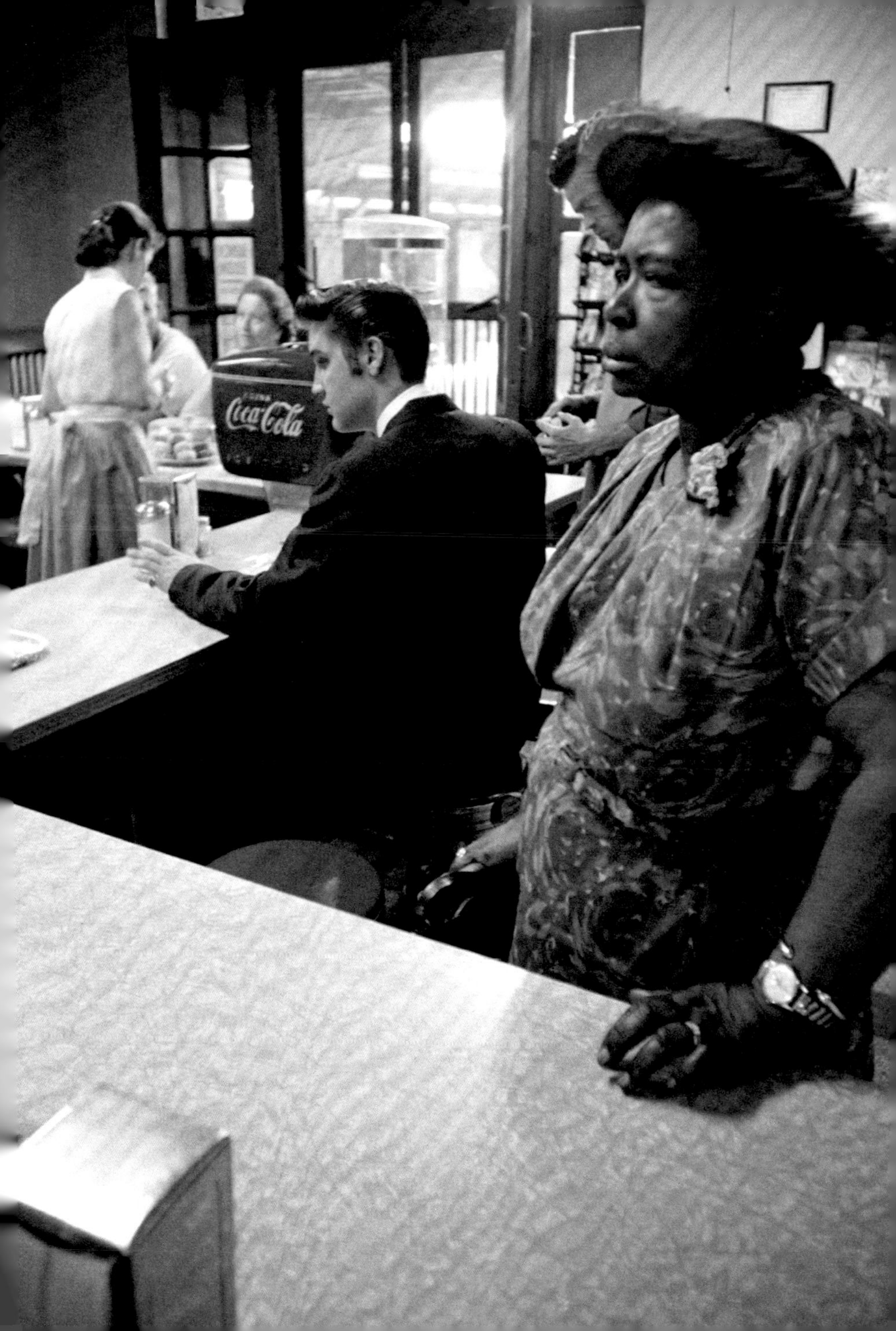
Coca-Cola

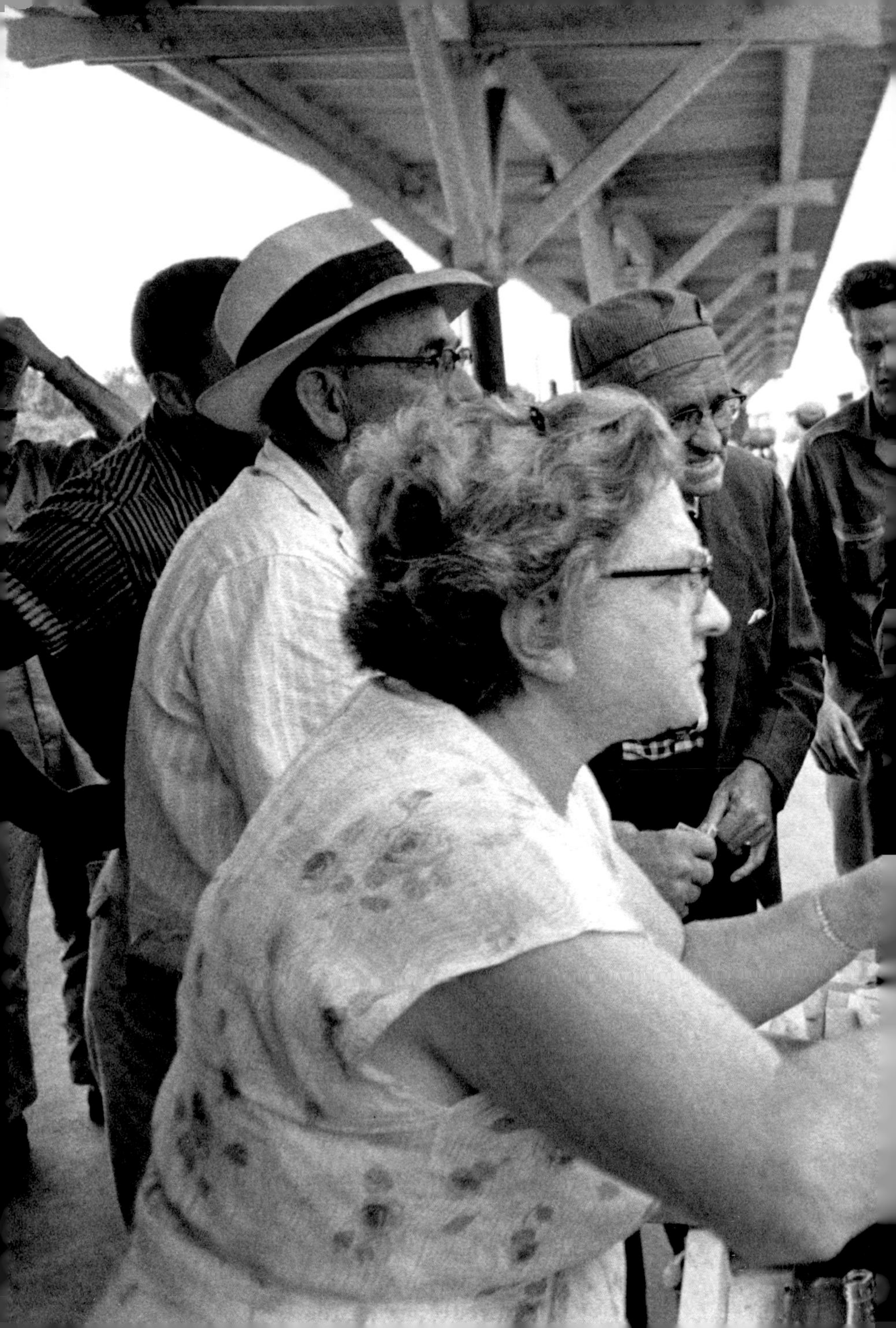

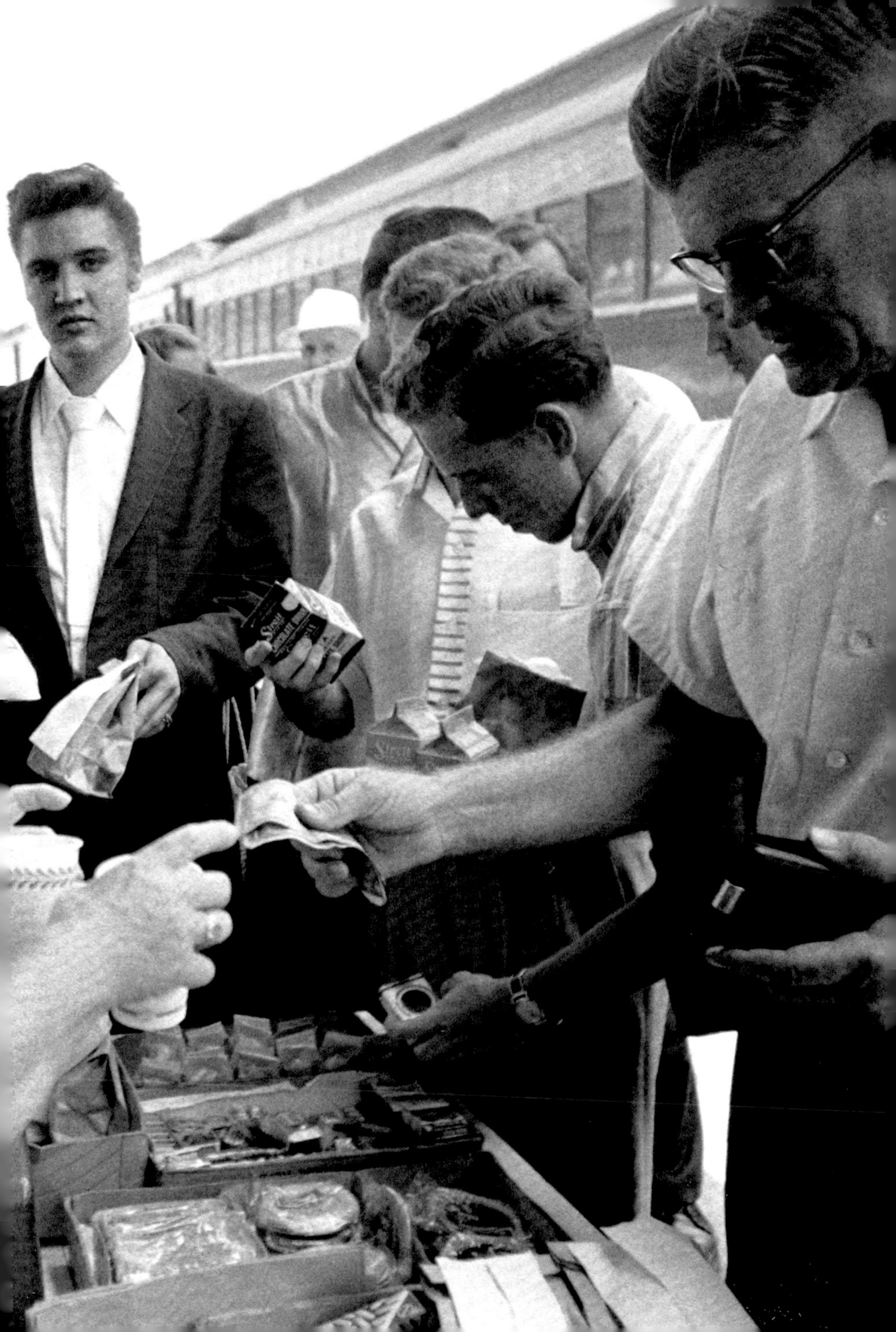

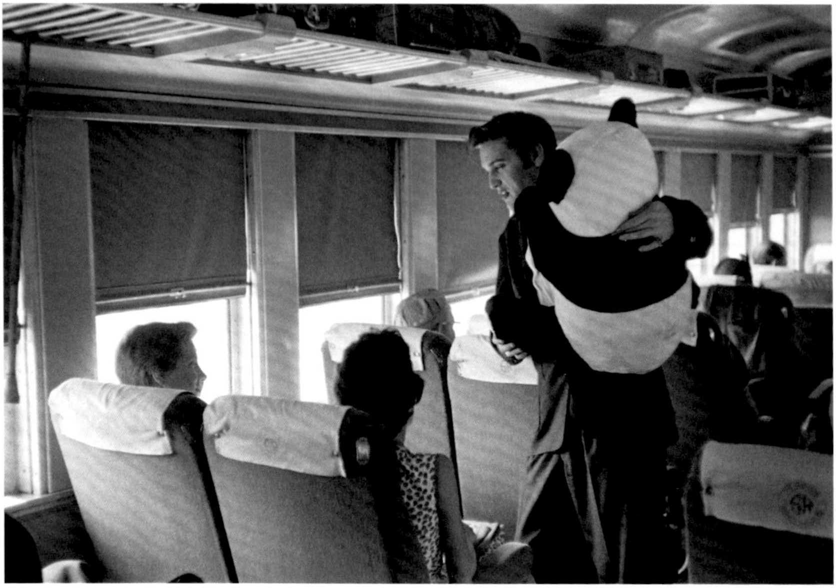

ABOVE & OPPOSITE
A three-foot-tall stuffed panda arrives mysteriously the first day of the train ride, and rumor has it the Colonel is responsible.

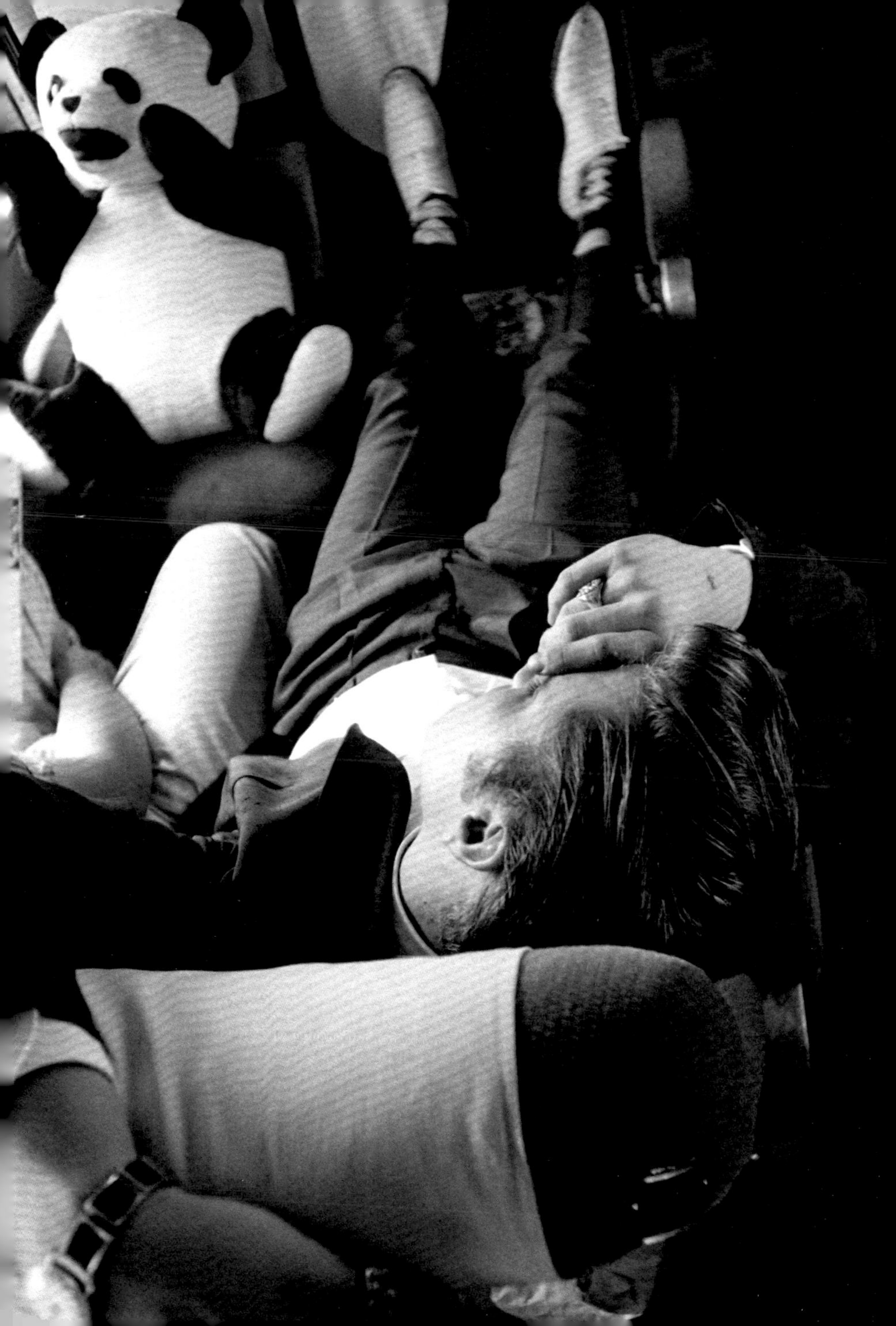

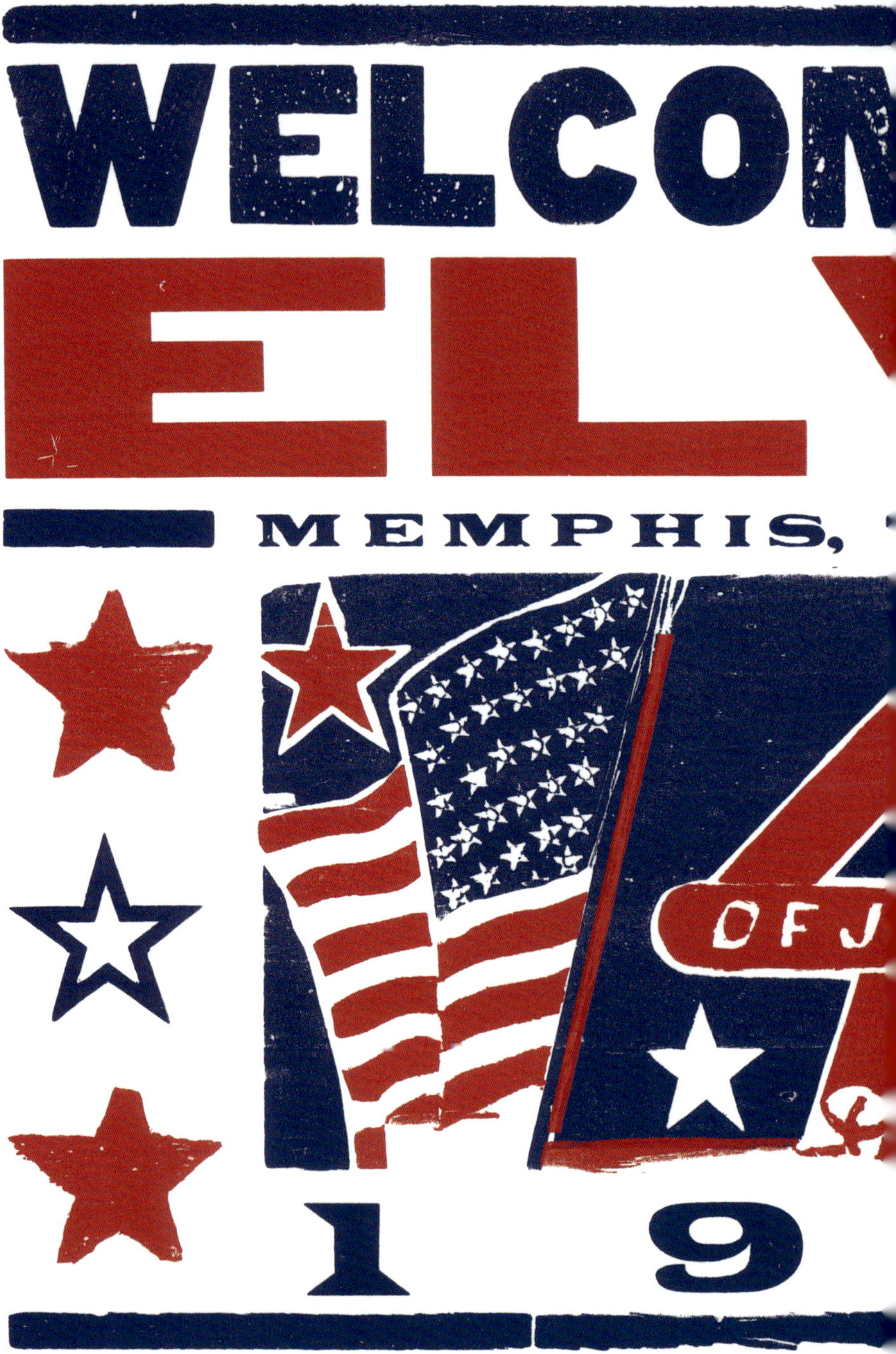
WELCOM
EL
MEMPHIS,
OFJ
1 9

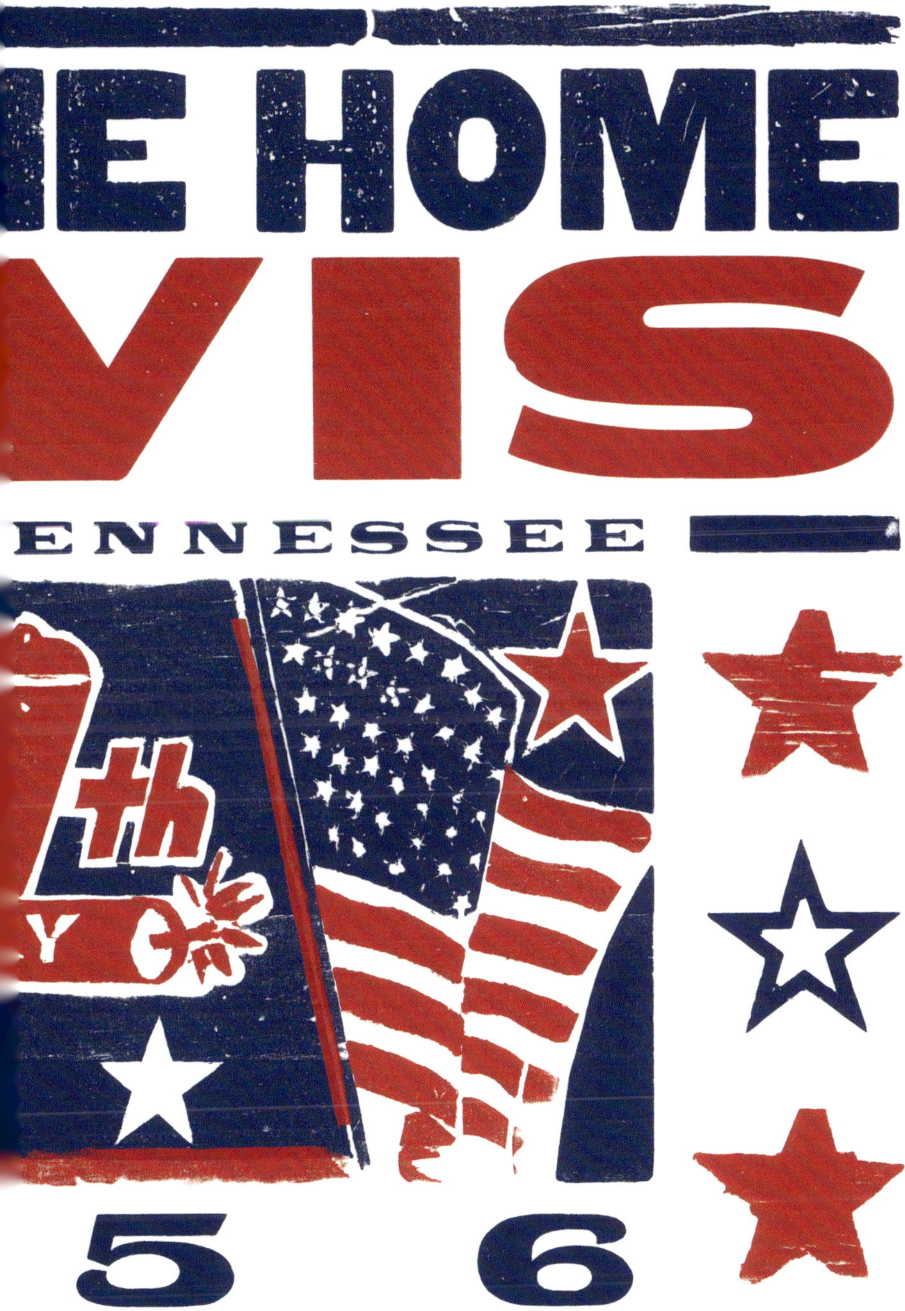
E HOME
VIS
ENNESSEE
th
Y
5 6

★ ★ ★

AS WE APPROACHED MEMPHIS, the Colonel had the conductor make a special stop at White Station, just outside Memphis. This allowed Elvis to take a shortcut to his family home at 1034 Audubon Drive and surprise them before the rest of us arrived. This would be one of the last times Elvis would walk down the street alone, like an ordinary person. There were around a hundred people from the neighborhood there to welcome Elvis home when I arrived, many teenage girls dressed in their holiday best. His mother, Gladys, greeted me, and I found the singer outside. After some confusion about getting his Harley started (it was out of gas) Elvis went for several rides, one with me on the back. I call these the best photographs I never got, because I ran out of film. Then Elvis decided to take a swim in the new pool with some of his cousins and friends. Six hours later the pool remained half filled (from a hose attached to the kitchen sink), and I finally got in, rather than keep shooting from above. The afternoon ended with Elvis and ex-girlfriend Barbara Hearn listening to his three new songs before he prepared for his concert that night at Russwood Park.

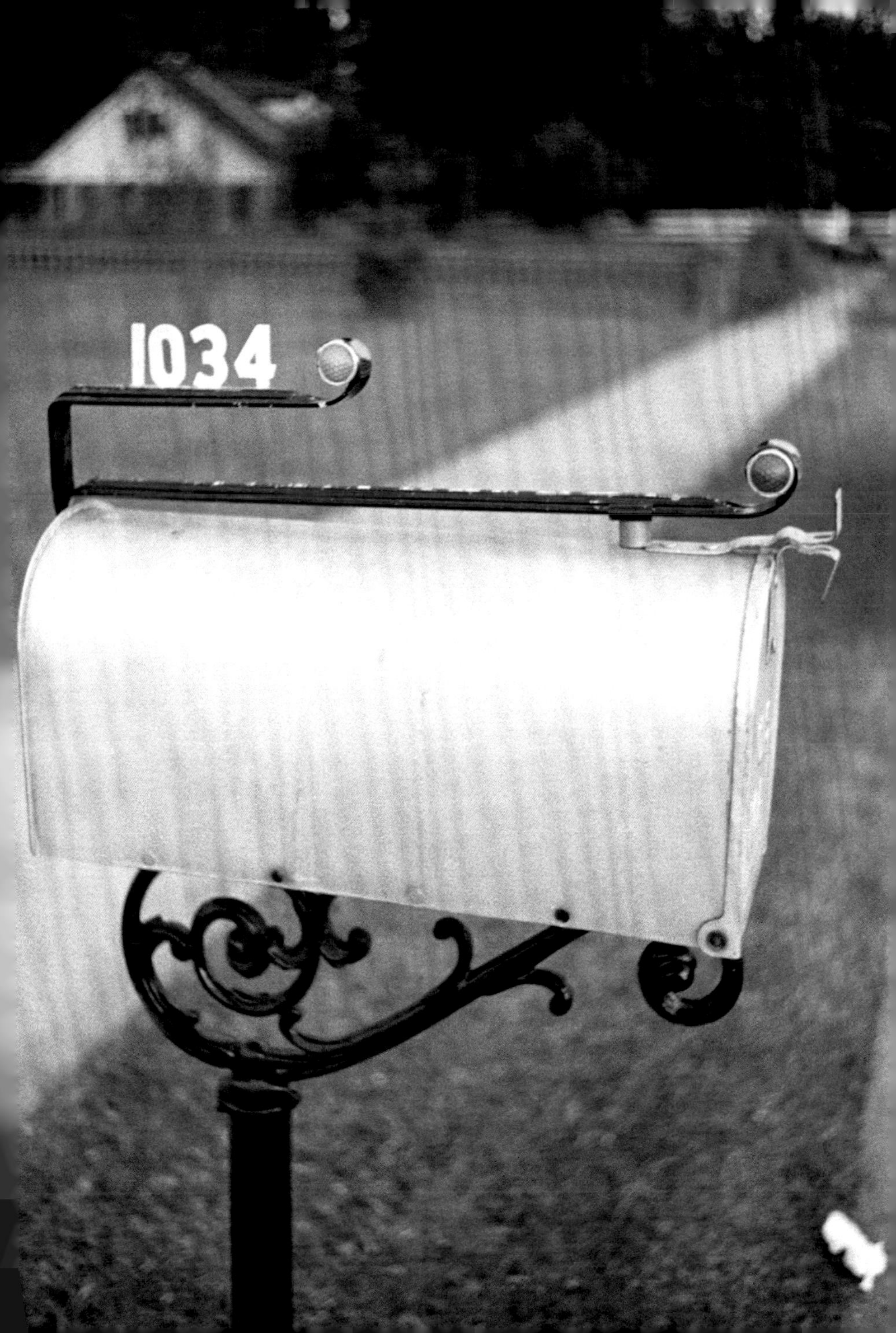
1034

He had difficulty building true friendships, and I had that difficulty, too. I have a lot of friends, but I am just not a person who builds relationships easily. Elvis was the same way. He was just, innately, a loner.

SAM PHILLIPS

PAGE 133
The mailbox at 1034 Audubon Drive, the Presley family home in Memphis, on the Fourth of July.

OPPOSITE
Eager to get home, Elvis prepares to hop off the train a few minutes outside Memphis on an unauthorized stop arranged by Colonel Tom Parker.

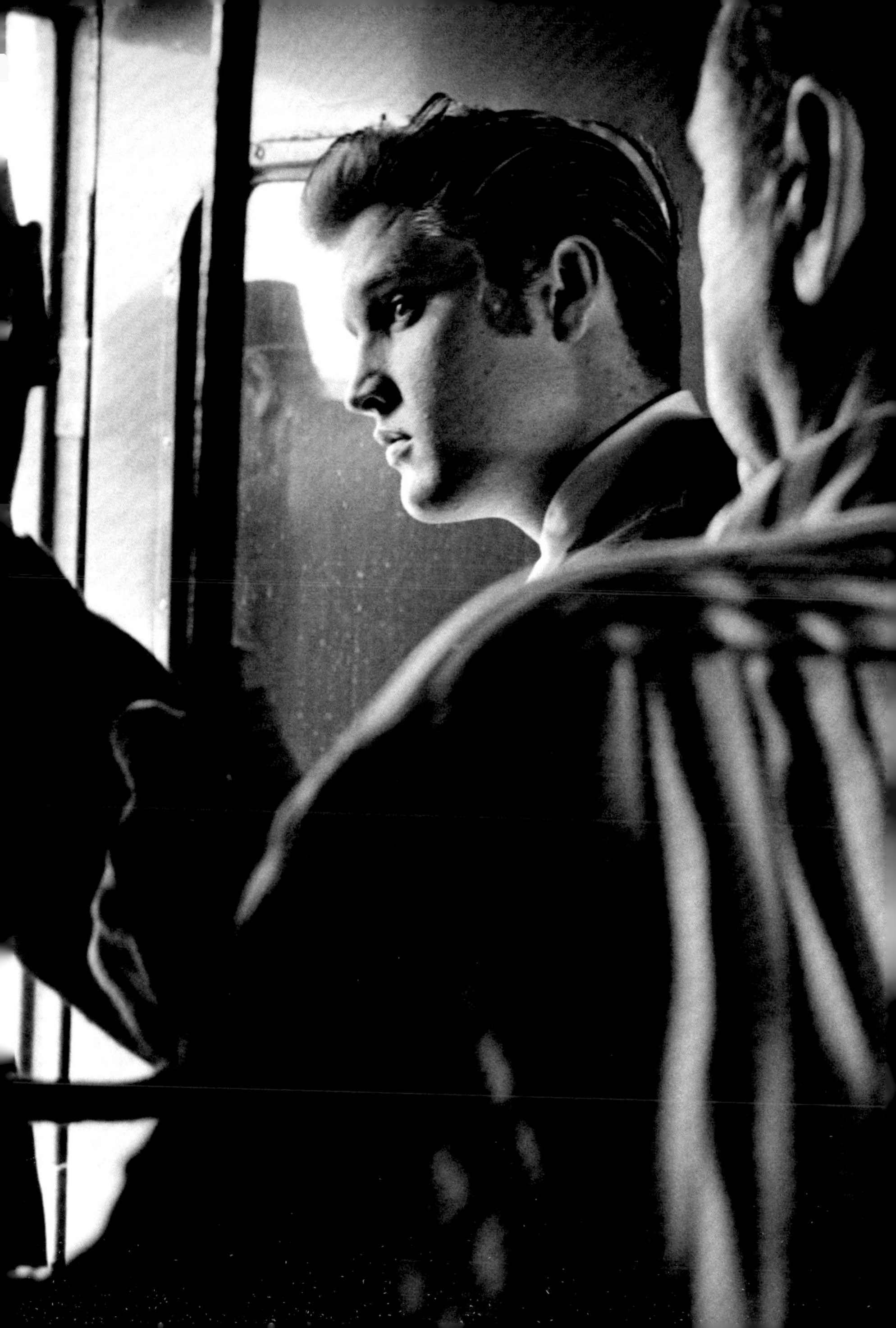

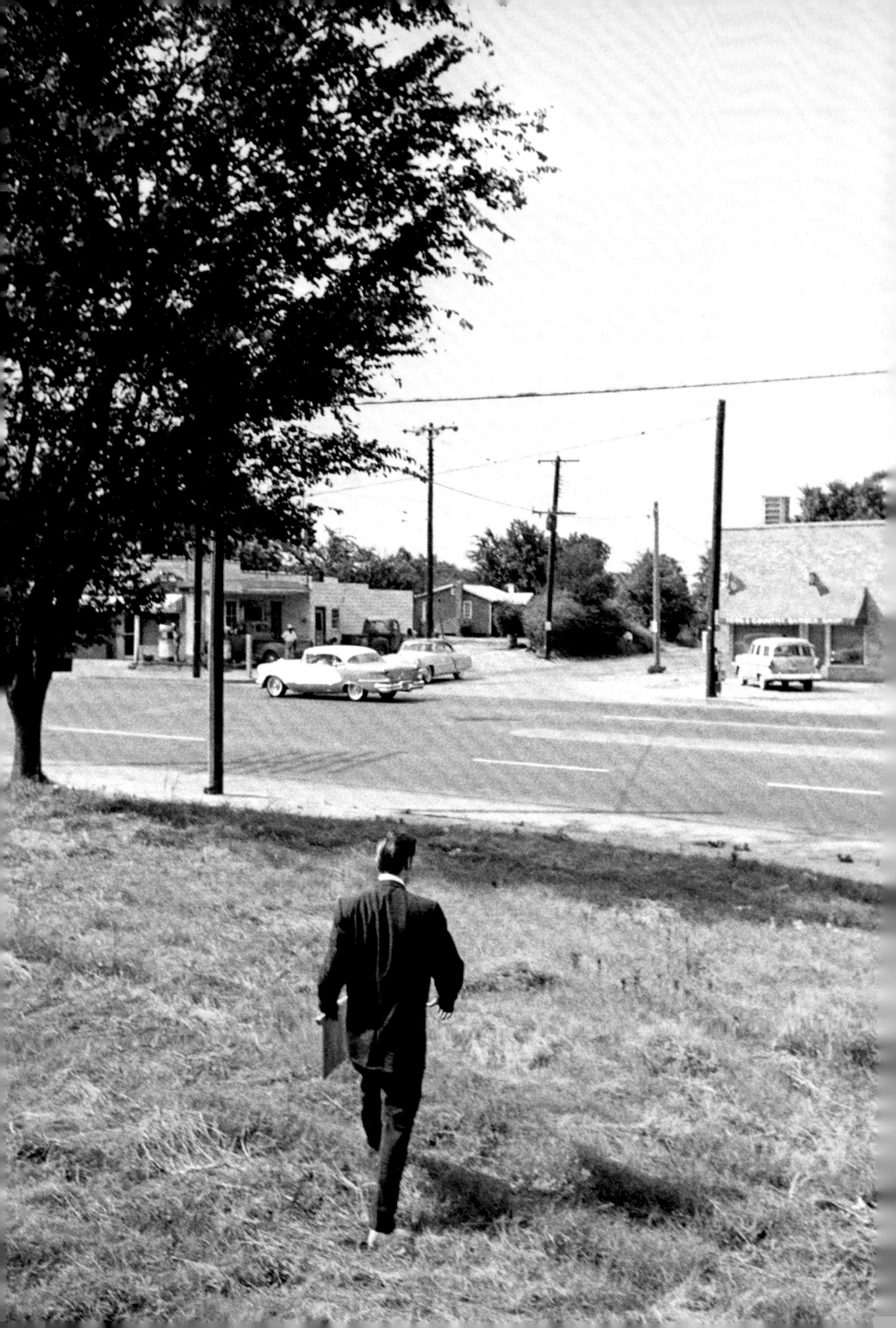

There were people that didn't like Jesus Christ. They killed him and Jesus Christ was a perfect man. And there's gonna be people that don't like ya regardless of who you are or what you do because if everybody thought the same way they'd be drivin' the same car, everybody'd be marryin' the same woman, and that wouldn't work out.

ELVIS PRESLEY

OPPOSITE
By stopping at the White Station rather than going on to Memphis Central Station and taking a taxi back to the suburbs, Elvis is able to save an hour getting home to see his family.

FOLLOWING SPREAD
Now off the train at White Station, he waves to the Colonel, Wertheimer, and the conductor; and travels down the street alone, probably the last time he can do so in his lifetime.

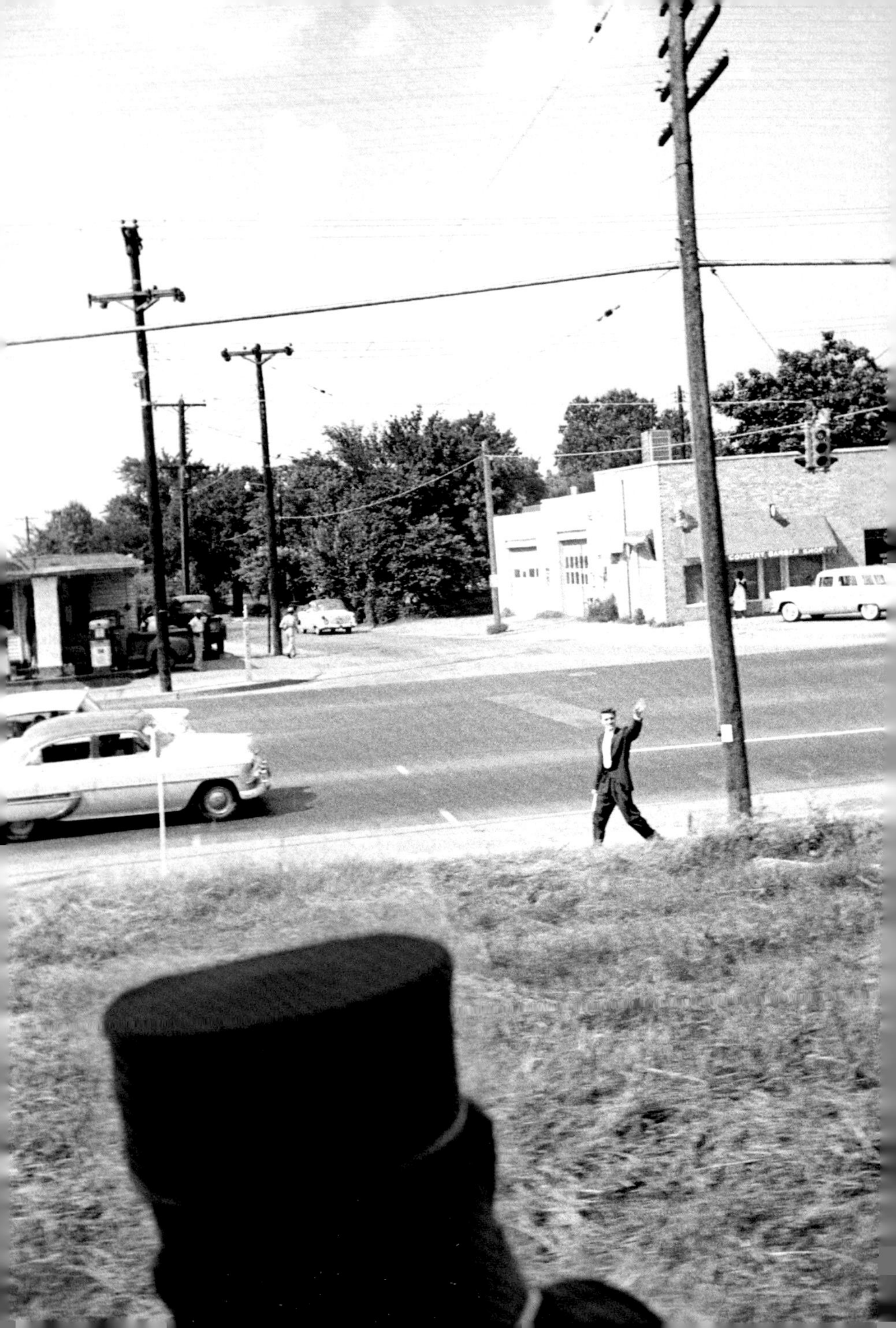

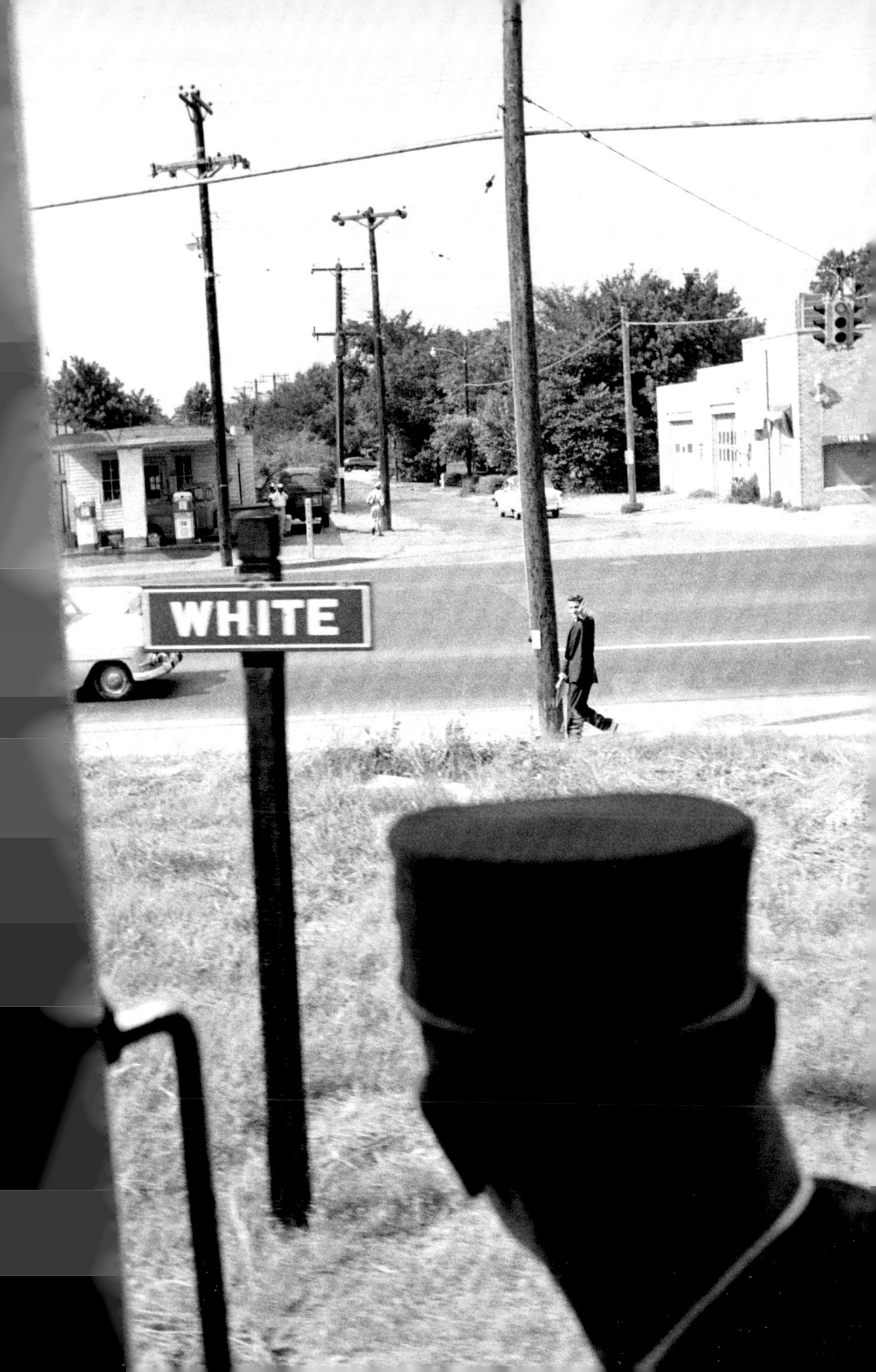
WHITE

When he was hardly four he'd tell me: "Don't worry, baby. When I'm grown up I'll buy you a big home and two cars. One for you and Daddy and one for me." All his life he'd say out loud what he was going to do for us...And you know, I believed him.

GLADYS PRESLEY
New York Daily News interview, September 23–27, 1956

OPPOSITE
No Gas in the Tank, Elvis on his Harley-Davidson, wondering why it won't start, Memphis, Tennessee, July 4, 1956.

FOLLOWING SPREAD
Friends and neighbors gather in the yard as Elvis tries to get his Harley running. Once they discover no gas in the tank, someone volunteers to get a Jerrycan of gasoline.

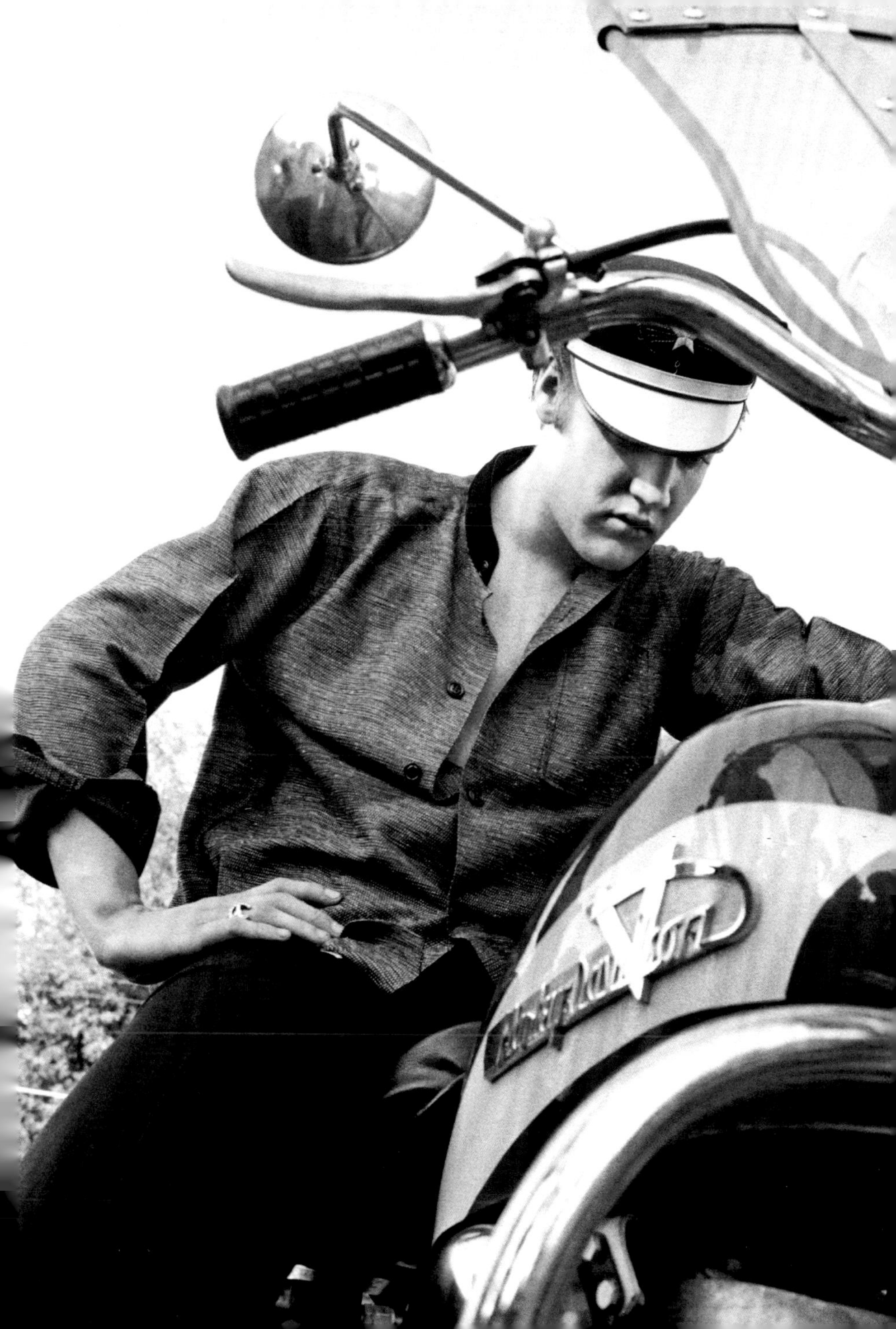

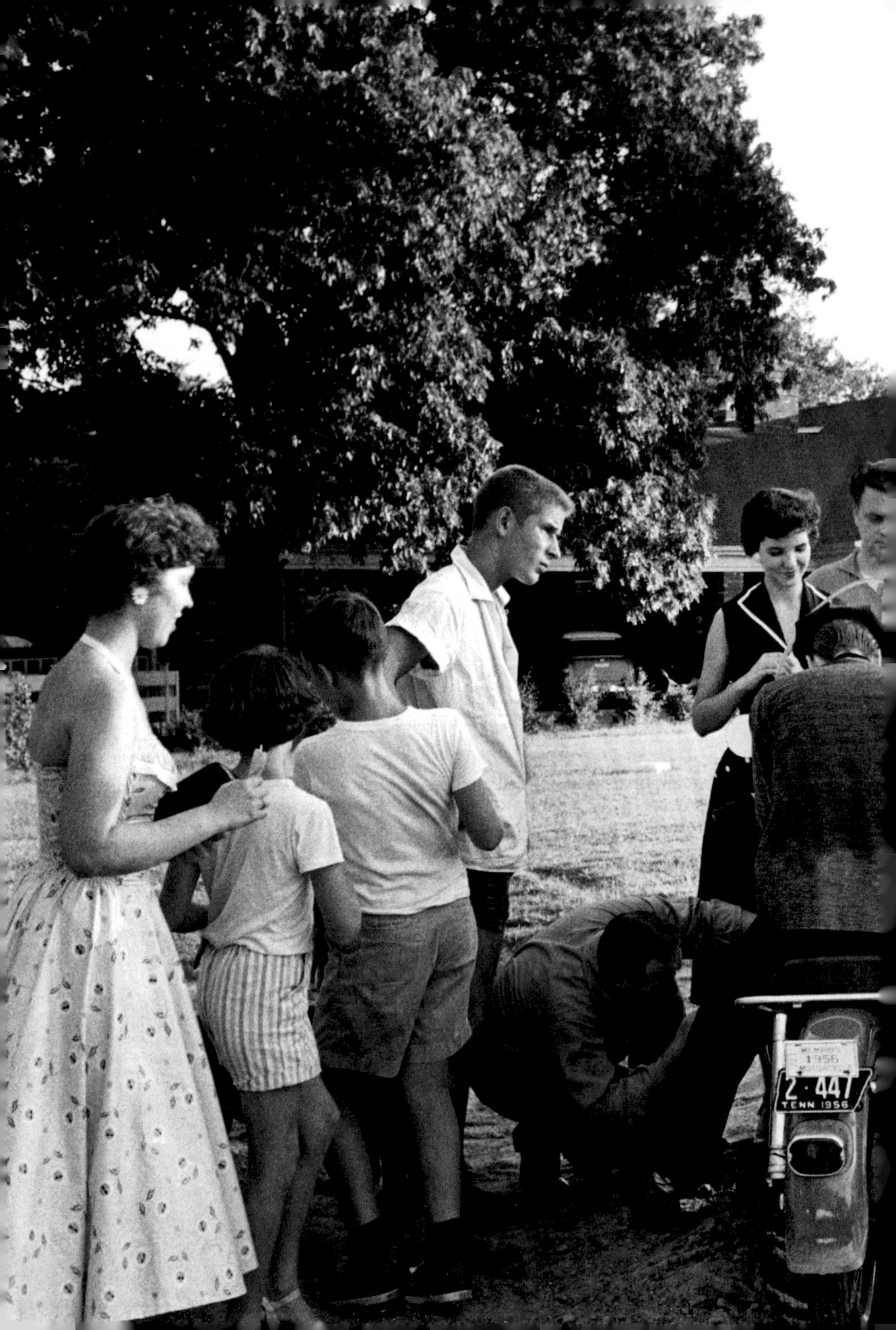
1956
2 · 447
TENN 1956

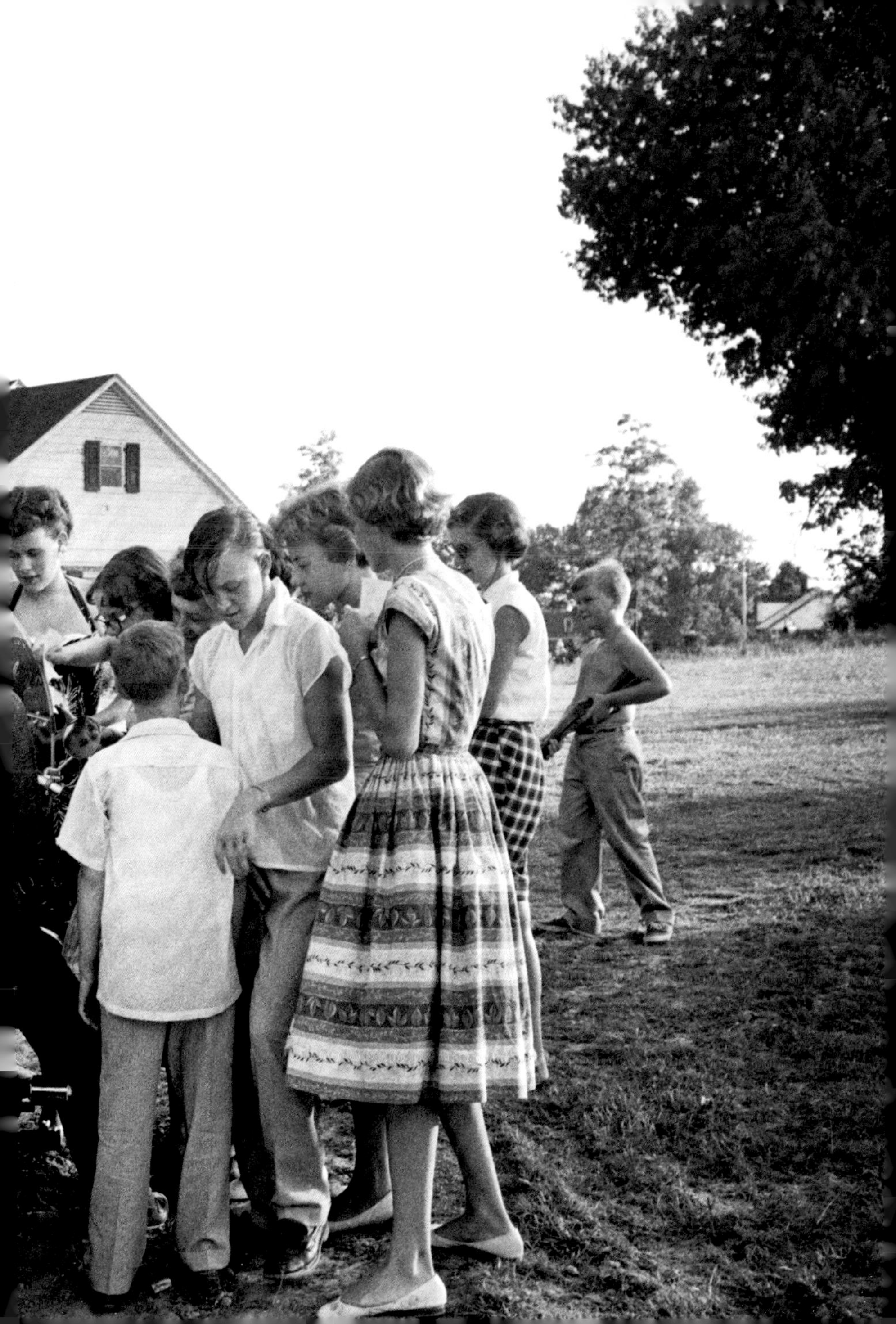

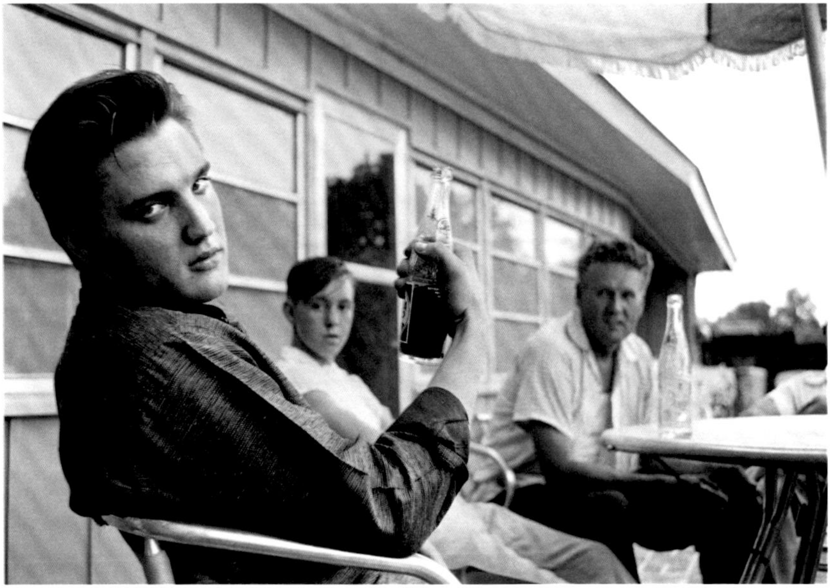

ABOVE
Before the concert at Russwood Park, Elvis relaxes on the back patio with his family and turns to give the photographer his patented stare.

OPPOSITE
A perplexed Elvis insists on cooling off in the pool on this hot July Fourth before his performance later that evening at Russwood Park. His father, Vernon, explains that a stuck valve is preventing the normal flow of water.

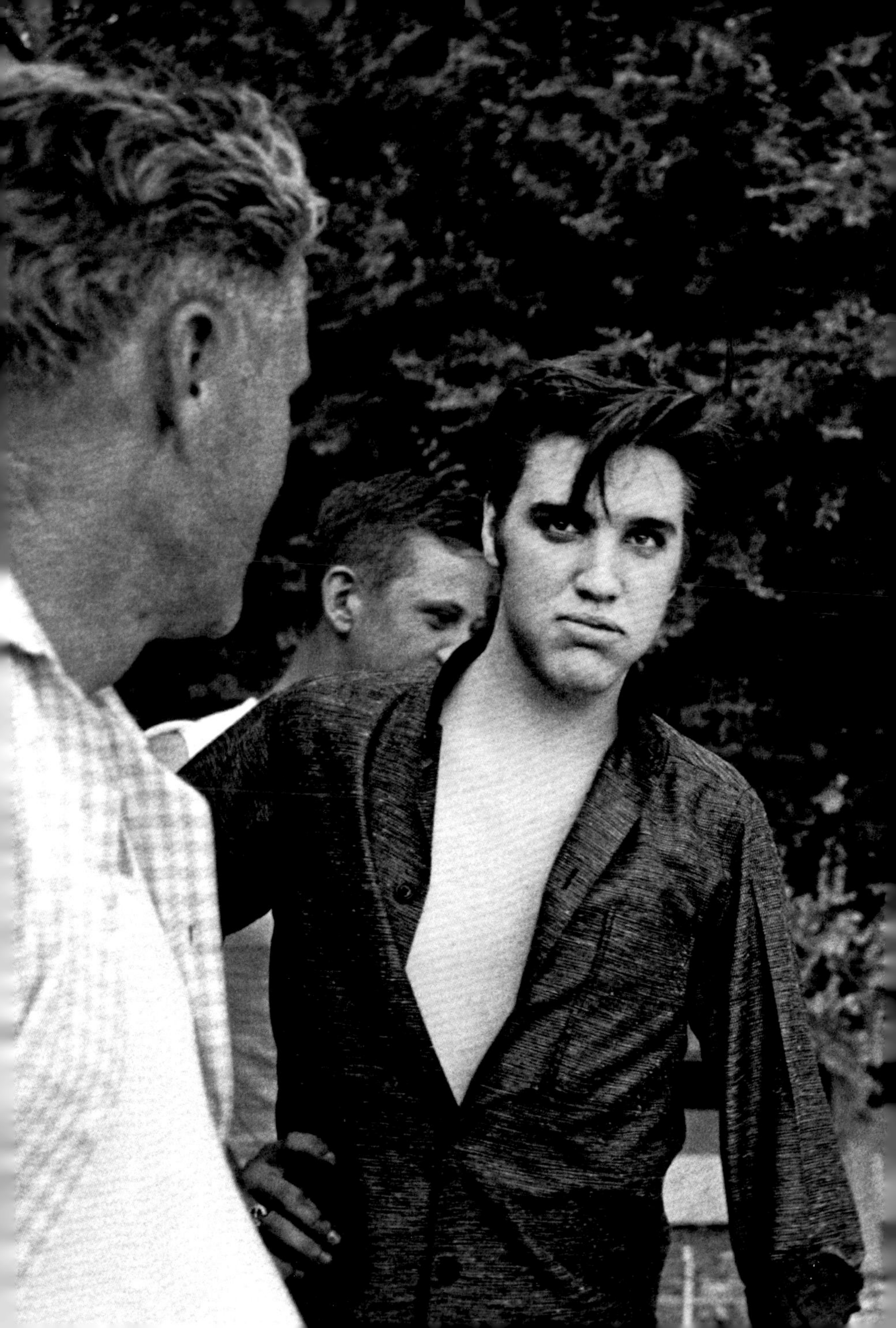

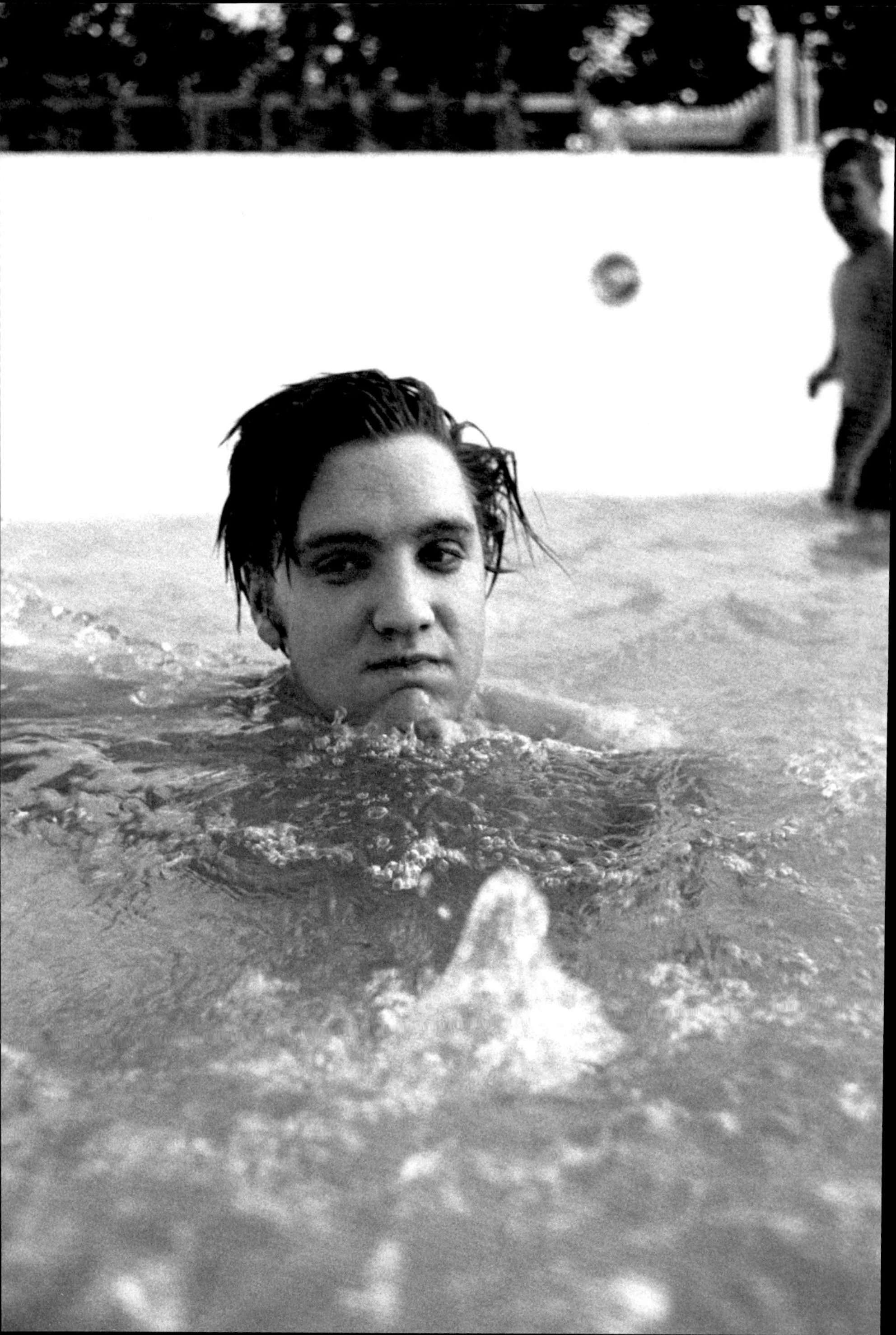

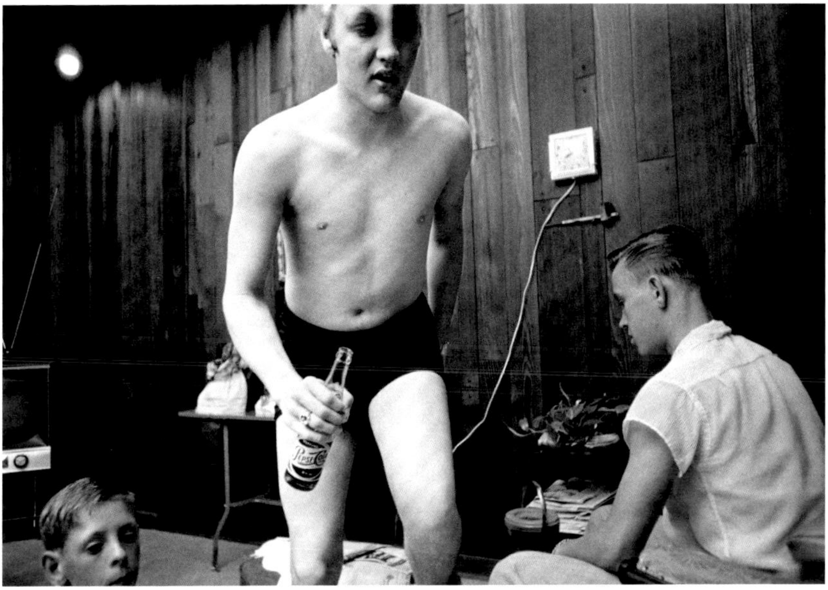

OPPOSITE
Since the valve is stuck, the pool is filled for hours with a garden hose attached to the kitchen sink. Six hours in, the pool is not even half full.

ABOVE
Elvis enjoys a Pepsi in the rec room with his cousins Billy and Bobby Smith.

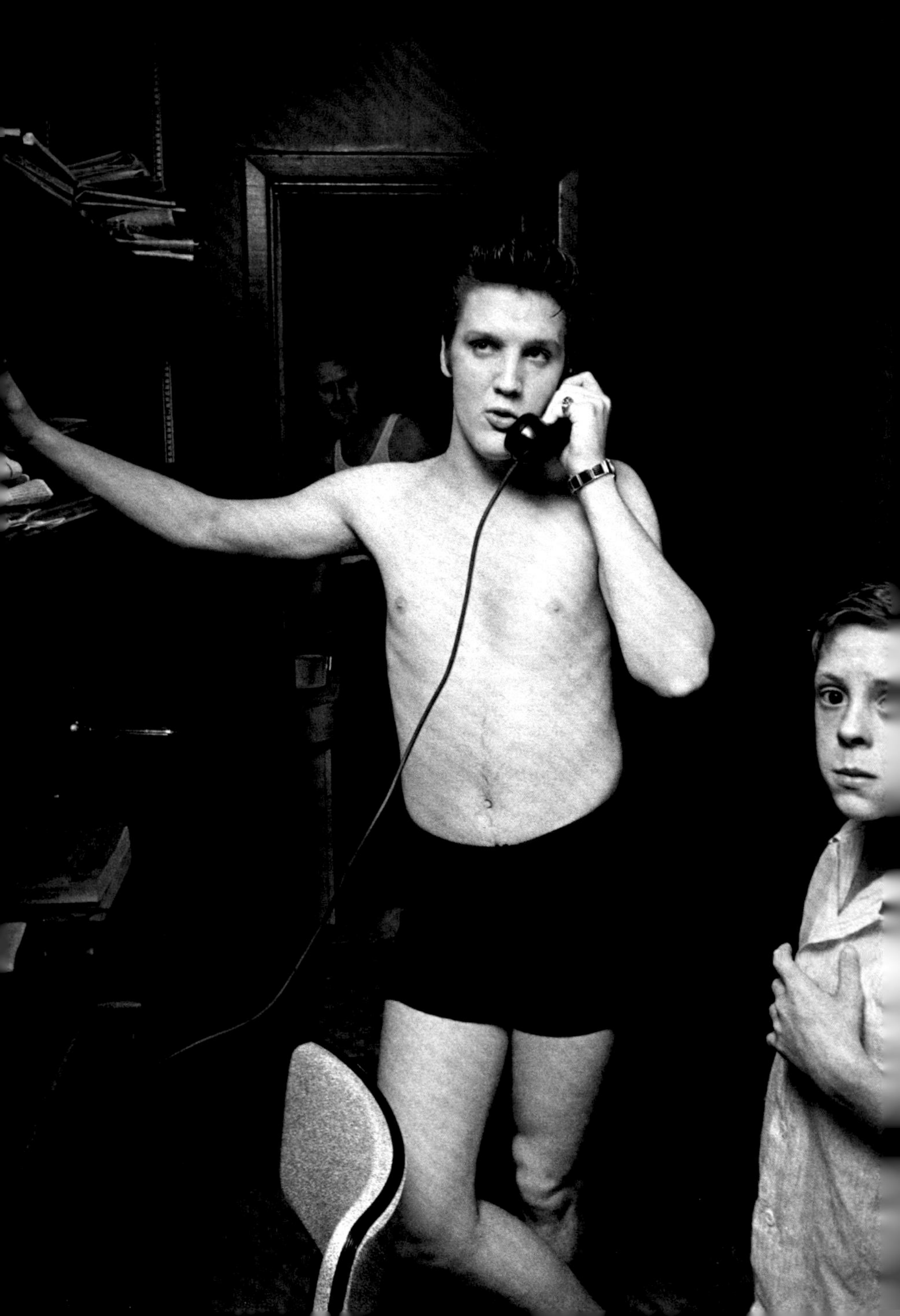

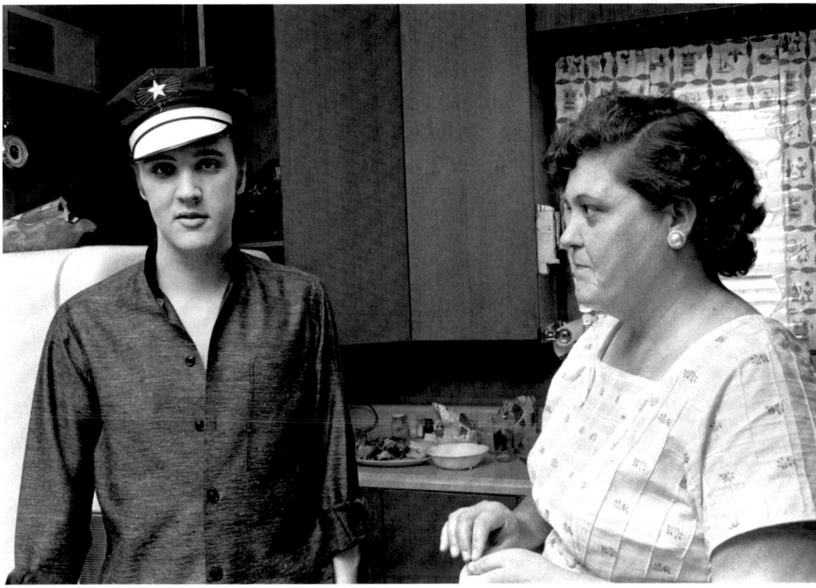

OPPOSITE
Talking on the phone at home,
his dad in the background shaving.

ABOVE
Elvis and his mom, Gladys,
in the kitchen of their new home.

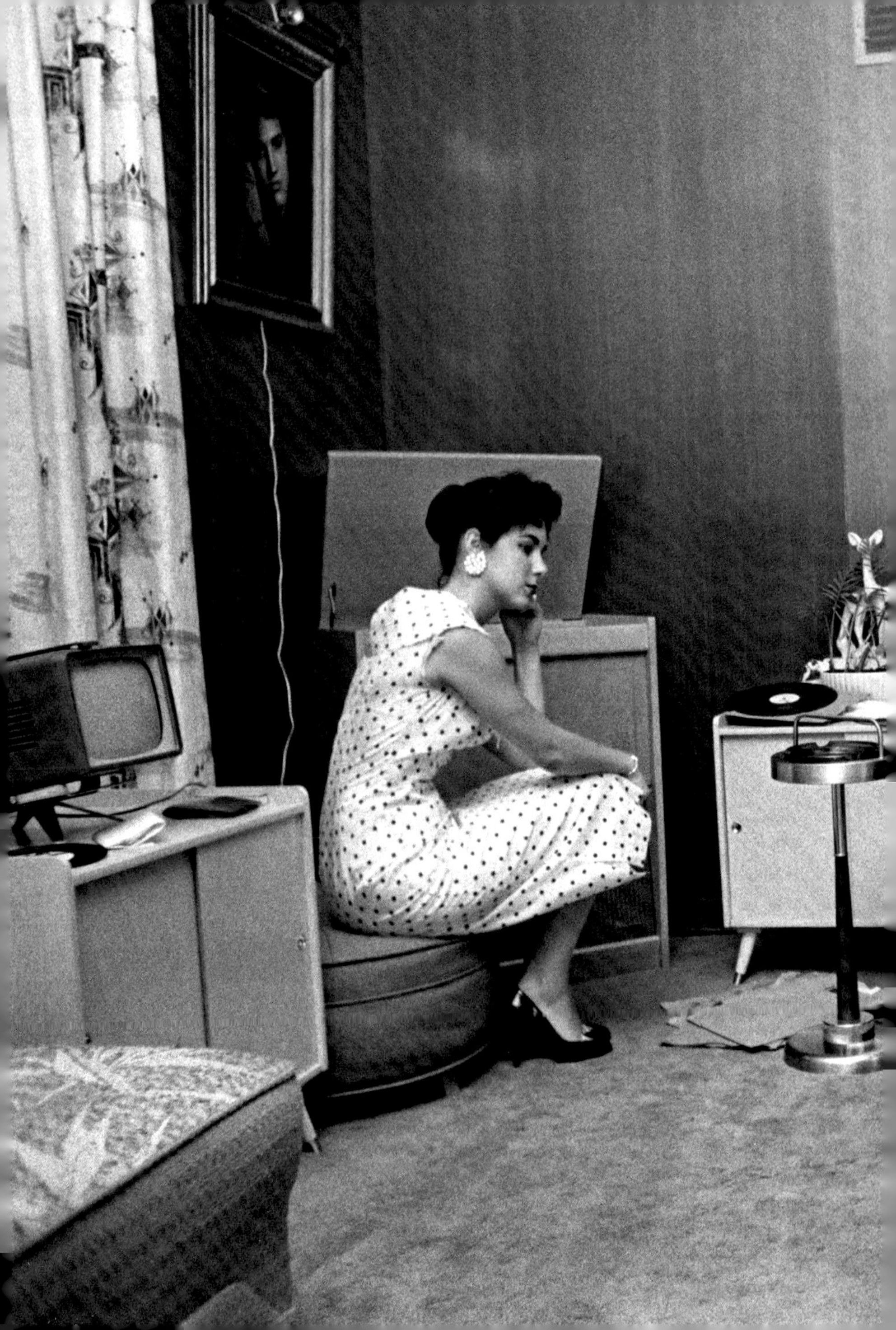

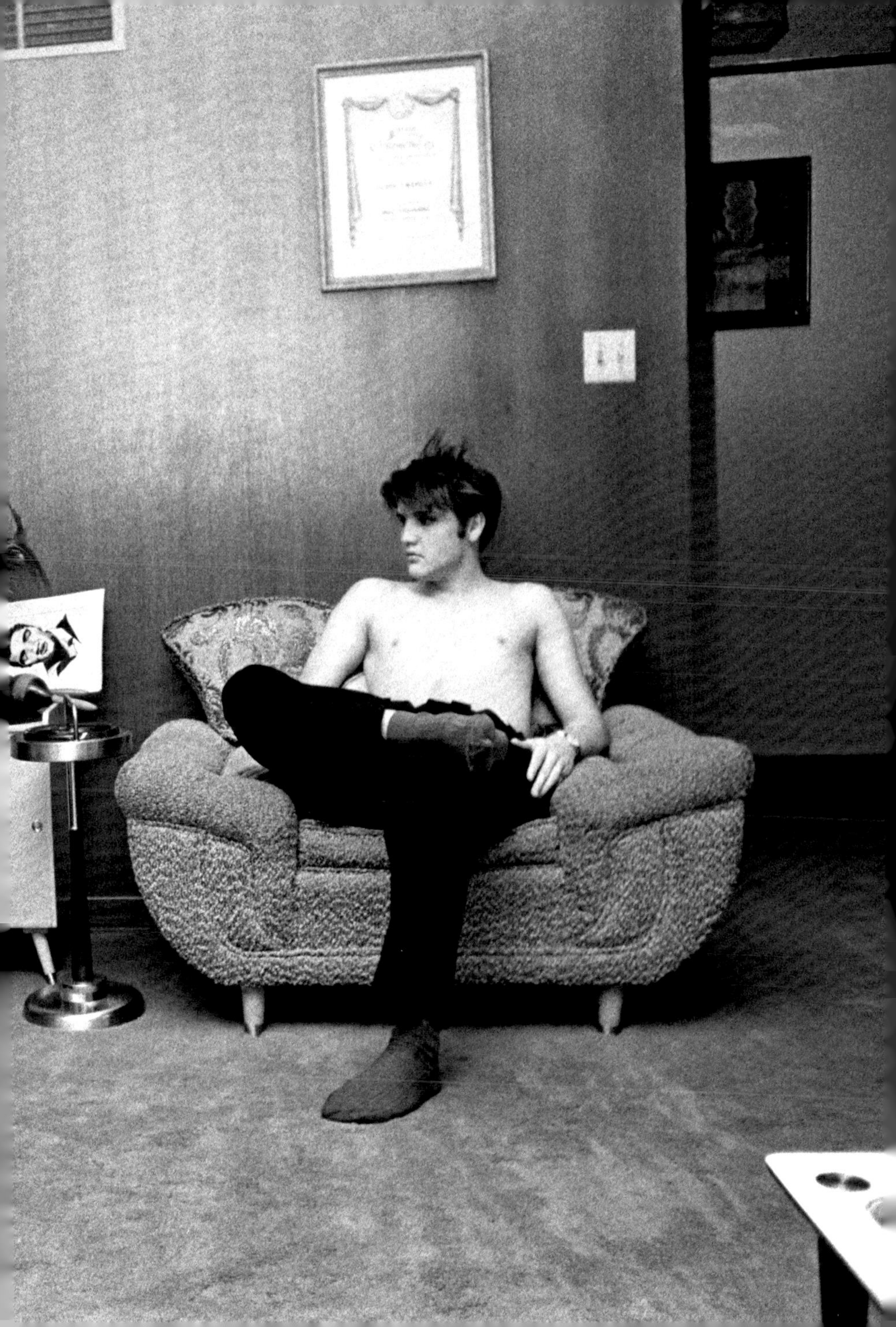

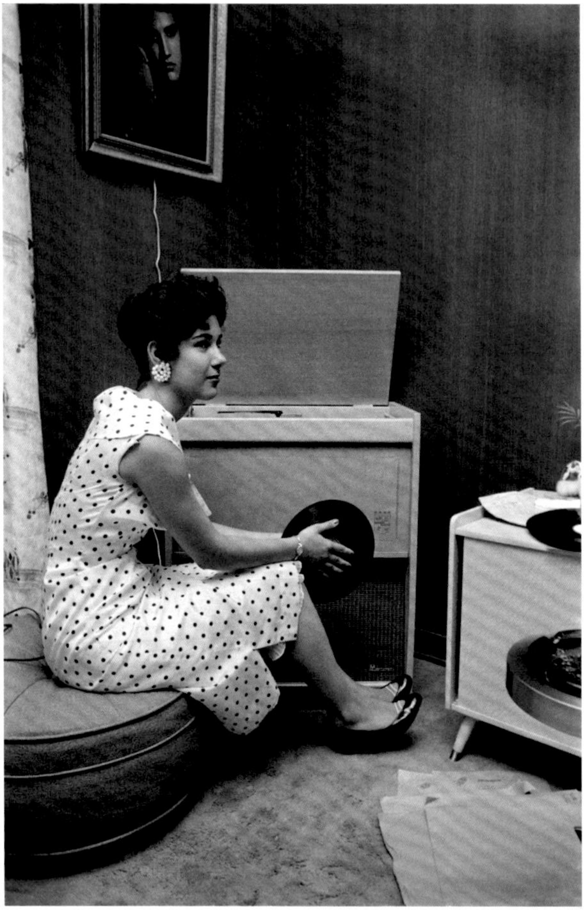

PREVIOUS SPREAD & ABOVE
High school sweetheart Barbara Hearn comes by the house before the concert, and listens to the quick acetate discs from the RCA Victor session a few days earlier.

OPPOSITE
Elvis asks her for a dance to see if the songs are "danceable."

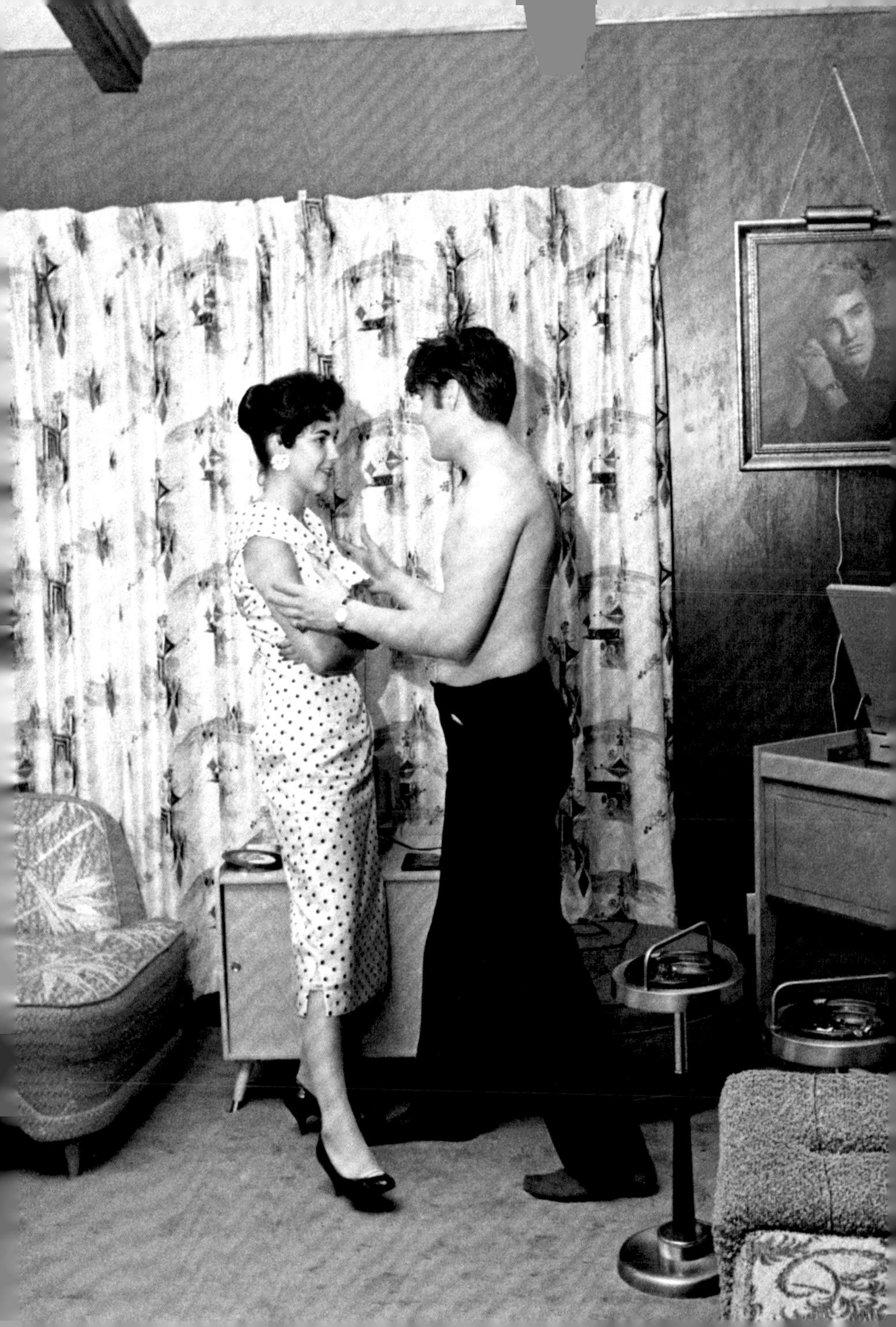

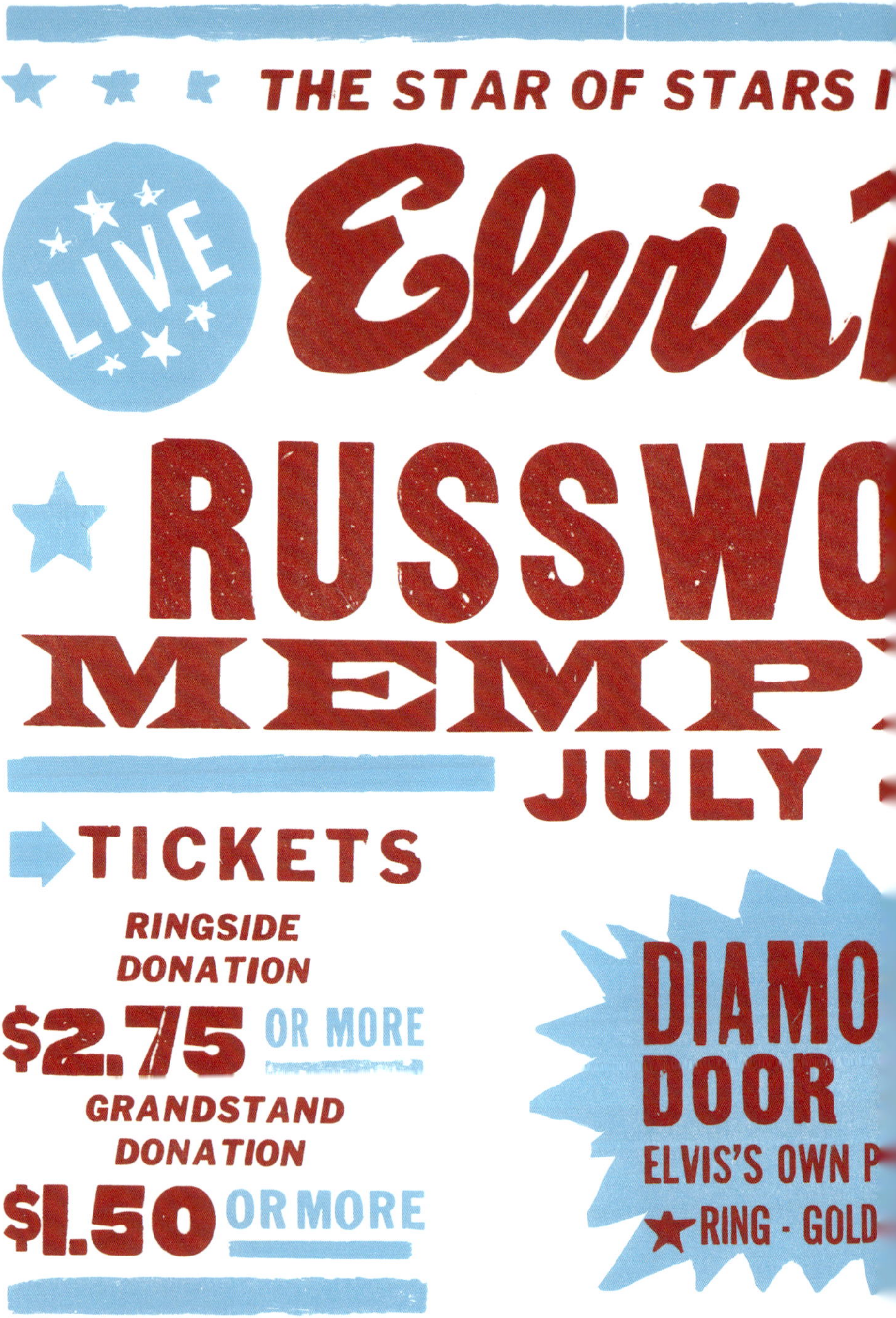
THE STAR OF STARS I
LIVE
Elvis
RUSSWO
MEMP
JULY
TICKETS
RINGSIDE
DONATION
$2.75 OR MORE
GRANDSTAND
DONATION
$1.50 OR MORE
DIAMO
DOOR
ELVIS'S OWN P
RING - GOLD

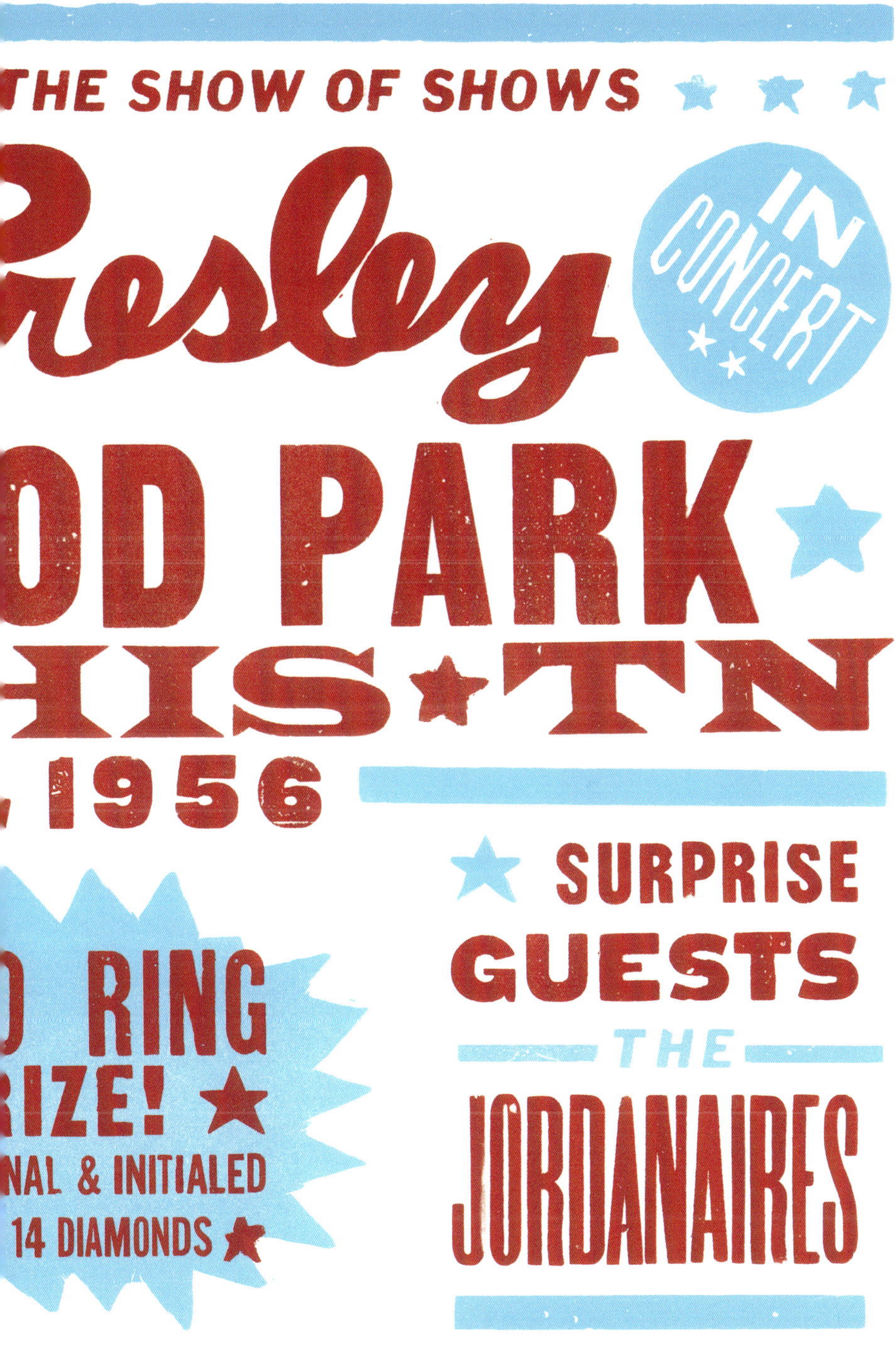
THE SHOW OF SHOWS
resley
IN CONCERT
OD PARK
HIS TN
1956
RING
RIZE!
NAL & INITIALED
14 DIAMONDS
SURPRISE
GUESTS
THE
JORDANAIRES

★ ★ ★

ELVIS PERFORMED THAT EVENING at Russwood Park in Memphis, a baseball stadium converted into a concert venue that would hold up to 14,000 fans. All the proceeds from the concert went to the Cynthia Milk Fund and the Variety Club's Home for Convalescent Children. Elvis, the Colonel, and I got a ride to the stadium with the sheriff in his police car. Escorted by the local police and Navy Shore Patrol, Elvis took the stage dressed all in black. Alluding to his scripted performance on *The Steve Allen Show* in which he sang to a live hound dog while wearing a tux, Elvis told the audience in Memphis, "Tonight you're going to see what the real Elvis Presley is all about." He proceeded to sing and gyrate and carry on all over the stage, to the delight of the crowd. Little did I know, as I got on the late-night train to New York that night, that it would be another two years before I would see Elvis again.

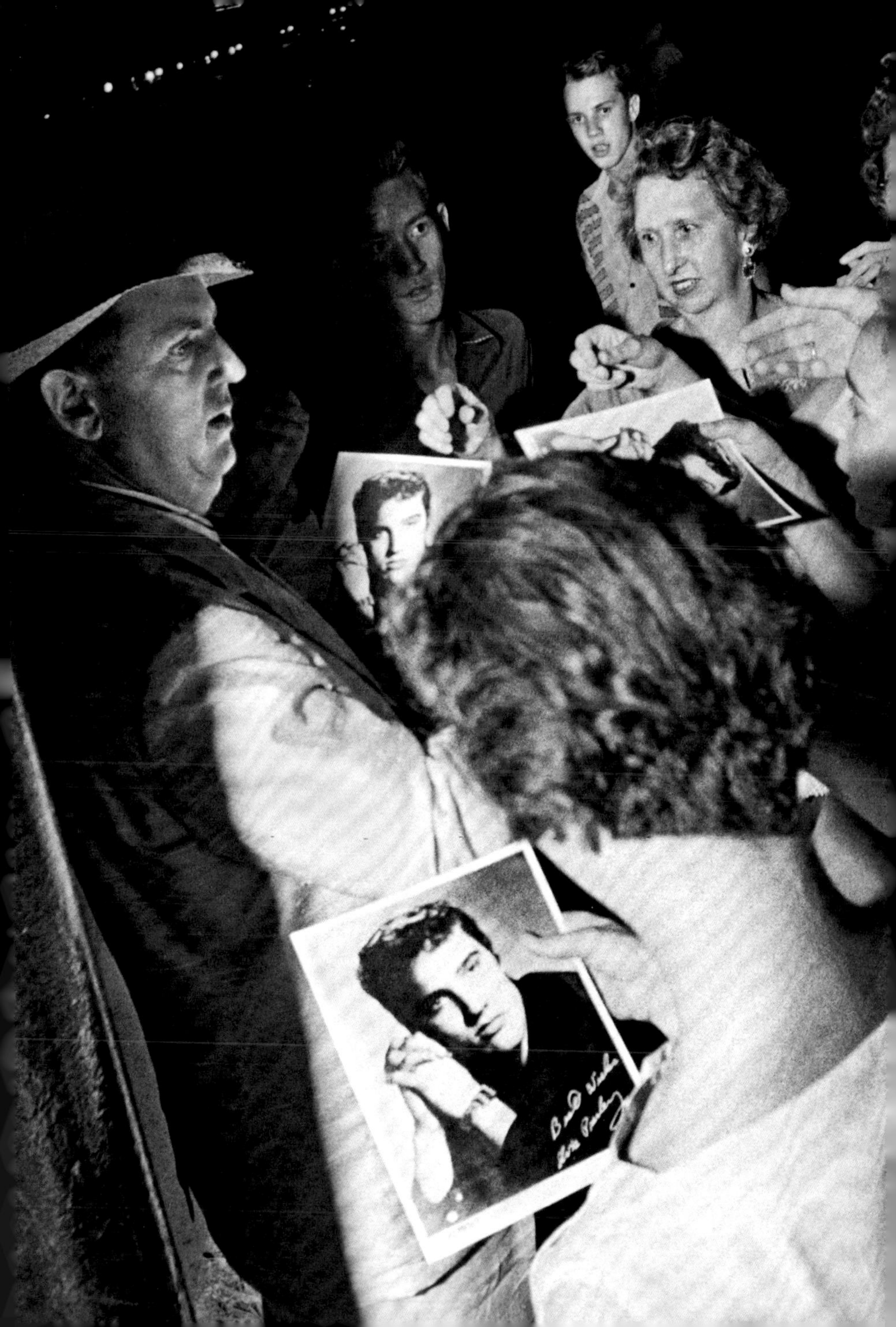
Best Wishes
Elvis Presley

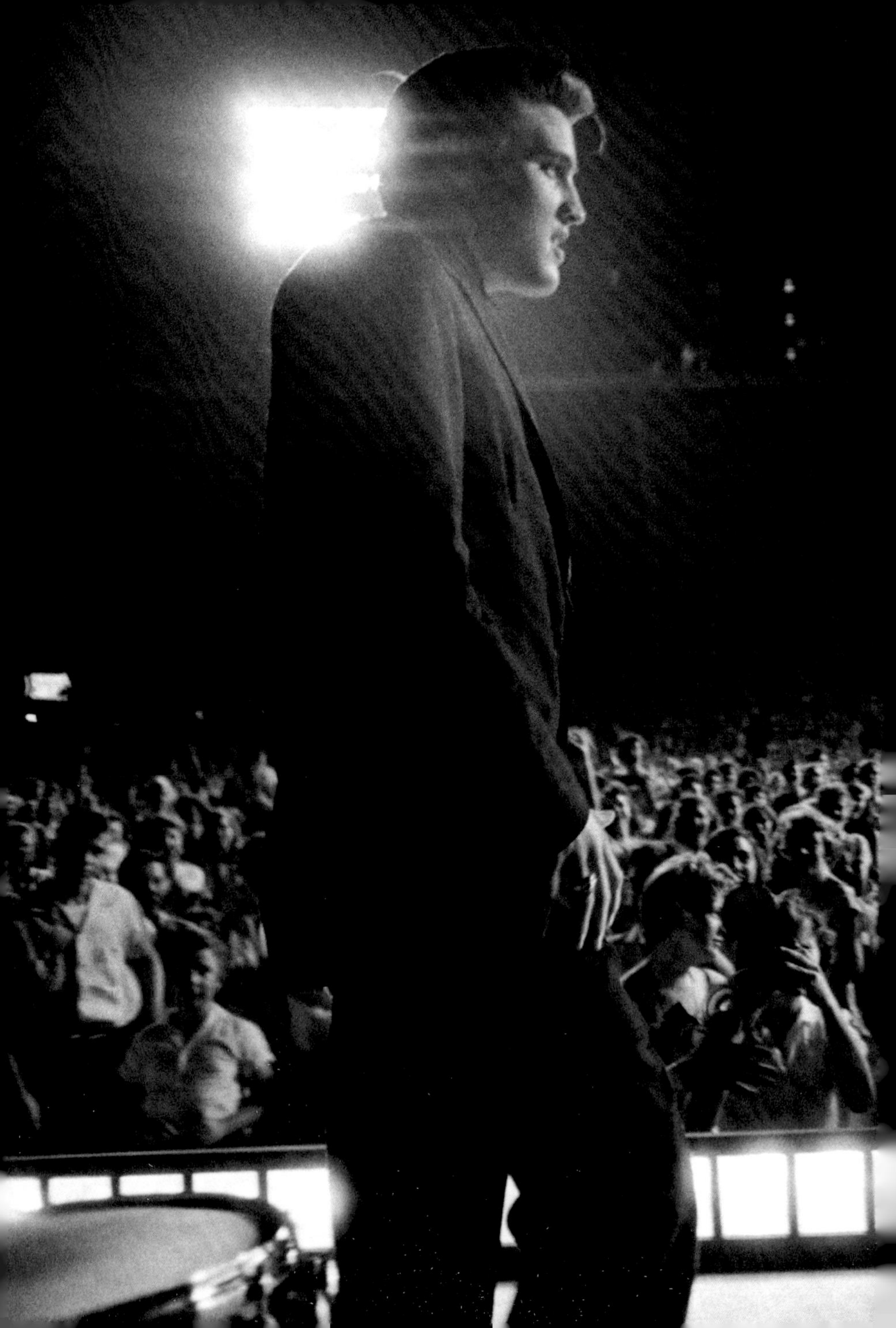

Elvis is a no-talent performer riding the crest of a wave of mass hysteria... He's drawing an average of two thousand kids a show and most of them are girls. Elvis can't sing, can't play the guitar.

HERB ROWE
Miami Herald, August 4, 1956

PAGE 157
Colonel Parker sells autographed photos for a dime a piece before the Russwood Park show, which was a concert to benefit the Cynthia Milk Fund and the Variety Club's Home for Convalescent Children.

OPPOSITE
Elvis takes the stage wearing all black except for his tie and his socks (both red).

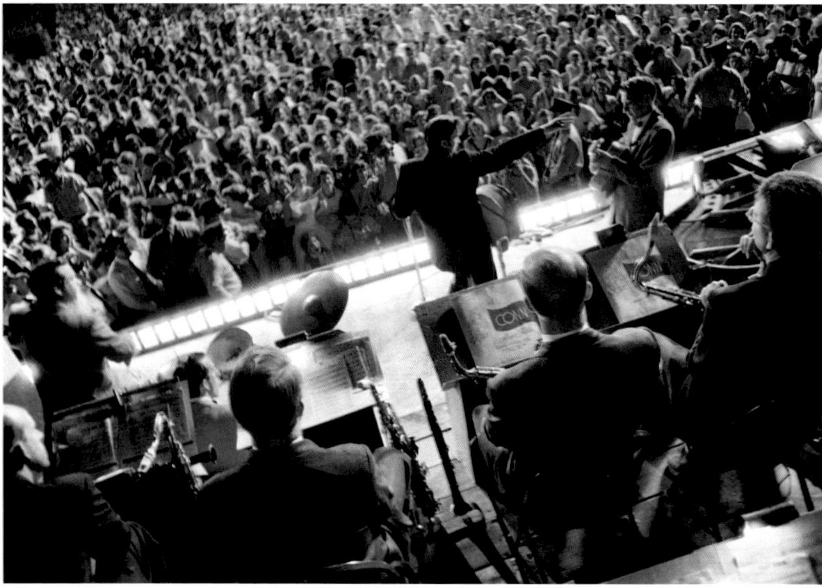

ABOVE

Referring to his tightly scripted performance on *Steve Allen*, Elvis readies the audience: "Tonight you're going to see what the real Elvis Presley is all about." Then he proceeds to gyrate all over the stage to their delight.

OPPOSITE

Starburst, Russwood Park, Memphis, Tennessee, July 4, 1956. A lucky accident, a flashbulb goes off in the crowd at the very moment the shutter of Wertheimer's camera opens, creating a magnificent spray of backlight.

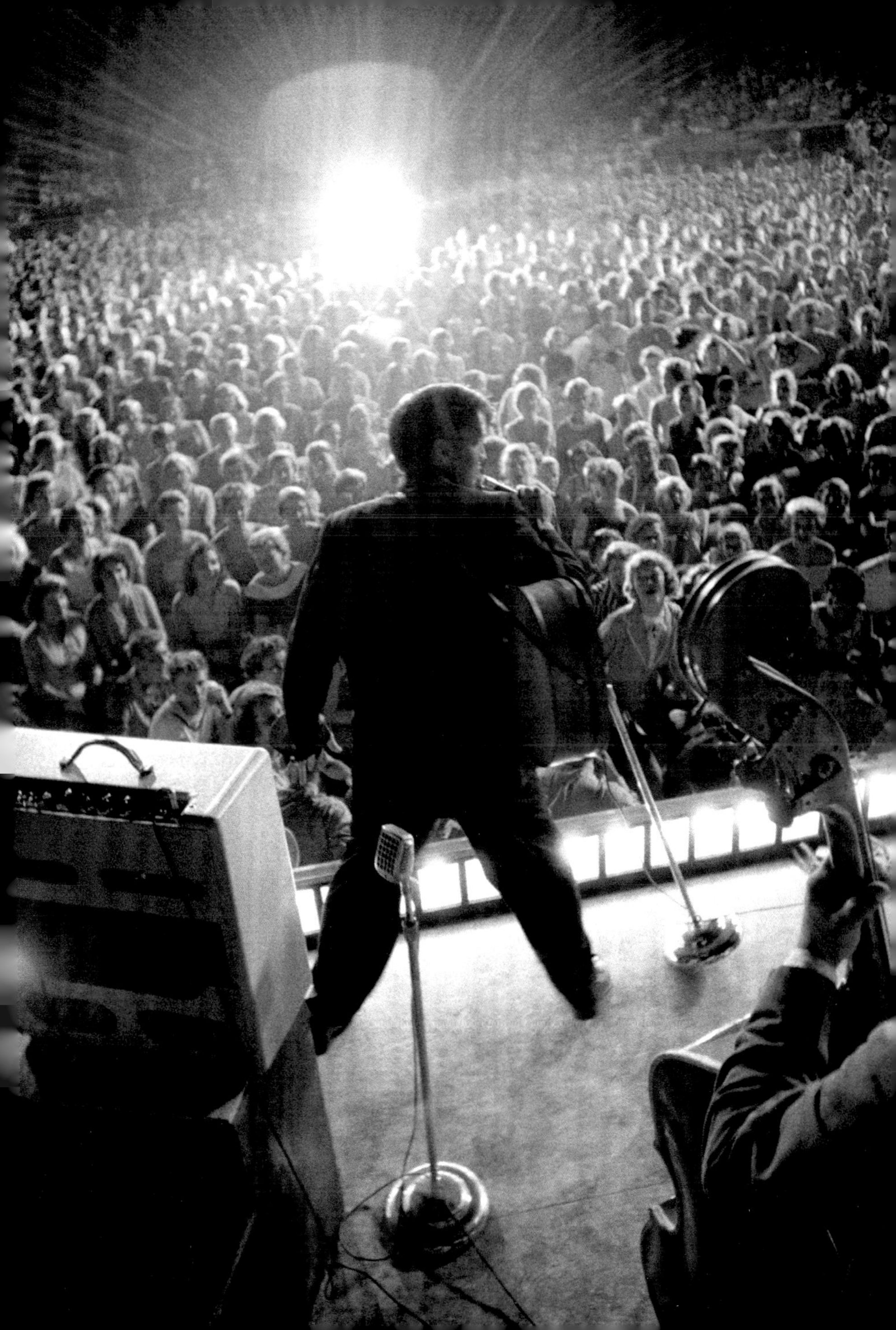

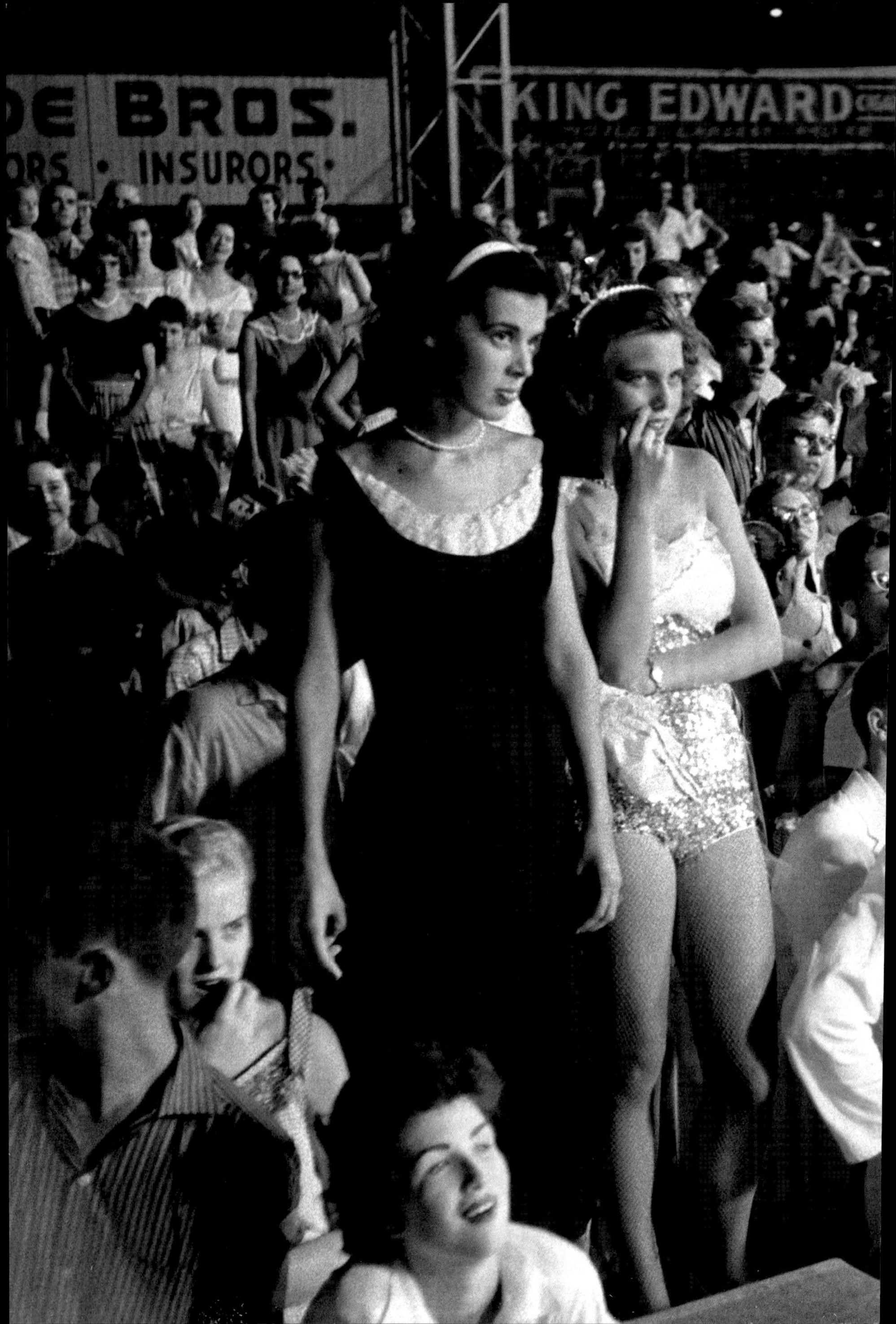
DE BROS.
ORS • INSURORS •
KING EDWARD

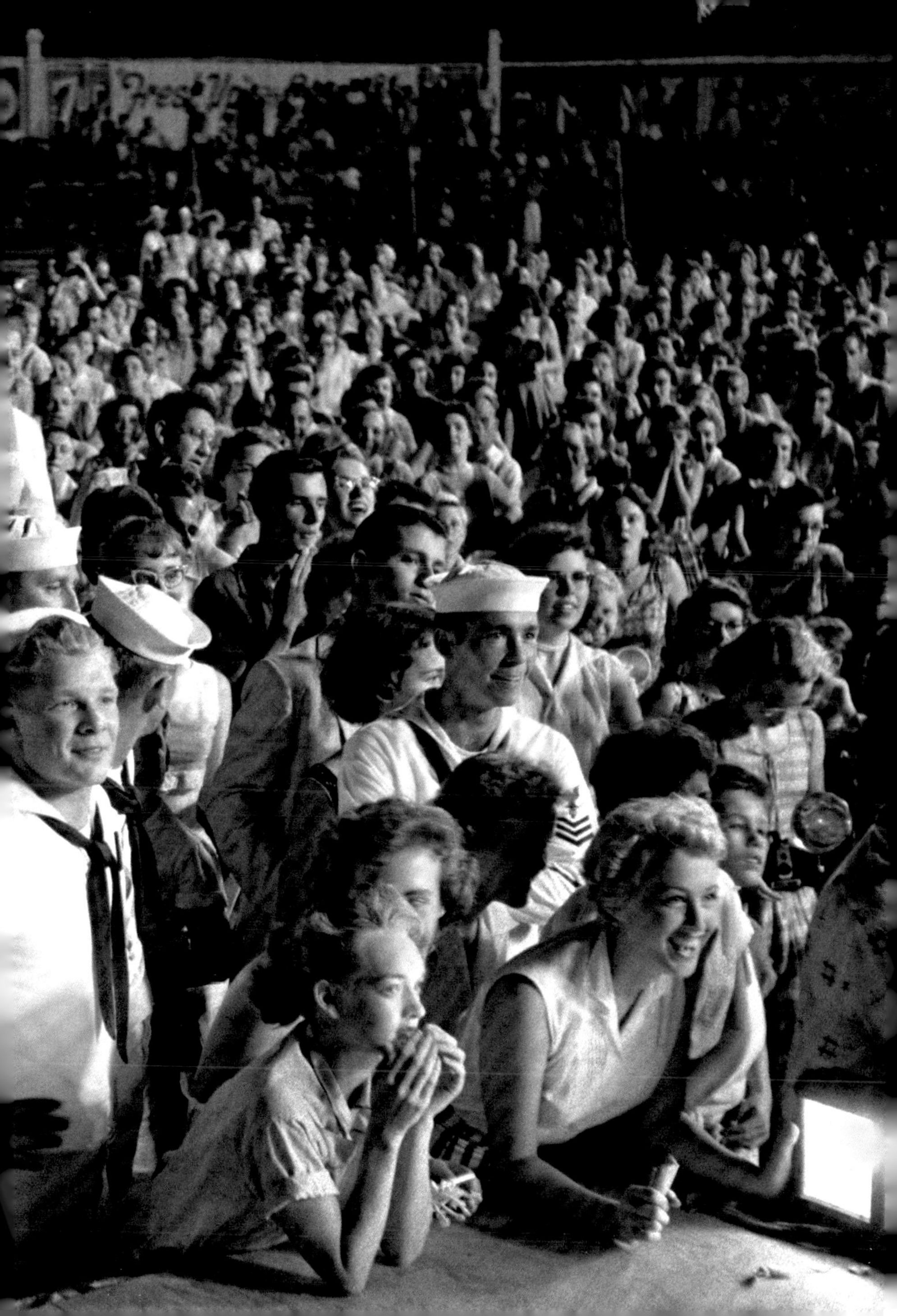

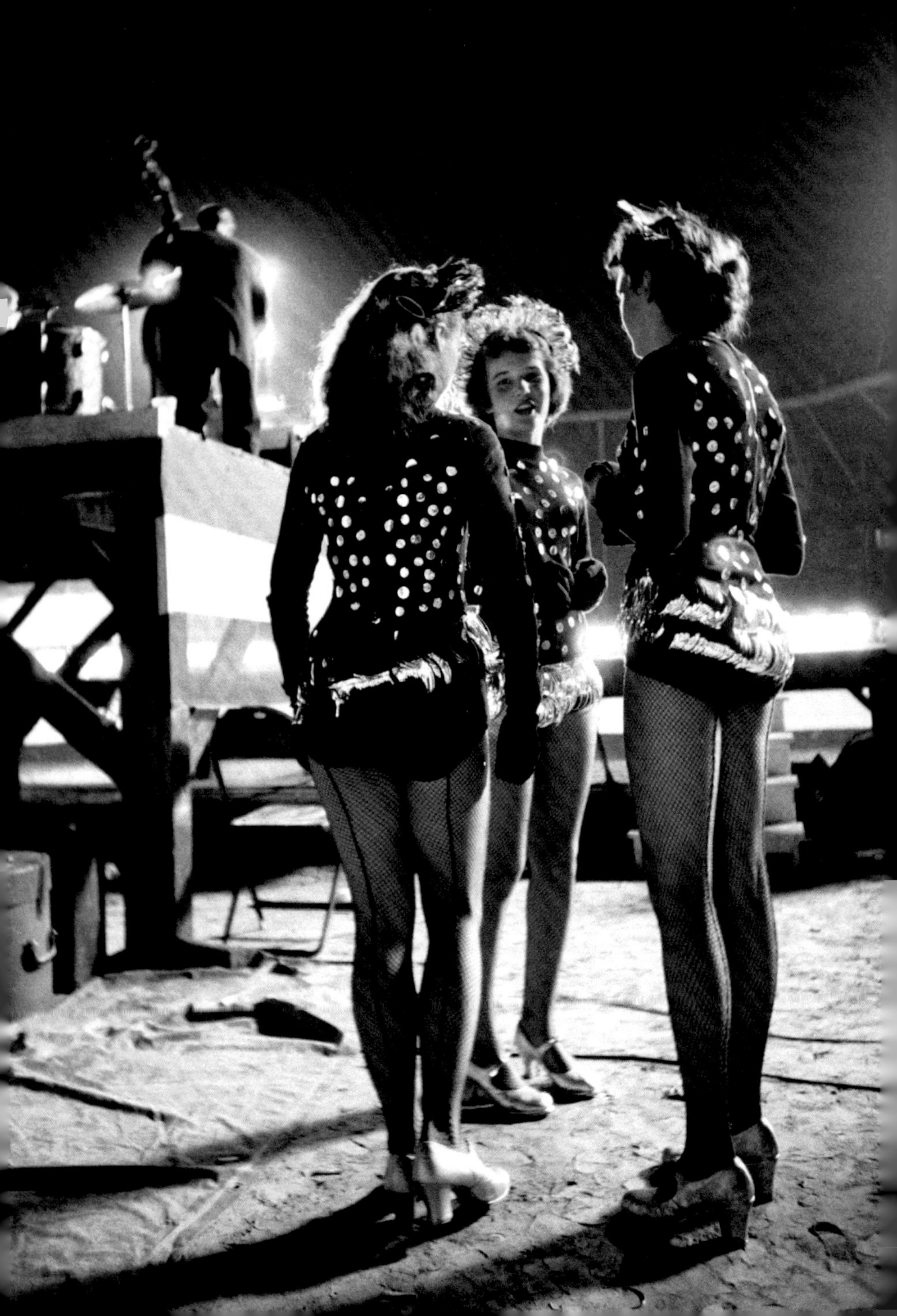

There's a big difference in singing on a record and singing for an audience. People can stay home and listen to records on the radio or phonograph and it doesn't cost 'em anything. But when they pay their money to come out and see you at a personal appearance, these people want to see a show.

ELVIS PRESLEY
Elvis Answers Back magazine,
August 28, 1956

PREVIOUS SPREAD
The next day, newspapers reported the Russwood crowd to number 14,000.

OPPOSITE
Over 100 performers were on stage that night for the benefit show, including tap dancers and baton twirlers.

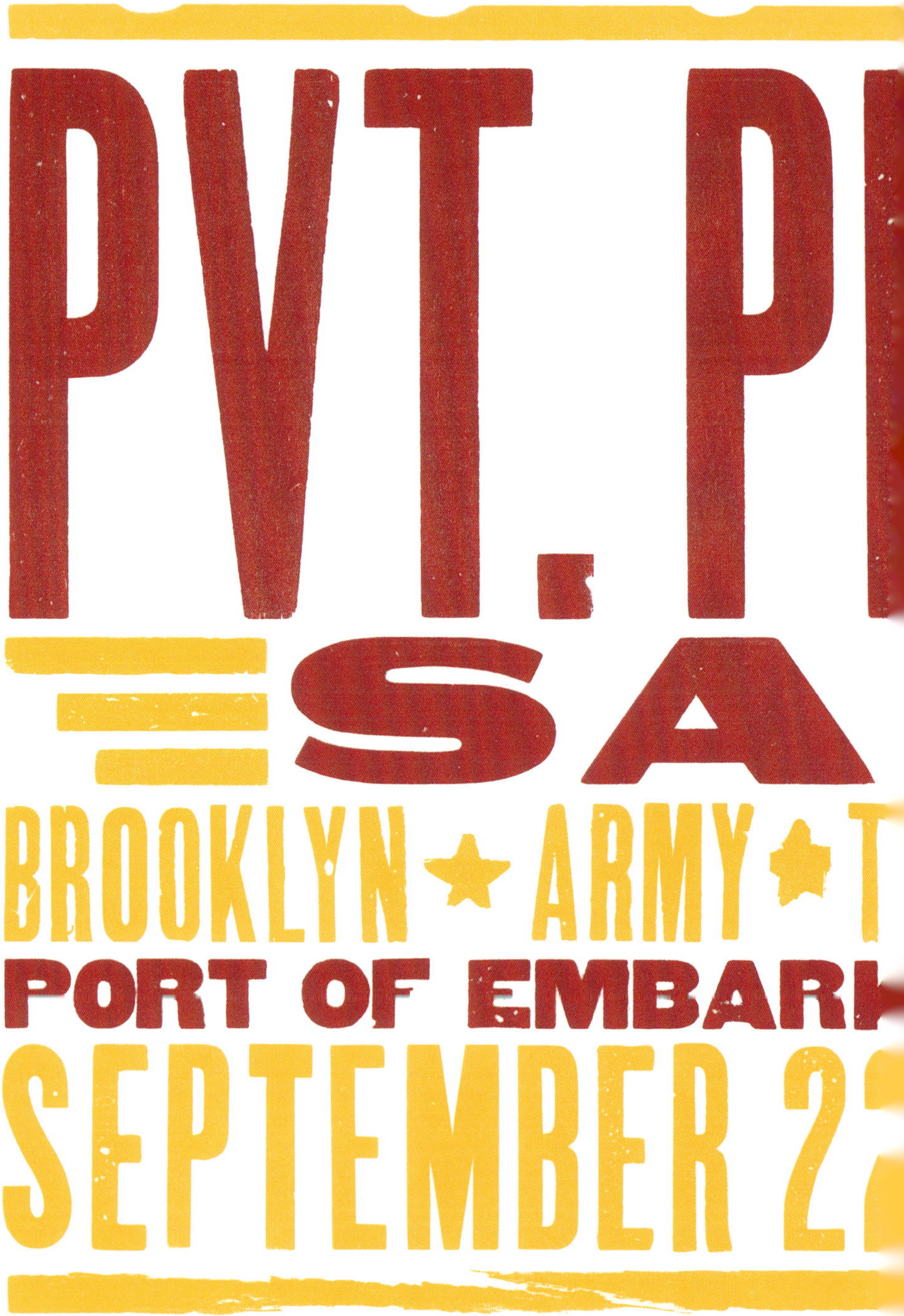
PVT.
BROOKLYN ARMY
PORT OF EMBAR
SEPTEMBER

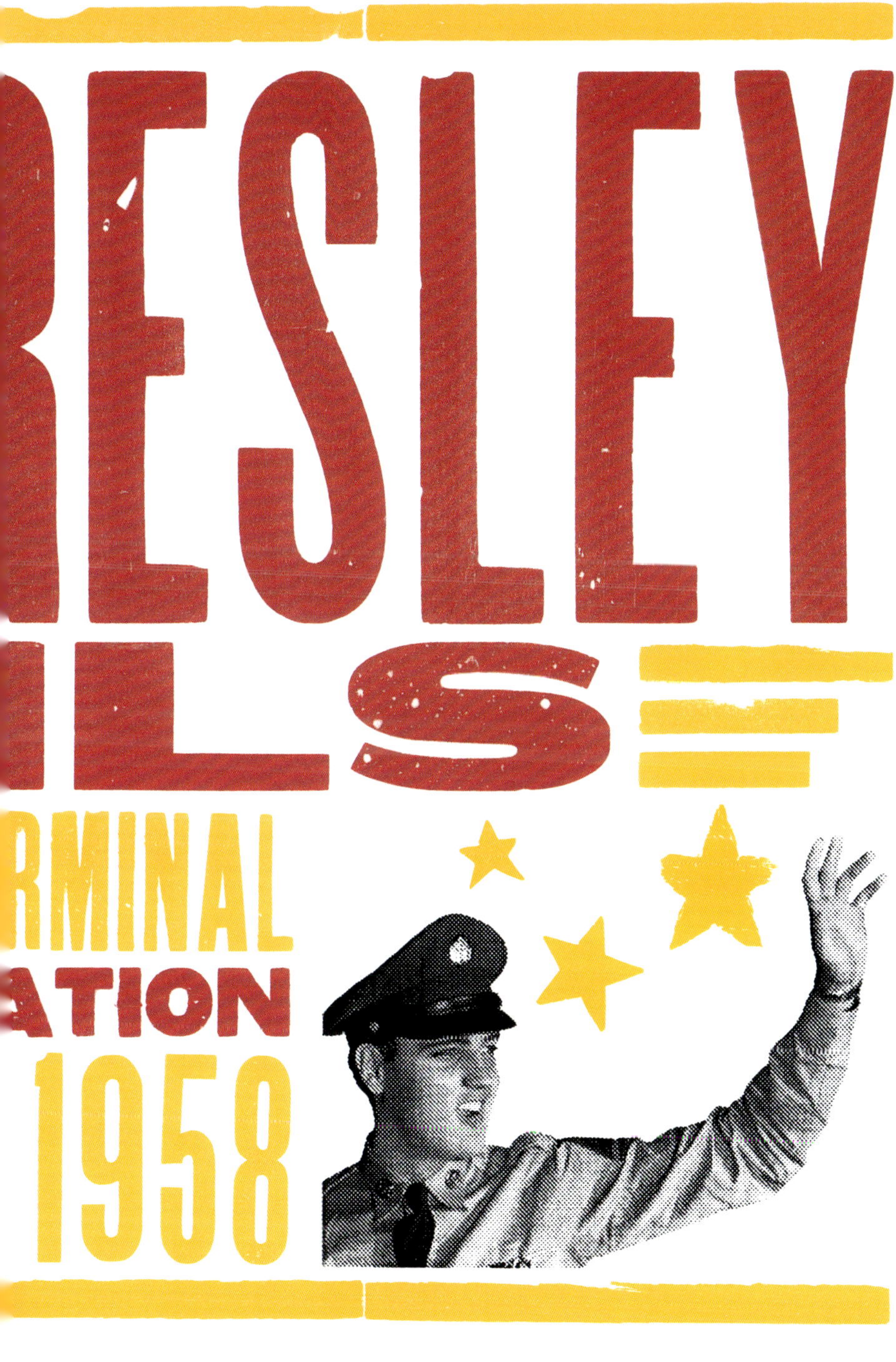
RESLEY
ILS
RMINAL
ATION
1958

★ ★ ★

A LITTLE LESS THAN A YEAR AFTER Elvis entered the U.S. Army, he arrived at the Brooklyn Army Terminal Port of Embarkation sporting a crew cut and normal sideburns, ready to do occupation duty as a soldier in Germany. A terrible and life-changing incident had happened five weeks earlier when his beloved mother, Gladys, passed away. It was announced that Private Presley was not being treated differently from other soldiers; however, he held a press conference in front of approximately 250 media people with recruiting posters hanging behind him prior to shipping out. I was warned by Anne Fulchino that Colonel Parker was going to be there—but I reassured her that I had nothing to fear. When I was at the podium he squeezed in beside me. After a moment he looked me in the face and said, "Wertheimer! Taking any good pictures?" And I said, "Always, Colonel, always," and he replied, "Very good, keep it up." Colonel Parker was always thinking ahead, providing the bandleader with sheet music of Elvis's hits, especially those from Sun Records. The Army band played many of Elvis's early songs as the USS *Randall* troop ship sailed out of New York Harbor with 6,000 soldiers aboard. That was the last time I ever saw him.

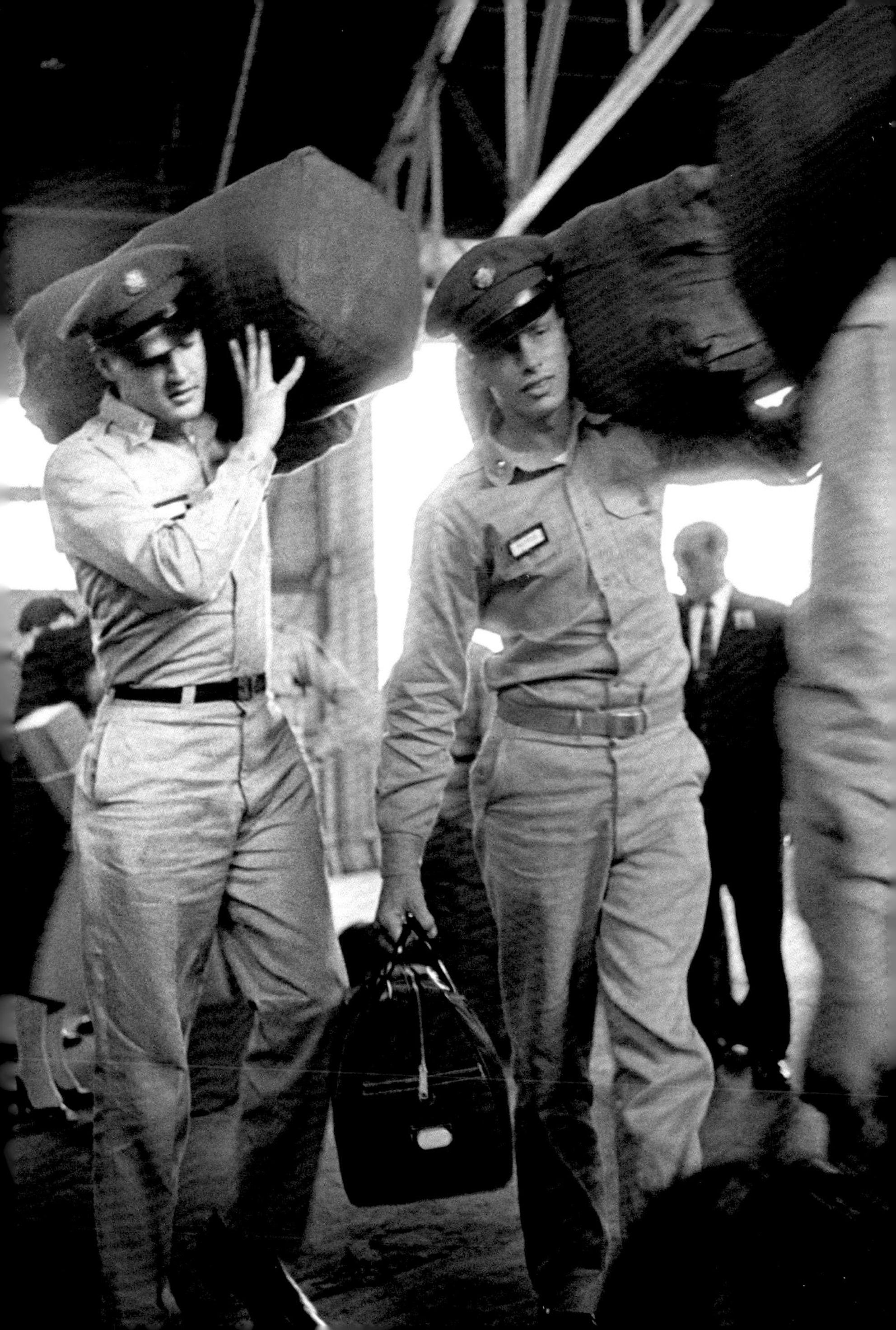

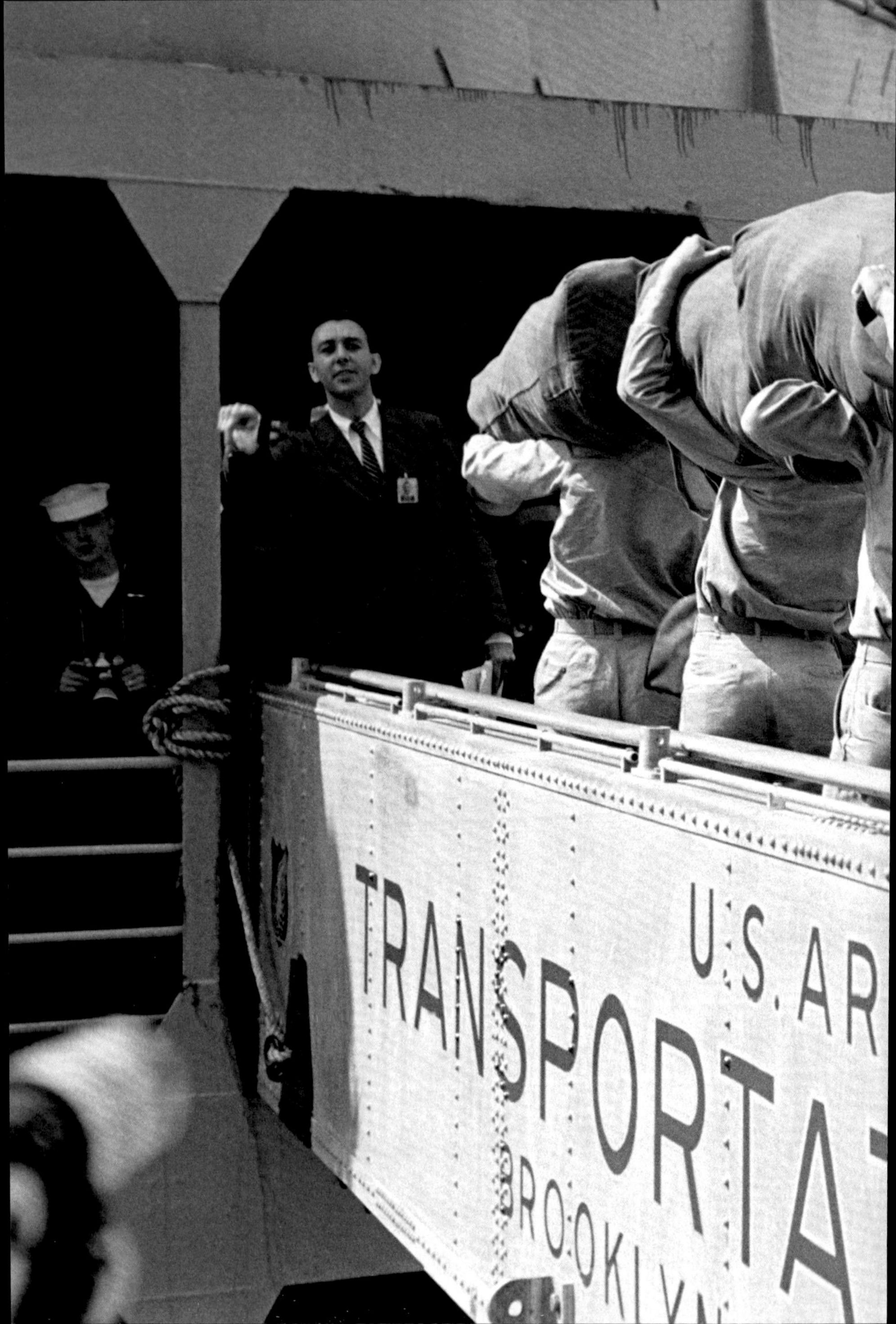
U.S. AR
TRANSPORTA
BROOKLYN

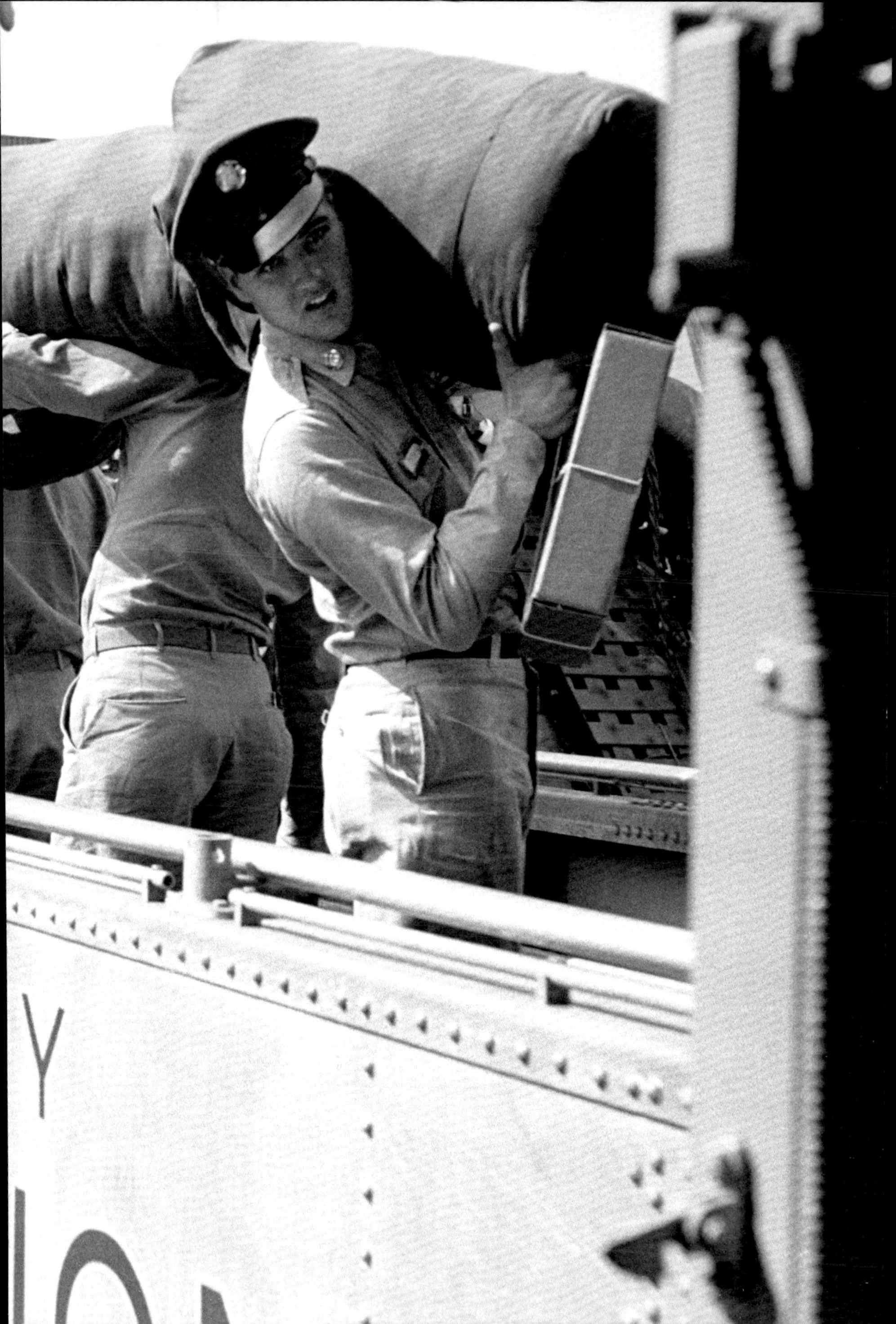

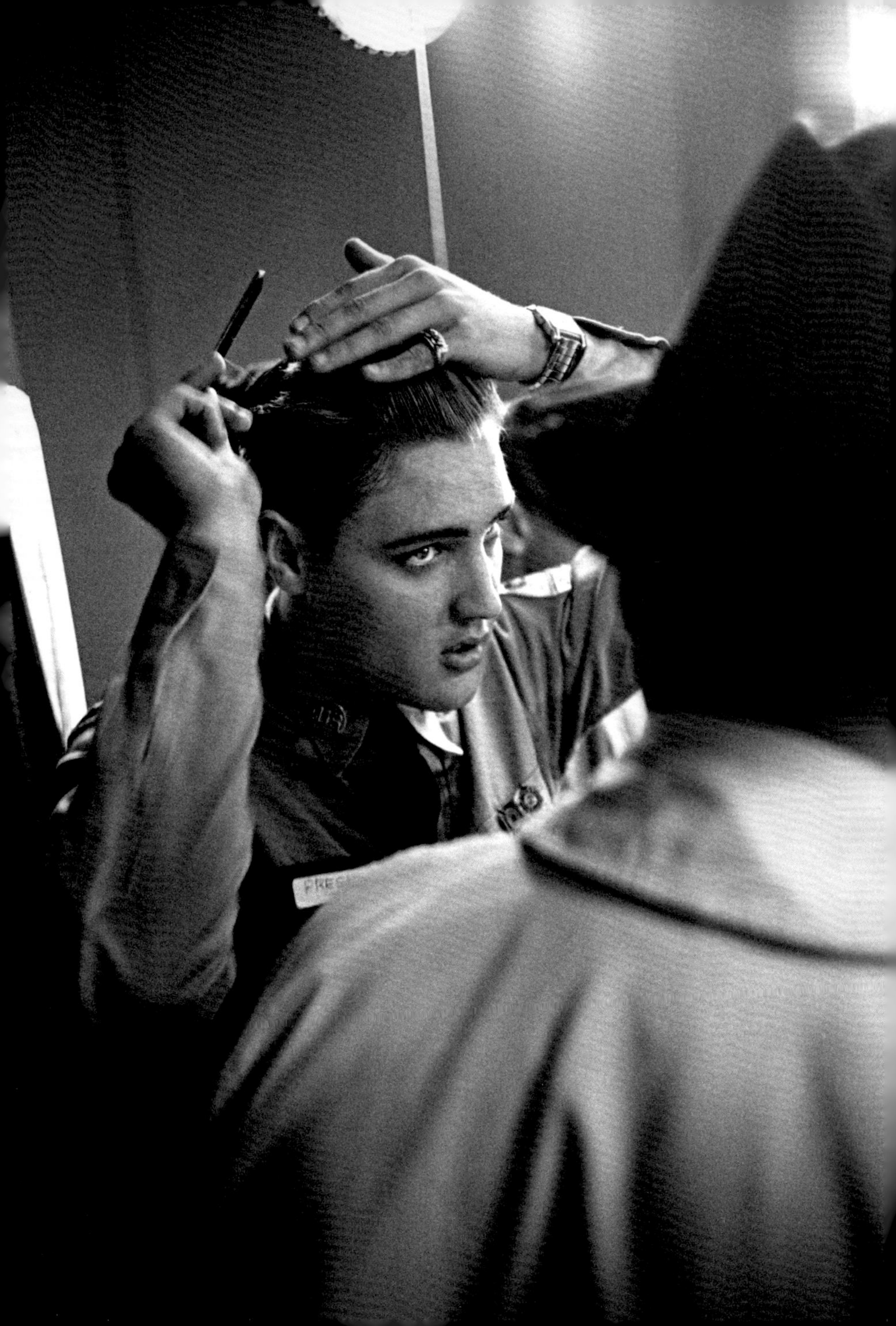

Pvt. Elvis Presley departed yesterday with 1,170 members of the Third Armored Division for an eighteen-month tour of duty in Germany. The entertainer said that if rock 'n' roll music died out during his stay in service, he would give up singing and try to become a good actor.

THE NEW YORK TIMES
September 23, 1958

PAGE 169 & PREVIOUS SPREAD
"Could we try that once more?" Elvis and fellow soldiers of Company D First Battalion 32nd Armor, Third Armored Division walk the gangplank of the USS *Randall* at the Brooklyn Army Terminal Port of Embarkation.

OPPOSITE
Combing his GI haircut.

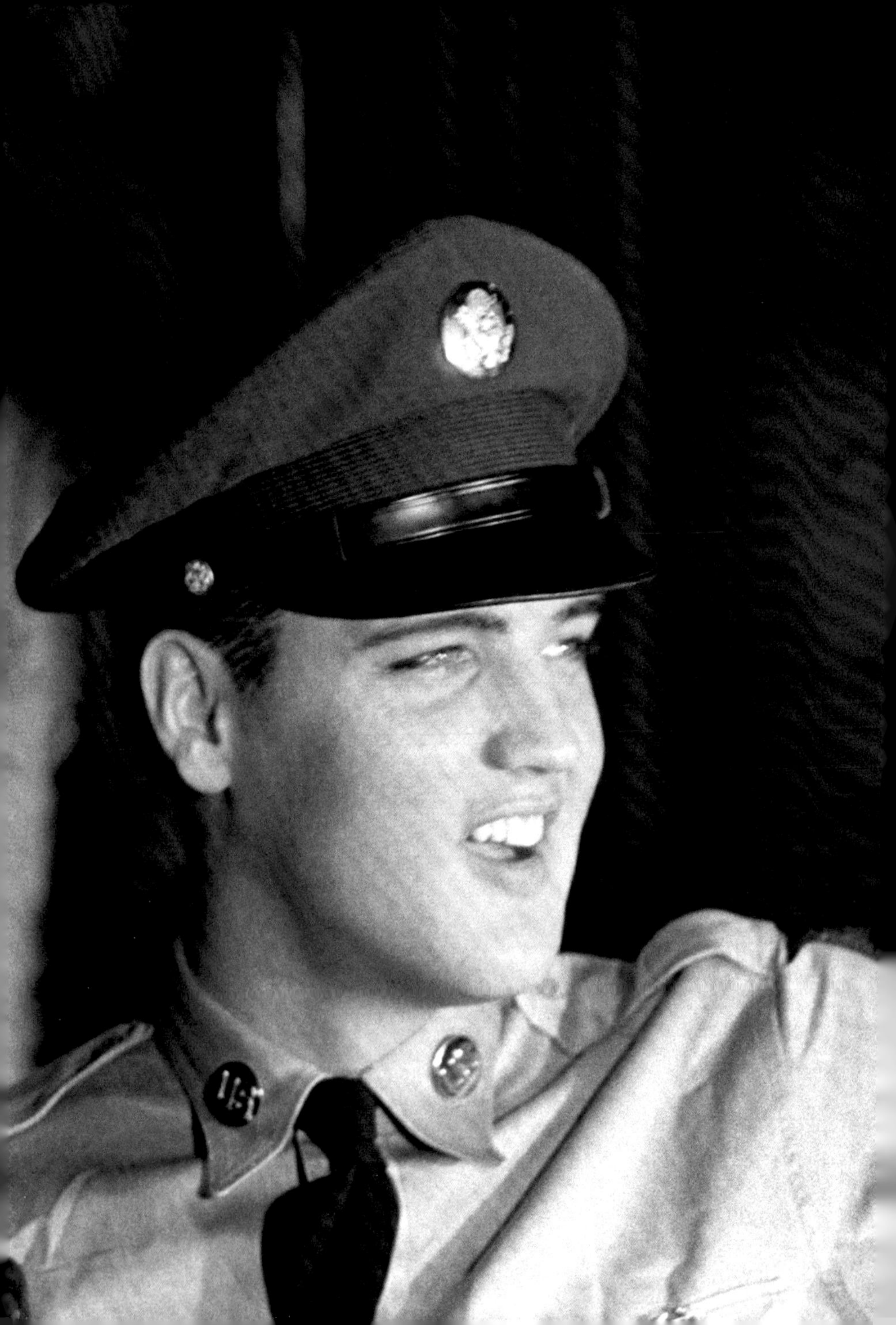

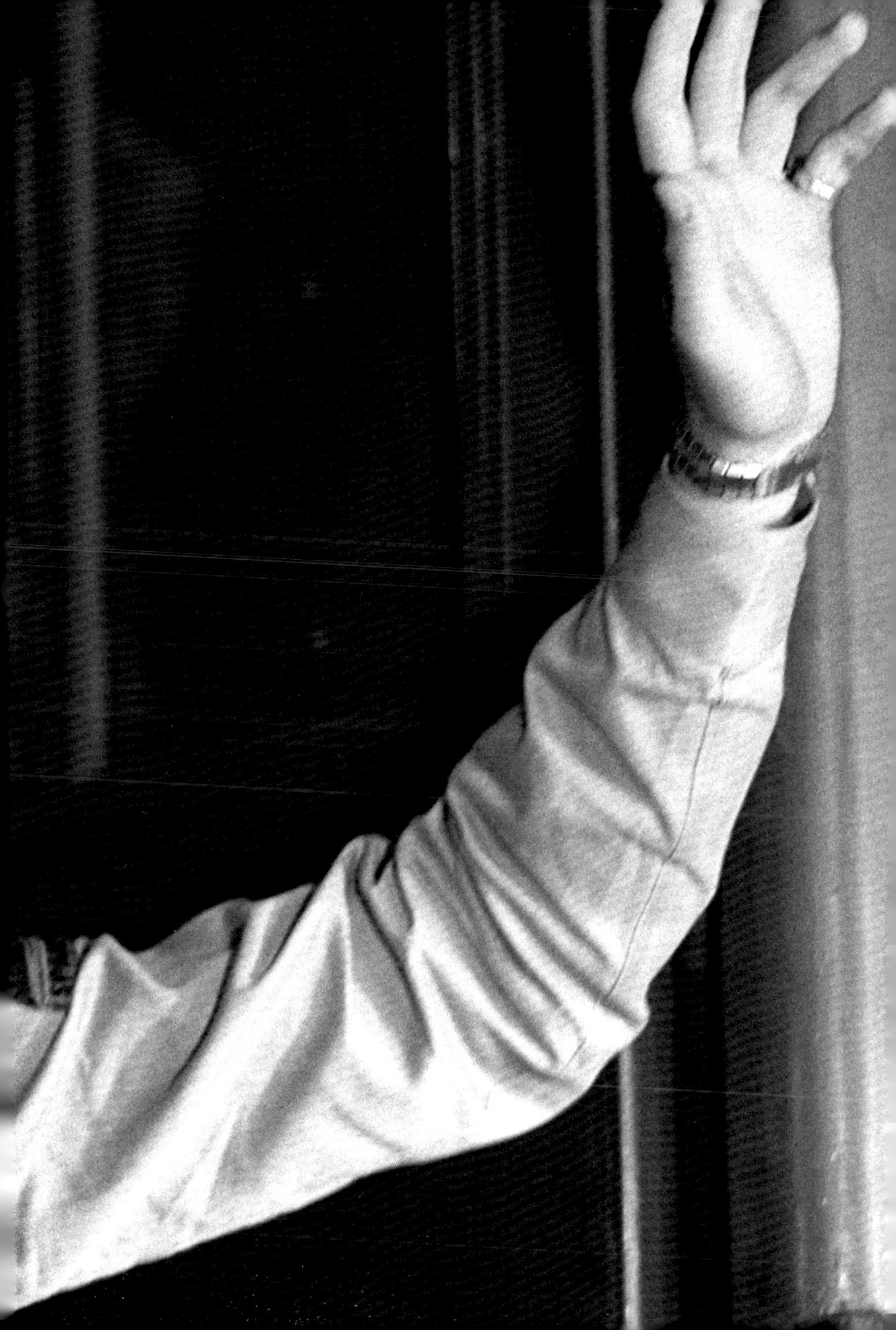

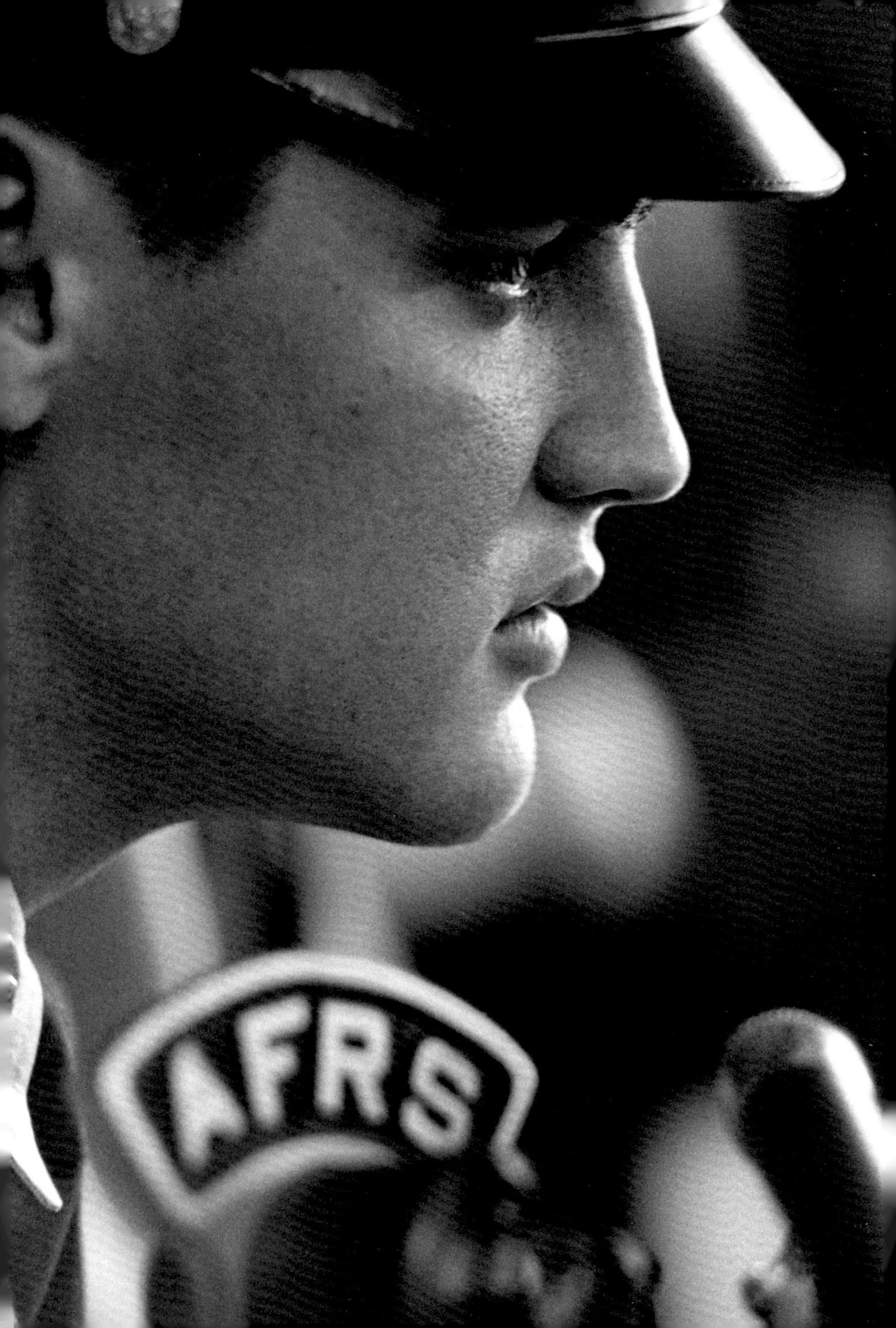
AFRS

It's rare when an artist's talent
can touch an entire generation of people.
It's even more rare when that same influence
affects several generations. Elvis made an
imprint on the world of pop music unequaled
by any other single performer.

DICK CLARK

PREVIOUS SPREAD
Private Presley, Brooklyn Army Terminal Port of Embarkation, September 22, 1958.

OPPOSITE
Elvis holds forth on the Armed Forces Radio Service, broadcasting his departure for Friedberg, Germany.

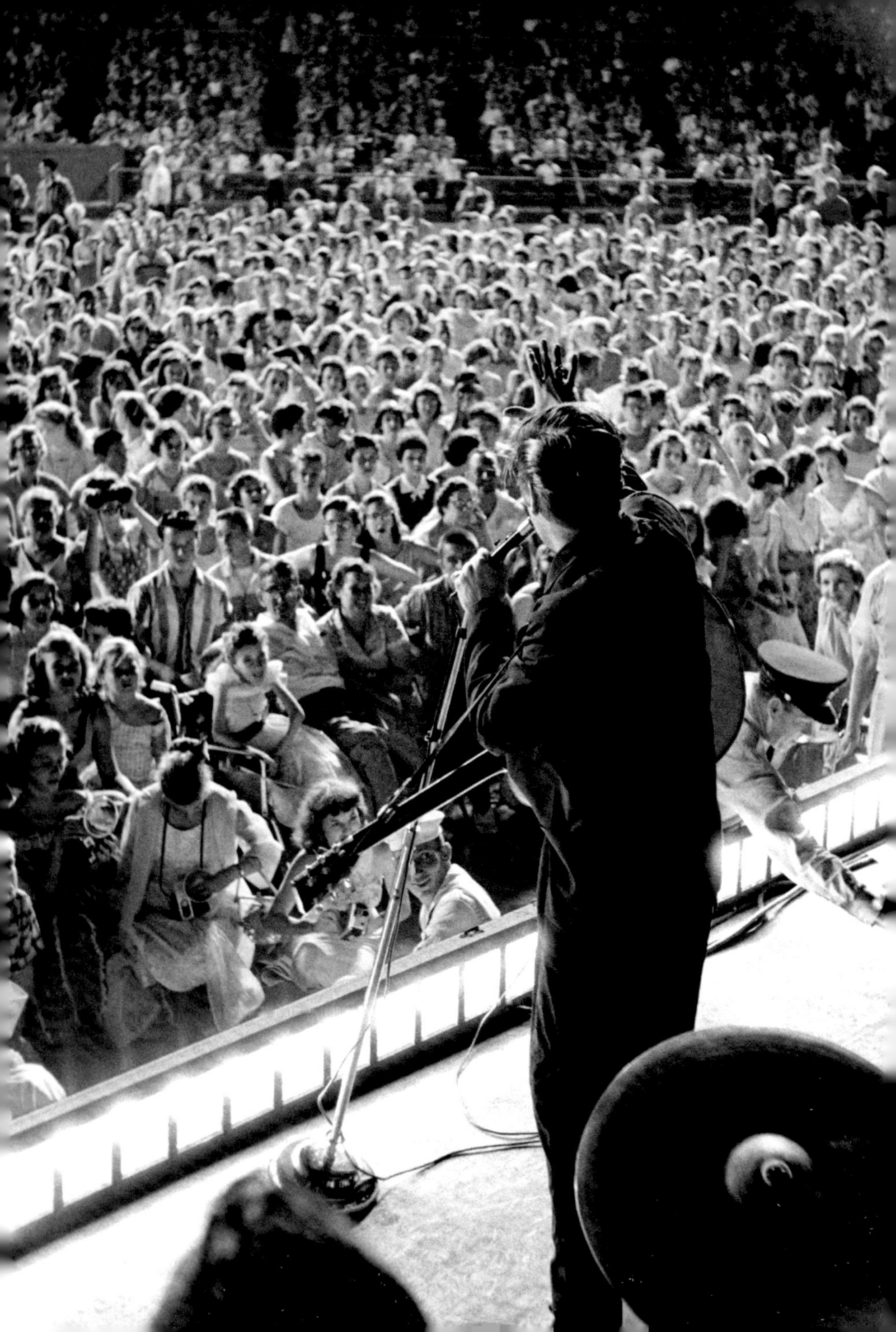

Just Another Assignment

★

CHRIS MURRAY

IT WAS A HOT SUMMER NIGHT in Memphis on July 4, 1956. A 21-year-old Elvis Presley had just returned home from a trip to New York City, where he had made several appearances on national television shows and recorded "Hound Dog," "Don't Be Cruel," and "Any Way You Want Me" at RCA Victor's Studio 1. "Hound Dog" and "Don't Be Cruel" would soon be released as A- and B-sides of a 45-rpm record ready to explode on radio airwaves. Elvis was to perform that evening in Russwood Park, a stadium in Memphis. The crowd was buzzing and in a mood of great anticipation, excited to see their hometown boy who had gone north and "made it big."

Photographer Alfred Wertheimer, just 26 years old himself, accompanied Elvis to his concert. The sheriff arrived at the Presley home in his police car. Elvis sat in the middle of the front seat, in between the sheriff and his manager, Colonel Tom Parker. Wertheimer sat in the backseat alone. When they arrived, Wertheimer photographed Elvis moving through a surging crowd that was trying to get as close to him as possible.

The air was electric when a black-clad Elvis took the stage, backed by Scotty Moore on the guitar, Bill Black on bass, and D. J. Fontana on drums. 14,000 people were on hand to celebrate this new liberating and thrilling music performed by one of their own. Alluding to the stiff script he'd followed just a few days earlier on *The Steve Allen Show*, he told the Memphis audience, "Tonight, you're going to see what the real Elvis is all about."

Benefit concert at Russwood Park, Memphis, Tennessee, July 4, 1956.

What followed was a mesmerizing, no-holds-barred performance. The fans loved it, and Wertheimer photographed it all. Within a few short months, Elvis Presley would soon be the most talked-about entertainer in the world.

Alfred Wertheimer's photographs of Elvis Presley are a unique visual record of the most exciting and influential performer of our time. They capture Elvis at the quintessential moment of his explosive appearance onto the cultural landscape, and no photographer ever again had the kind of access to the star that Wertheimer experienced. Wertheimer has described his photographs as "the first and last look at the day-to-day life of Elvis Presley." Apart from Elvis's own recordings from this period, Wertheimer's photographs are the most compelling vintage document of the singer in 1956, a very special year for a young man from Memphis who was about to shake up the world. They are an extra-ordinary record of how these two storytellers' lives came together, a 21-year-old singer on the verge of fame and fortune crossing paths with a 26-year-old photographer about to document a legend.

AT THE AGE OF SIX, in 1936, Alfred Wertheimer left Germany with his father, Julius, his mother, Katy, and his brother, Henry. Julius was a kosher delicatessen butcher with a little shop in Coburg, Germany. After leaving their home behind, young Alfred and his family came to New York City and after several moves rented an apartment at 842 Nostrand Avenue in Brooklyn. Julius got a job at Carmel Kosher Provision, and the Wertheimer family settled in to a new life in America.

Wertheimer graduated from high school in 1947 and spent a year at City College studying drawing before being accepted at Cooper Union, a school of art and engineering in Manhattan. Cooper Union was tuition-free, and he describes himself as "one of the lucky 90," as only 90 students were admitted that year. At Cooper Union, Wertheimer took his first photographs with a camera Henry had given him. Using available light, he photographed his classmates and teachers, and was delighted to see his photos published in the school newspaper.

In 1951 Wertheimer graduated with a major in advertising design, and the following year he was drafted into the U.S. Army, where he worked as a military photographer from 1952–54. While in basic training, he became the first and only photographer to cover a unit's transition from civilian life to military or GI (government issue) property. At the end of the 16 weeks, he put together what he felt was a good portfolio showing what it took to go

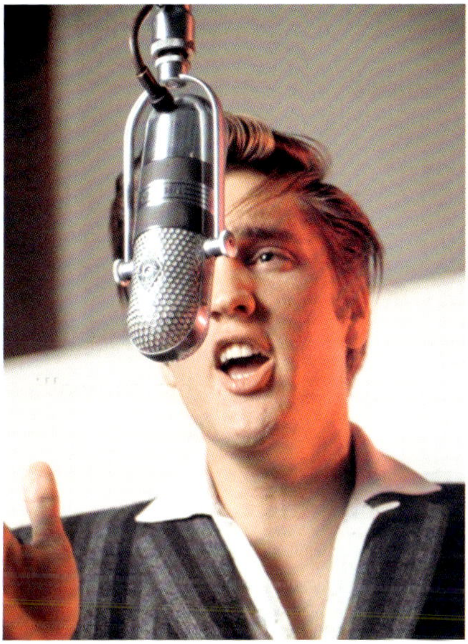

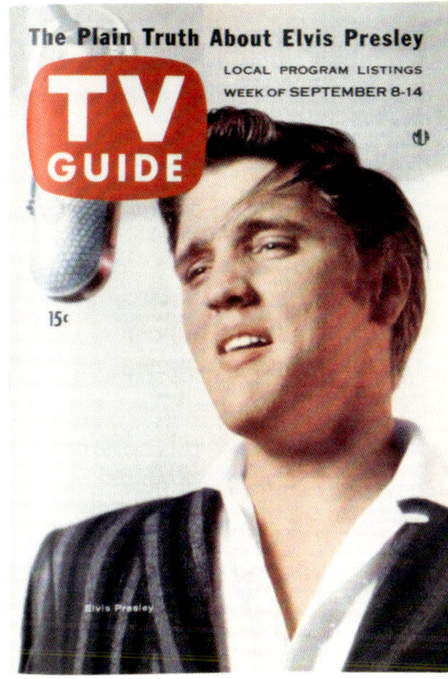

from a civilian to a soldier. He presented it to the captain of his company with the hope of influencing him to change his job title from a mortar base plate carrier. The captain complimented his work, and Wertheimer said, "I appreciate that, sir. Is there any possibility of you changing my job classification to that of photographer?" The captain said that would require the general's approval, which was soon granted.

After finishing his service in 1954, Wertheimer returned to New York City, where he found a job with fashion photographer Tom Palumbo, who worked on assignment for *Harper's Bazaar* magazine under the legendary art director Alexey Brodovitch. Wertheimer learned much under Palumbo, developing film, printing photographs, setting up and cleaning the studio, keeping track of negatives and his music library, assisting at shoots, and going to the colorlab for processing.

After about a year, he started his own business as a freelance photographer. Though he worked independently, he shared studio space with a group of photographers at Dave Linton's studio at Third Avenue

Elvis at the microphone, RCA Victor Studio 1, July 2, 1956.
The September 8–14 issue of *TV Guide*, featuring one of Wertheimer's portraits from that historic session, was the first of many Elvis covers for the publication.

and 74th Street. His good friend Paul Schutzer, a talented photojournalist, also worked there and introduced Wertheimer to the publicist at RCA Victor's pop record division, Anne Fulchino. Fulchino hired him to photograph RCA acts like Perry Como, Lena Horne, Julius La Rosa, Arthur Rubinstein, Nelson Eddy, Jeannette MacDonald, and others. In March 1956 she asked him to come take some pictures of RCA's latest acquisition. While Wertheimer had never heard of this new singer, in just a few months the whole world would know the name Elvis Presley.

ALFRED WERTHEIMER HAS OFTEN SAID, "My photographs speak for themselves." That they resonate so splendidly is a result of his awareness and sensitivity as a skilled photographer, qualities that complemented his charismatic subject, Elvis Presley. For no matter who else he photographed in the years to come, including his later work as a documentary cameraman for television, no assignment would ever come close to matching the Elvis job. About his experience revealing Elvis's environment and how he lived in it, Wertheimer has remarked, "I was a reporter whose pen was a camera."

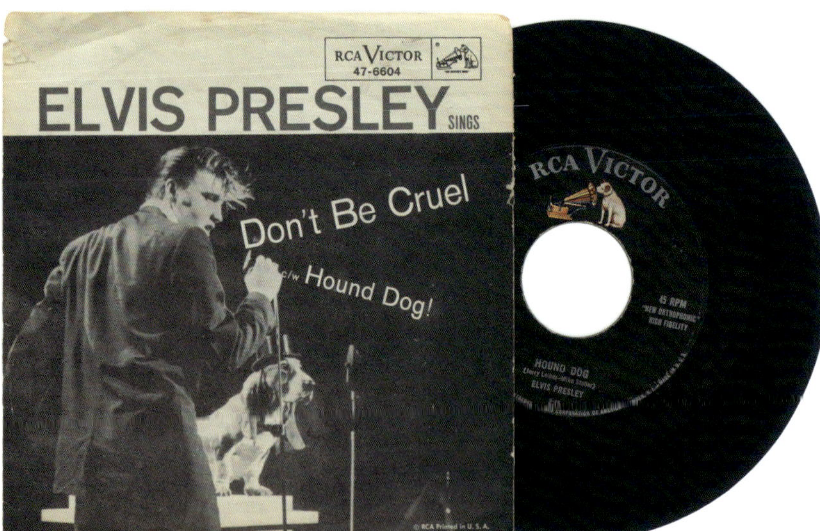

Don't Be Cruel/Hound Dog, 45 rpm cover, 1956.
The RCA Victor release featured one of Wertheimer's photographs from the set of *The Steve Allen Show.*

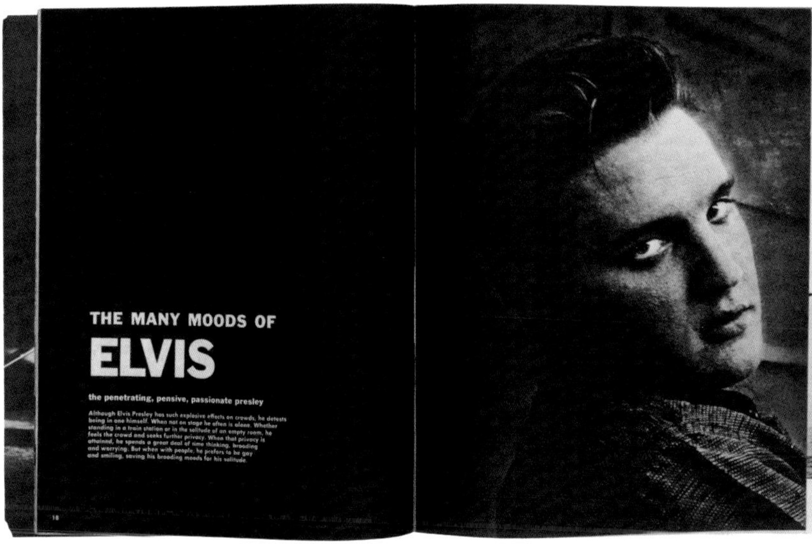

THE MANY MOODS OF
ELVIS
the penetrating, pensive, passionate presley
Although Elvis Presley has such explosive effects on crowds, he detests being in one himself. When not on stage he often is alone. Whether standing in a train station or in the solitude of an empty room, he feels the crowd and seeks further privacy. When that privacy is attained, he spends a great deal of time thinking, brooding and worrying. But when with people, he prefers to be gay and smiling, saving his brooding moods for his solitude.

Steeped in the distinguished tradition of photojournalists, Wertheimer embraced an aesthetic that was simultaneously classic yet innovative. Wertheimer was not a rock-and-roll photographer. After all, that genre of photography did not even exist yet. However, his photographs of Elvis would set a standard for all photographers who would go on to document musical artists.

In 1958 Elvis Presley was drafted into the U.S. Army and reported to the draft board on South Main Street in Memphis, Tennessee, for his physical on March 24. A few days later, Elvis was assigned to the Third Armored Division at Fort Hood, Texas. After his basic training, advanced tank training, and basic unit training, he was ready to ship out to Germany and join a scout platoon called Company C. On Friday, September 19, he boarded a troop train in Killeen, Texas, headed to the Brooklyn Army Terminal Port of Embarkation, and arrived in New York at 9 a.m. on Monday, September 22.

Elvis Presley was at the height of his fame when he was drafted. Like many young men, he was anxious about leaving behind friends, family, and career, but more significantly, he was still deeply affected by the loss

Interior, *The Amazing Elvis Presley*, September 1956.
Produced by Alfred Wertheimer under the imprint Renal Corporation,
the fanzine sold 400,000 copies at 35 cents apiece.

of his beloved mother, who had died just five weeks before he was to ship out from New York. Although his father and grandmother were going to accompany him to Germany, Elvis was clearly unsettled. Considering all of the changes of the past three years and his incredible rise to fame and fortune, Elvis had a lot on his mind. This day in Brooklyn was surely a turning point in his life.

When Alfred Wertheimer arrived at the Brooklyn Army Terminal to photograph Elvis shipping out, he was not the only photographer this time. There were dozens of photographers, film and TV crews, and reporters on hand. But Wertheimer knew Elvis, his entourage, the Colonel, and the representatives from RCA Victor. Having served in the Army only a few years earlier, Wertheimer was familiar with that environment and photographed the events surrounding the embarkation with an insider's point of view. These photos of Elvis's departure tell the story of that day and are the last photographs Wertheimer ever took of Elvis.

To some, Elvis's departure in 1958 marks the end of the most exciting and compelling period of his career as a performer and musical artist. Wertheimer's 1956 photographs of Elvis documented that golden period for us all. These last photos of Elvis shipping out are Wertheimer's goodbye to the Elvis he knew.

Wertheimer's photographs capture Elvis at a crossroads of culture. Elvis went on to unprecedented fame and fortune as a musical artist, but it is Alfred Wertheimer's photo-graphs that remind us of a time in America when a young man from Mississippi could change the world with a song. These photographs of Elvis Presley are without a doubt the most important and compelling images ever taken of the greatest rock-and-roll icon of all time. No other photographer has ever come closer to catching Elvis Presley's magic than Alfred Wertheimer.

WERTHEIMER CONTINUED TO WORK as a freelance photographer after taking his last photographs of Elvis Presley on September 22, 1958. Throughout the late '50s he photographed Eleanor Roosevelt, Perry Como, Nina Simone, Paul Anka, Nelson Eddy, and many others, and shot for magazines like *Life*, *Pageant*, and *Paris Match*. "But some of the best assignments are my own assignments," Wertheimer says. And his fondness for being the "fly on the wall" led to photo essays on religious sects in New York (Sweet Daddy Grace's United House of Prayer for All People, Hasidim, Jehovah's Witnesses) and life inside Bellevue Psychiatric

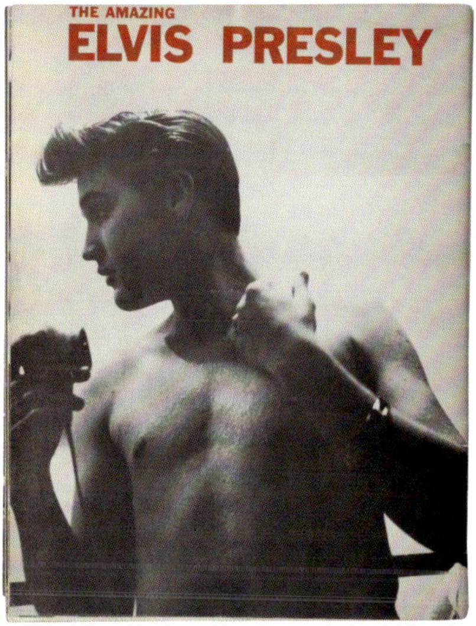

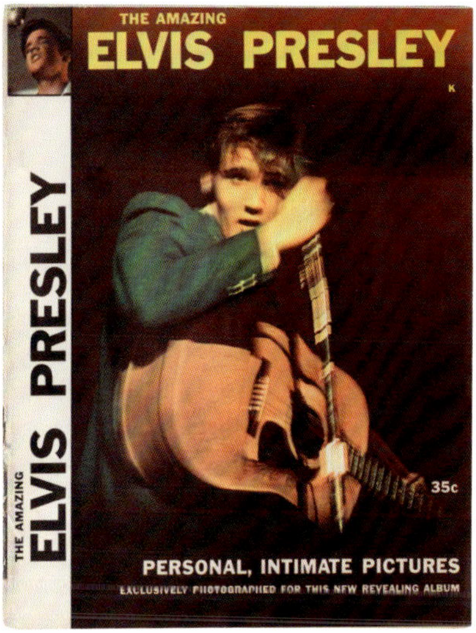

Hospital. "I'm basically a curious person, and want to know how things evolved and why," he says. "And I like to do it visually."

But by the early '60s he was no longer interested in making still pictures. In 1964 he became a cameraman and filmmaker for Granada TV in the UK. Producing segments for the weekly show *World in Action* took him from Bolivia on a hunt for Che Guevara to Harvard and Yale, where professors were doing research on flying saucers. In 1969 he was hired as one of the principal cameramen on the Mike Wadleigh film *Woodstock*. The straight man in a sea of 300,000 hippies, he shot the famous mudslide scene. More prepared than the rest of the crew, Wertheimer had arrived on location with his own equipment. When he noticed that Wadleigh had rented every Éclair camera in New York City for the job, the idea for a new business began to form in his mind...

He soon bought a Steenbeck editing machine, then another, and before he knew it he had 28 Steenbecks and a staff of four to service them in a 12,000-square-foot office in midtown Manhattan. Catering to networks such as CBS News and ABC Sports, Cinergy Communications became the go-to place for many creative cinematographers and editors

Back and front cover, *The Amazing Elvis Presley*, September 1956, with photographs by Wertheimer.

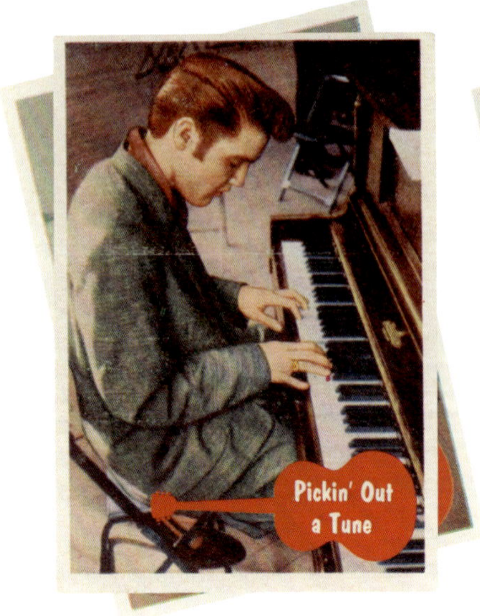

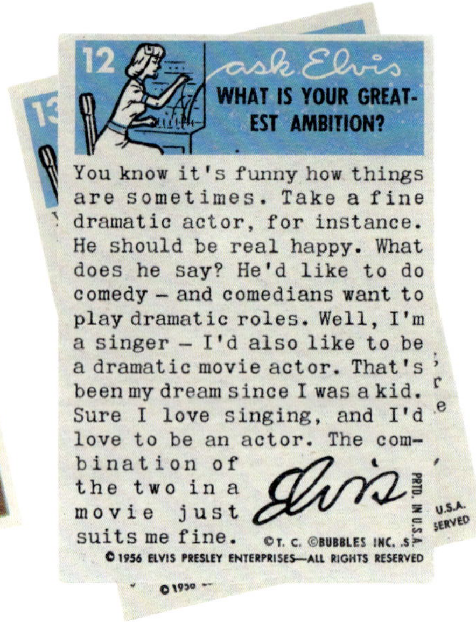

of that time, including documentary filmmakers like Ken Burns. Wertheimer ran the business for 20 years, but as digital technology began transforming the filmmaker's world, he decided to sell his analog Steenbeck business and return to photography.

In the early '90s Wertheimer began to focus for the first time on his vast archive of personal photographs, publishing books of his work and exhibiting his photographs of Elvis Presley, starting with a one-man show at my gallery in Washington, D.C., Govinda Gallery. His work has been exhibited at the Fondation Cartier pour l'art contemporain in Paris; the Rock and Roll Hall of Fame and Museum in Cleveland, Ohio; the Experience Music Project in Seattle, Washington; Domus Artium in Salamanca, Spain; and the Jule Collins Smith Museum in Auburn, Alabama. And Wertheimer's exhibition, *Elvis at 21*, co-organized by the Smithsonian Institution and Govinda Gallery, has traveled to 14 museums, including the Grammy Museum in Los Angeles and the National Portrait Gallery in Washington, D.C.

ABOVE
Elvis trading cards produced by Colonel Tom Parker, using Wertheimer's photographs, released June 29, 1956.

OPPOSITE
Time to play a few gospel songs before rehearsal for *The Steve Allen Show*, June 29, 1956.

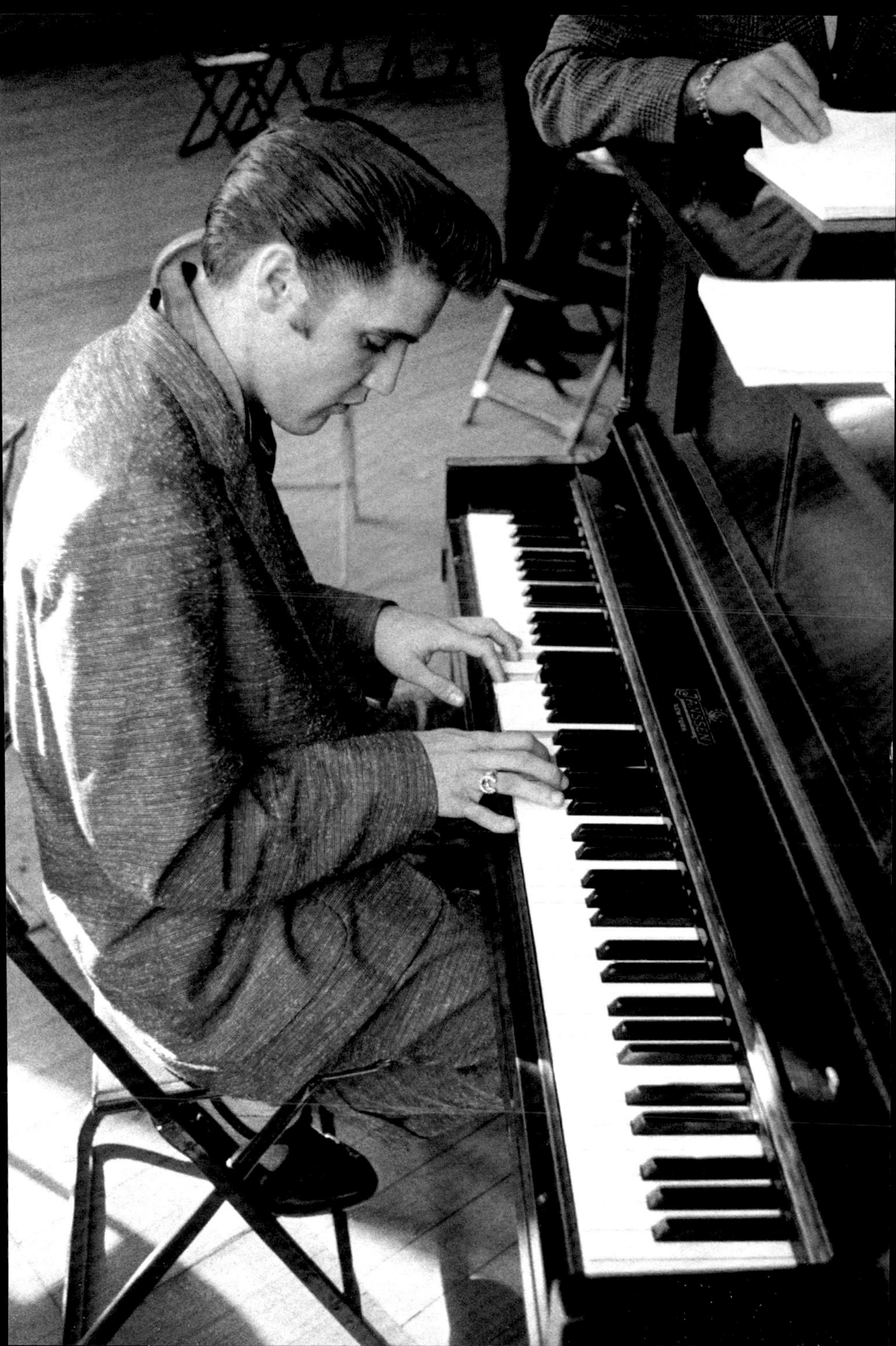

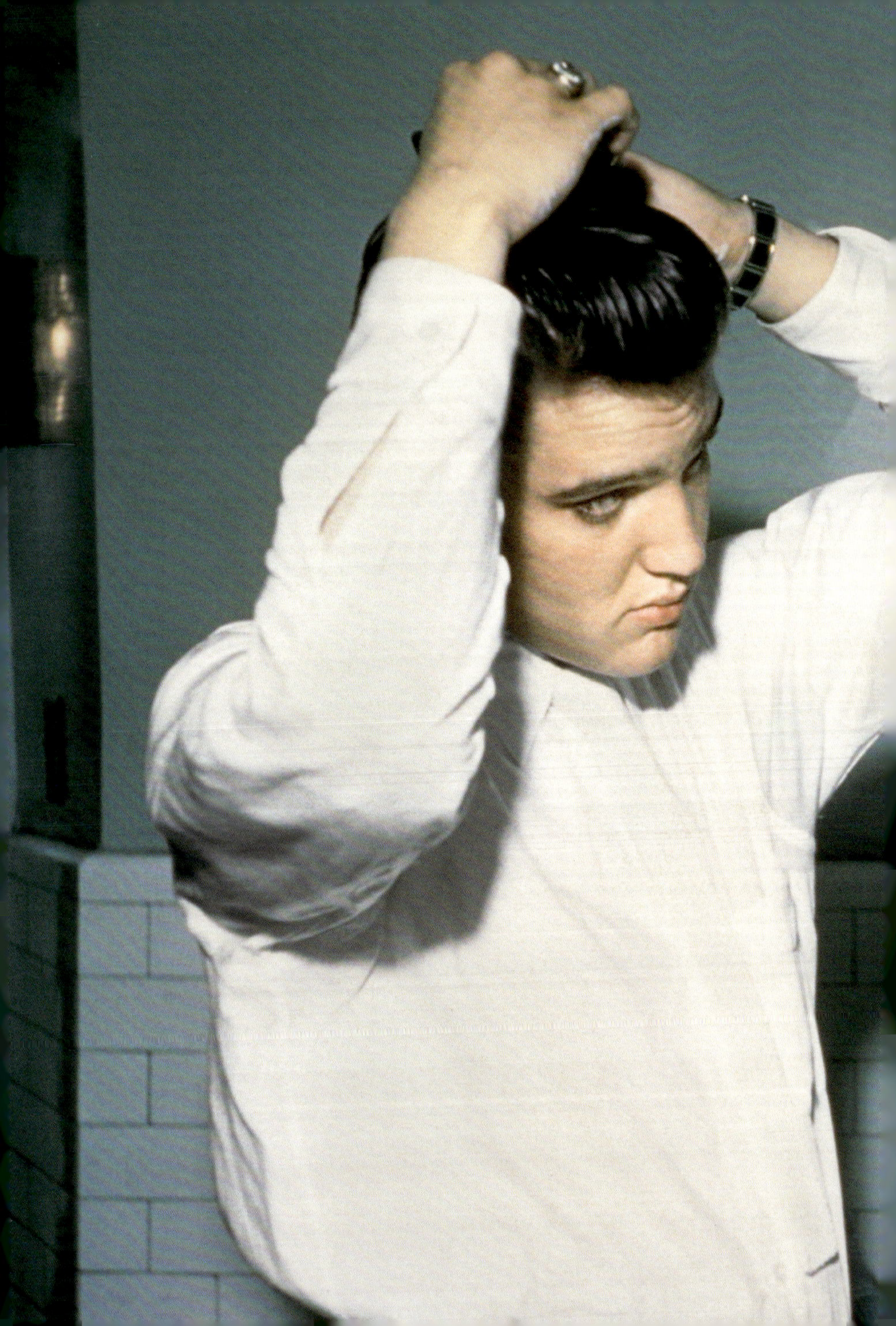

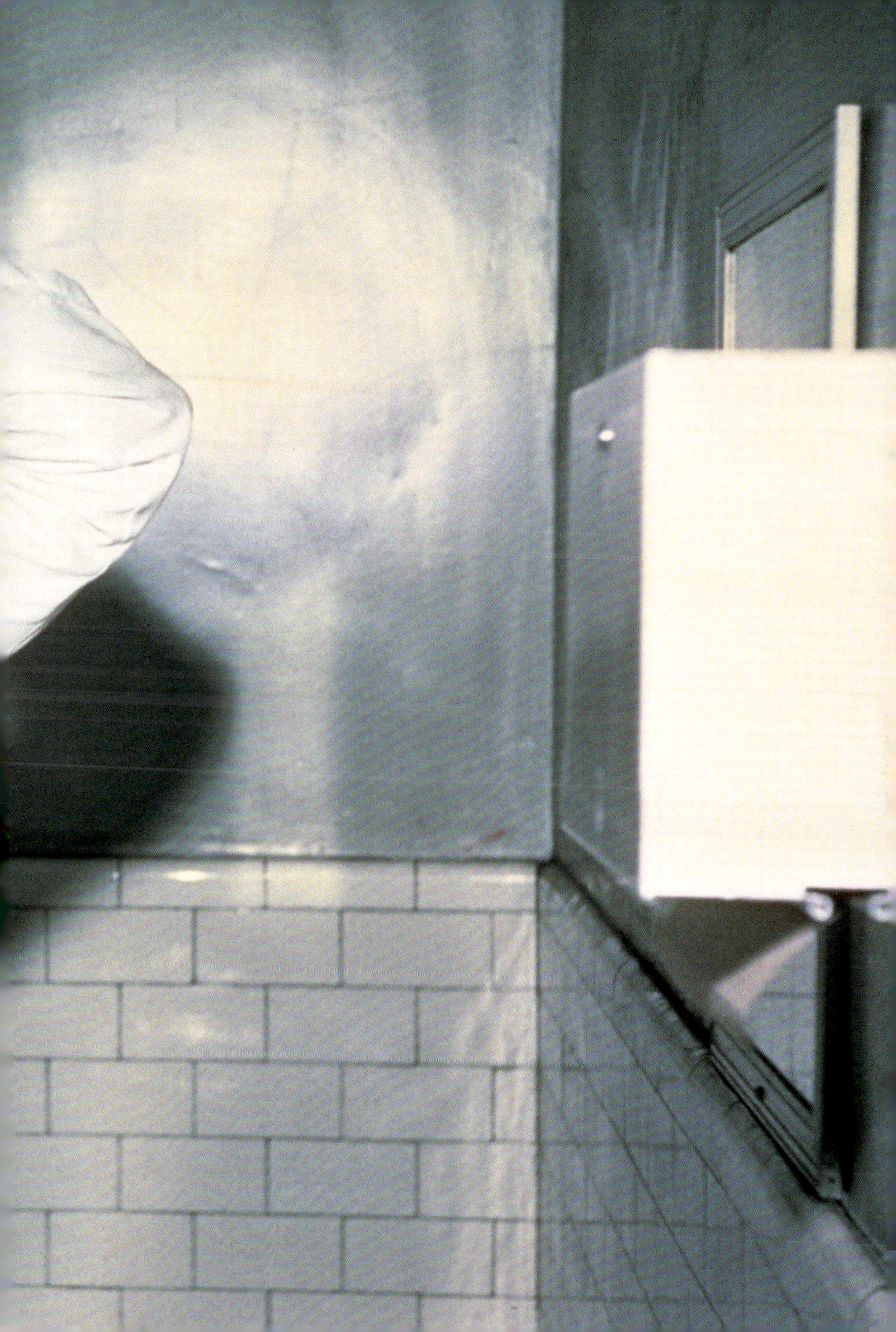

FRONT COVER Portrait study in color: the 8 P.M. show at the Mosque Theater.

PAGE 1 Portrait at the Jefferson Hotel coffee shop lunch counter, Richmond, Virginia, June 30, 1956.

PAGE 2 AND BACK COVER
Going Home, July 4, 1956, aboard the Southern Railway local train to Memphis, Tennessee.

PAGE 7 Elvis's Martin guitar, with a tooled leather cover, stands upright against the wall during the recording session of "Hound Dog" and "Don't Be Cruel," RCA Victor Studio 1, New York City, July 2, 1956.

PREVIOUS SPREAD Elvis combs his hair in the men's room of the Mosque Theater, which was used as a dressing room for all of the male performers of *The Elvis Presley Show*, Richmond, Virginia, June 30, 1956.

OPPOSITE Elvis bows to the applause of a studio audience at the end of a performance on *Stage Show*, March 17, 1956.

PAGE 192 As the USS *Randall* pulls out into New York Harbor a screaming fan expresses her dismay that "Elvis has left the country," September 22, 1958.

Want to see more? Visit *taschen.com* to view our current publications, browse our latest magazine, and subscribe to our newsletter.

All photos and text
© MUUS Collection unless otherwise noted. All Rights Reserved.

"Just Another Assignment"
© 2015 Chris Murray.
"Elvis: The Life and Legacy"
© 2015 Robert Santelli.

The original letterpress poster art throughout this book was created by Hatch Show Print in Nashville, Tennessee, by designers Jennifer Bronstein, Carl Carbonell, and Jim Sherraden, with project management by Celene Aubry.

EACH AND EVERY TASCHEN BOOK PLANTS A SEED!
Each year, we offset our annual carbon emissions with carbon credits at the Instituto Terra, a reforestation program in Minas Gerais, Brazil, founded by Lélia and Sebastião Salgado. To find out more about this ecological partnership, please check: *www.taschen.com/institutoterra*.
Inspiration: unlimited.
Carbon footprint: (almost) zero.

© 2026 TASCHEN GmbH
Hohenzollernring 53
50672 Köln, Germany
www.taschen.com

Original edition:
© 2013 TASCHEN GmbH

Printed in Italy
ISBN 978-3-8365-9708-1

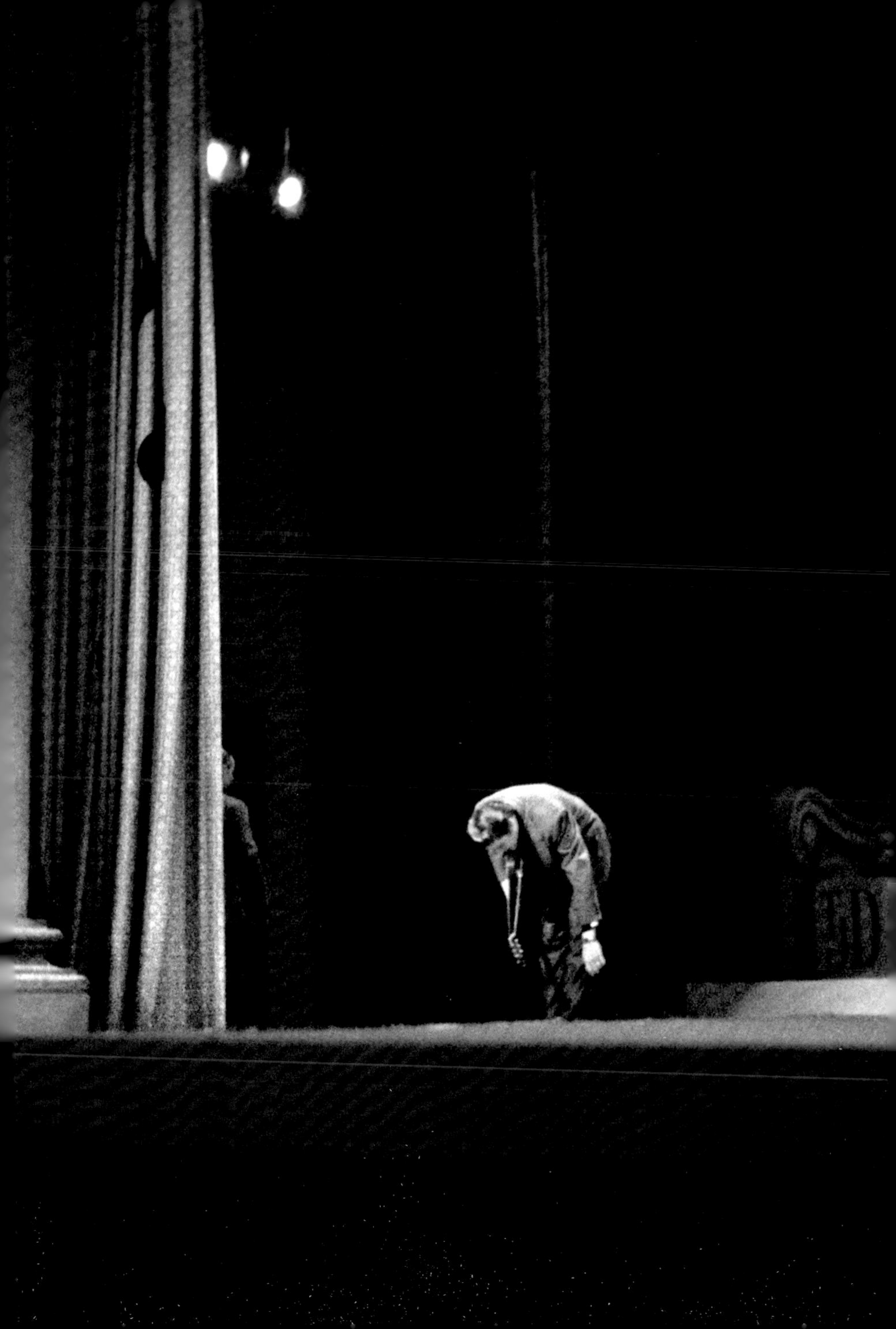

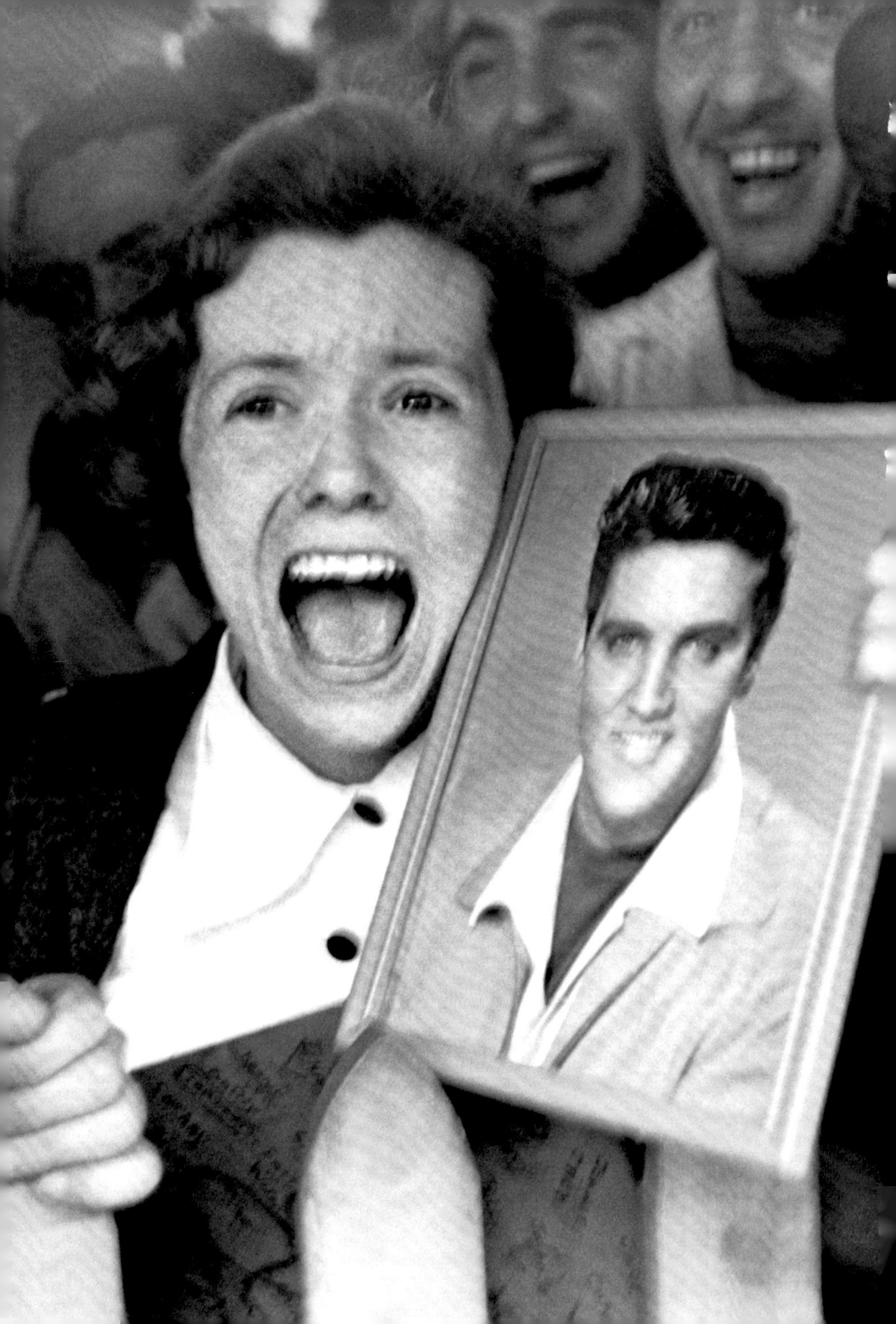

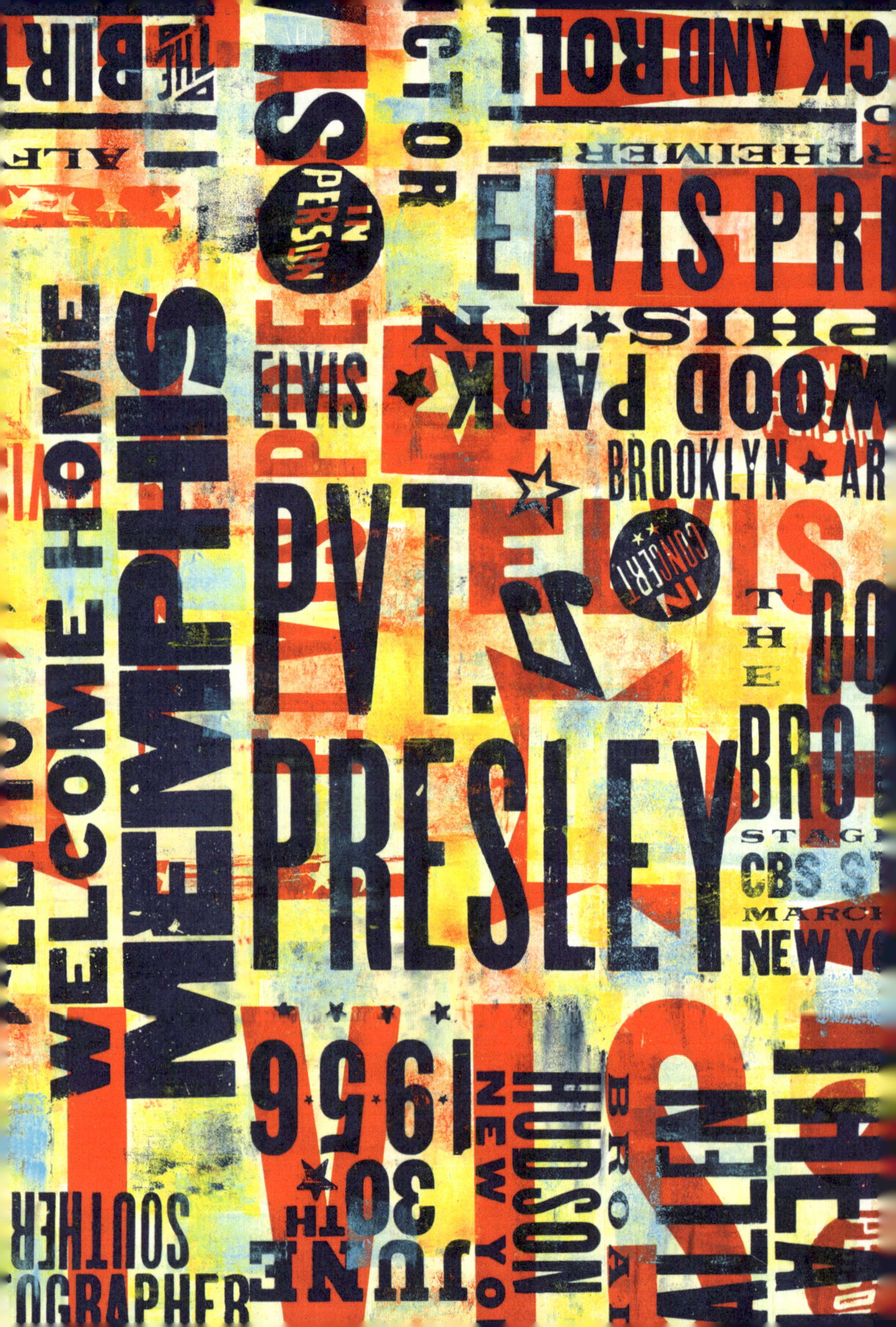

ELVIS PRI
ELVIS
BROOKLYN ★ AR
IN CONCERT
PVT.
PRESLEY
BRO
STAG
CBS S
MARC
NEW Y